7/88

Beyond Minimalism

Beyond Minimalism

BECKETT'S LATE STYLE
IN THE THEATER

Enoch Brater

New York   Oxford
OXFORD UNIVERSITY PRESS
1987

Oxford University Press

Oxford   New York   Toronto
Delhi   Bombay   Calcutta   Madras   Karachi
Petaling Jaya   Singapore   Hong Kong   Tokyo
Nairobi   Dar es Salaam   Cape Town
Melbourne   Auckland

and associated companies in
Beirut   Berlin   Ibadan   Nicosia

Published by Oxford University Press, Inc.,
200 Madison Avenue, New York, New York 10016

Oxford is a registered trademark of Oxford University Press

Library of Congress Cataloging-in-Publication Data

Brater, Enoch.
Beyond minimalism.

Bibliography: p.
Includes index.
1. Beckett, Samuel, 1906–   —Criticism and
interpretation.   I. Title.
PR6003.E282Z5767   1987   842'.914   86-12829
ISBN 0-19-504167-4 (alk. paper)

2 4 6 8 10 9 7 5 3 1

Printed in the United States of America
on acid-free paper

In memory of
Adolf Klarmann
1904–1975

VLADIMIR: You should have been a poet.

ESTRAGON: I was. (*Gesture towards his rags.*) Isn't that obvious?

Silence.

— *Waiting for Godot*

Preface

When I first thought of writing a book about Beckett's plays of the seventies and eighties, it seemed to me that the playwright had embarked on the exploration of an entirely new dramatic mode—new, at least, for him. Gone were the very recognizable moods of *Waiting for Godot* and *Endgame,* plays with which my generation had grown up. *Footfalls* and *What Where* were "really" avant-garde, but now that I have written this book I realize that that is how an earlier generation of theatergoers must have felt about the currently familiar territory of Gogo and Didi and Hamm and Clov. Habit is a great deadener.

Beyond Minimalism is an attempt to place Beckett's late theater style, "that MINE," in the context of his earlier drama. My title needs explaining. Minimalism, an abstract and by some measure even a geometric art form, at best aims to do more and more with less and less. And that's how *Not I* struck me when I saw it performed at Lincoln Center in 1972, though at the time I wasn't quite sure if in this instance less wasn't simply less. It now seems to me that Beckett's plays demonstrate an aesthetic which goes far beyond the limited and often dehumanized sphere we recognize in the chilling reticence of minimalist art. In these late plays Beckett reaches for something far more concrete: what remains in the theater, live and palpable and real, after so much has been taken away, how much doesn't have to happen onstage for a lyrical dramatic moment to expand and unfold.

In making this argument I have been steadily enriched and encouraged by the work of my colleagues in the field. Martin Esslin, Marty Fehsenfeld, Hersh Zeifman, Jim Knowlson, Linda Ben-Zvi, Ro-

sette Lamont, Kristin Morrison, and Stan Gontarski have left their mark
on *Beyond Minimalism* in ways that the book should make self-evi-
dent. Jill Levenson, Sidney Homan, Rubin Rabinovitz, and Normand
Berlin read the manuscript constructively and sympathetically: "For
this relief much thanks." To one final reader, Ruby Cohn, who must
remain for every Beckett critic *il miglior fabbro,* I wish to express my
continuing gratitude for her pioneering scholarship and warm friend-
ship.

I want to thank, as well, the editors of *Modern Drama, Twentieth
Century Literature,* and *Modern Language Quarterly* for permission
to reprint here in revised form material that was always intended for
a book. My students at the University of Michigan, both in class and
seminar, have raised questions (and contributed insights) which have
left me more indebted to them than they to me. William P. Sisler and
Henry Krawitz, my patient and cheerful editors at Oxford University
Press, have been, once again, everywhere unstinting and straightfor-
ward in bringing this project to fruition. Liz, Jessica, and Jonathan,
who gave me the warm support every writer needs, already must know
how their spirit cheered me on.

Ann Arbor and London   E.B.
Fall 1986

Contents

Beyond Minimalism

CHAPTER ONE

Genre Under Stress

To speak of Beckett's late style in the theater is to come to grips with the need for a new kind of critical vocabulary. Drama, narrative, and poetry, the conventional categories a literary tradition has imposed on chapter and verse, seem in this instance tangential and inconvenient. Genre is under stress. The theater event is reduced to a piece of monologue and the play is on the verge of becoming something else, something that looks suspiciously like a performance poem. All the while a story is being told, a fiction closely approximating the dramatic situation the audience encounters in the theater. It is no longer possible to separate the dancer from the dance. Theater technology, too, is called upon to strut and fret its hour upon the stage—more likely, in this case, limited to fifteen or twenty minutes. Lighting, "Faint, though by no means invisible,"[1] and especially mechanical recording devices, frame the action, advance the plot, and function more like dramatic principals than incidental side effects. Something is taking its course, but this particular course, in such efficient stage terms, is one that has not been taken before.

To a certain extent theater has been from the start a collaborative art. Performance, that ritual of communion the audience has with the voice of the playwright, has always been a much more complicated business than a term like "mediation" implies. One might even go so far as to say that without this rite of passage there is no play, though there may be a script. I have intentionally avoided using the word "text," for Beckett's late work in the theater, with its precise and schematic stage directions for lighting, movement, and sound, focuses our

3

attention very deliberately on the practical elements of making a stage image concrete. "Can you stage a mouth?" Beckett asked one sympathetic critic when he began to formulate his seed image for *Not I*. "Just a moving mouth, with the rest of the face in darkness?"[2] In theater terms it is the physical, not the metaphysical, that preoccupies the playwright. Or to state it another way, without Beckett making his theater space new, there is no possibility of the physical apparatus achieving metaphysical resonance. Beckett's dramatic "text," leaving out all the nonessentials, is therefore a specific mandate for a specific staging. The performance becomes the play. The job of the director, whether it is Beckett himself or someone else, is, as Alan Schneider pointed out, "to make sure that the nonessentials don't creep back in."[3]

"Text," then, at least as Beckett has been redefining it since *Not I*, collapses our traditional way of thinking about drama as something separate and distinct from performance. In the later Beckett the two have become one, for only in this way has it become possible for the playwright to communicate his private image in the public forum that is theater. Though in a work like *Footfalls* the actress, the vocal quality, the dramatic posture, and the resultant emotional intensity (among other things) will change from production to production, every version of this work, true "to the letter and to the spirit,"[4] will *look* remarkably like every other version. And though every staging calls for an original lighting concept and costume design, it must be remembered that the blocking has been diagramed in advance ("seven eight nine wheel"):

```
 r    |    r    |    r    |    r    |    r    ←
L ─────────────────────────────────────────── R
 →    |    r    |    r    |    r    |    r    |
```

The playwright has similarly framed his images in *Rockaby*, *That Time*, and *Not I*. Compared to the range of possibility for the sets in Ibsen, Pinter, Shepard, or Shakespeare, there can be only a relatively low threshold of change from one rocking chair to the next, one disembodied head to another ("*long flaring white hair*" notwithstanding), and last, though by no means least, one mouth to the next "godforsaken hole."[5] "How do you act a mouth?" asked Jessica Tandy, who performed it in the world premiere of *Not I* at Lincoln Center in 1972. "I'd like to do a musical next."[6]

The absence of any acceptable boundaries distinguishing play from performance reality signals the breakdown of other generic distinctions as well, ones which will prove far more problematic in terms of the development of Beckett's dramatic structure. "Joyce was a synthesizer," he told Martin Esslin. "I am an analyzer."[7] In the context of Beckett's late style in the theater, a style whose impact on the audience has been designed to be immediate and visceral, one does not wish to overintellectualize the practical domain of the playwright's stagecraft. Nevertheless, any student of Beckett's early work seems bound to notice an ever-increasing awareness on the playwright's part of the not-so-exclusive territories separating fiction and poetry from dramatic opportunity. Let us look for a moment at Beckett's most famous play, *Waiting for Godot*. Estragon, who claims to be a poet and who happens to have a nodding acquaintance with the early Yeats ("The wind in the reeds"), thinks in images: he is so bound up by his simile of the leaves that he hardly hears his partner at all. Savoring the sound as much as the sense of "like leaves," his vain attempt at onomatopoeia takes on an independent life of its own. For one brief shining moment, at least until Vladimir succeeds in calling him back to what Beckett called "the local situation" at hand, this "muckheap" of waiting for Godot, Estragon fancies himself with the poets, not the bums, of eternity.[8] Hope springs eternal. Language can work wonders—especially when it has been so specifically crafted to do so. But let us not forget that it is this same Gogo who mixes the logic of his own metaphors. It is not the philosopher Didi, but this same sidekick poet who commits the unforgivable blooper, "Let us strike the iron before it freezes."[9]

Yet the poetic dimension in *Godot* functions in a far more incremental way than any comic fumbling with clumsy imagery implies. The dialogue of this play, which in terms of allusion and texture has been flirting with verbal lyricism all along, will finally break forth in a stunning dramatic metaphor to carry the full force of the play's rising action:

> POZZO: (*suddenly furious*). Have you not done tormenting me with your accursed time! It's abominable! When! When! One day, is that not enough for you, one day he went dumb, one day I went blind, one day we'll go deaf, one day we were born, one day we shall die, the same day, the same second, is that not enough for you? (*Calmer.*) They give birth astride of a grave, the light gleams an instant, then it's night once more. (*He jerks the rope.*) On!
>
> —*Waiting for Godot*, p. 57

Without the exercise of scanning the lines for us (though they could, of course, *be* scanned), Beckett has given Pozzo the appropriate speech

to sum up the dramatic climax we have been waiting for. Stage dialogue becomes the language of poetry and heightens the dramatic moment by encapsulating it in the words that will haunt us from this play.
Vladimir, a "crritic" as well as a philosopher, is so impressed by real
poetry when he hears it that he will refer to these lines again for us
before the curtain comes down:

> VLADIMIR: Was I sleeping, while the others suffered? Am I sleeping now?
> To-morrow, when I wake, or think I do, what shall I say of to-
> day? That with Estragon, my friend, at this place, until the fall
> of night, I waited for Godot? That Pozzo passed, with his car-
> rier, and that he spoke to us? Probably. But in all that what
> truth will there be? . . . Astride of a grave and a difficult birth.
> Down in the hole, lingeringly, the grave-digger puts on the for-
> ceps. We have time to grow old. The air is full of our cries.
> (*He listens.*) But habit is a great deadener. (*He looks again at
> Estragon.*) At me too someone is looking, of me too someone
> is saying, He is sleeping, he knows nothing, let him sleep on.
> (*Pause.*) I can't go on! (*Pause.*) What have I said?
>
> —*Waiting for Godot,* p. 58

What we are tempted to call the poetic in *Godot,* however, is
placed within the broader context of a play which borrows so many
of its other elements from burlesque, commedia dell'arte, silent film,
and even the music hall. Our final image of this piece will not be of
lyric incantation, but of pants falling down. Gogo pulls his back on,
followed by the striking stage direction: "*They do not move.*" In this
play, as so many critics have noticed, the poetic alternates with the
comic, creating a pattern whose hilarious adagios are as memorable as
Pozzo's lyricism.[10] *Waiting for Godot* therefore offers us a poetic moment which competes for our attention with the comic vitality that
makes this work so attractive in production. Finally, however, it will
be the lines of Pozzo's speech that contain the dramatic tension of the
play, resolving it by making us see the poetic in the comic. Beckett's
late style in the theater is ultimately a greater concentration on the
staying power of such moments, stretching them out to encompass the
entire range of the drama itself.

Beckett has been similarly analytical in his use of fictional narrative. An early work like *Endgame* will feature Hamm's "prolonged
creative effort," a father-son tale with overtones not merely archetypal,
but curiously autobiographical as well. As we have come to expect in
Beckett, dramatis personae tell stories. Hamm's "chronicle" in *End-*

game is such an obviously made thing that our attention inevitably falls, as it does in the novel *Malone Dies,* on the teller rather than the tale. It is the narrator who is being narrated here.[11] Set initially on Christmas Eve, Hamm's fiction takes place on "an extra-ordinary bitter day . . . zero by the thermometer." A few lines later the opening has been changed to "a glorious bright day . . . fifty by the heliometer, but already the sun was sinking down into the . . . down among the dead." Such emendations are only beginning. Before long the same tale has shifted to "a howling wild day, I remember, a hundred by the anenometer" and then to "an exceedingly dry day . . . zero by the hygrometer. Ideal weather for my lumbago."[12] Which day is it, the same day or any day or the day that is forever being created in the fiction of its own fictivity? What Hamm's "narrative tone" displays is not permanence but the difficult process of its own becoming.

As we shall later see in *Company,* Hamm's fictional enterprise is a "fable of one fabling of one with you in the dark."[13] Yet the darkness here is by no means the same darkness we encounter in novels like *Malone Dies* or in works like *Company.* Hamm's "story time" is presented to us live, onstage, and for one time only. In this instance the metaphorical darkness has been lit—and by nothing less than stage lights. This story, whose only existence can be in performance, depends for its life on the presence of an actor reciting that which keeps him on the boards, the dialogue. Narrative time has been subsumed within the production limits of stage time. *Endgame,* then, makes fiction, especially that part of getting itself written, an integral element of Beckett's dramatic process. But the fiction within *Endgame,* like the highly imaged dialogue in *Waiting for Godot,* is only one element among many others. This play, too, will come to rely on the heightened language of poetry for a central climactic moment:

> CLOV (*as before*): I say to myself—sometimes, Clov, you must learn to suffer better than that if you want them to weary of punishing you—one day. I say to myself—sometimes, Clov, you must be there better than that if you want them to let you go—one day. But I feel too old, and too far, to form new habits. Good, it'll never end, I'll never go.
> (*Pause.*)
> Then one day, suddenly, it ends, it changes. I don't understand, it dies, or it's me, I don't understand, that either. I ask the words that remain—sleeping, waking, morning, evening. They have nothing to say.
> (*Pause.*)

> I open the door of the cell and go. I am so bowed I only see
> my feet, if I open my eyes, and between my legs a little trail
> of black dust. I say to myself that the earth is extinguished,
> though I never saw it lit.

—*Endgame*, pp. 80–81

What Clov recites here is a sort of confessional poetry, a personal
statement we understand immediately, for as members of the audience
we have shared with this character the brutal reality of his own psychological endgame. There is no exit, only an agonizing "presentness." Something more than the language of fiction is suddenly called
for. Beckett therefore gives Clov the necessary monologue his recognition scene requires, providing him with a genuine lyricism to communicate his moment of personal insight.

What is important to notice in *Endgame* is how relatively easy it
is for us to locate the elements of poetry and fiction within the overall
structure of Beckett's drama. Such generic distinctions will be far more
difficult to make in *Krapp's Last Tape,* a single character play which
builds its dramatic emphasis from the coincidence of poetry, fiction,
and drama. In "Box . . . thrree . . . spool . . . five," the electronic
tape Krapp will play for us this evening in the theater, it is impossible
to say where memory ends, fiction begins, and poetry takes over. The
particular passage Krapp searches for on this recording is a combination of all three, so moving as a testament to the past that he will
wind his machine backward and forward in order to listen for it again
and again:

> *Krapp switches off, winds tape back, switches on again.*
> —upper lake, with the punt, bathed off the bank, then pushed
> out into the stream and drifted. She lay stretched out on the
> floorboards with her hands under her head and her eyes closed.
> Sun blazing down, bit of a breeze, water nice and lively. I no-
> ticed a scratch on her thigh and asked her how she came by it.
> Picking gooseberries, she said. I said again I thought it was
> hopeless and no good going on, and she agreed, without open-
> ing her eyes. (*Pause.*) I asked her to look at me and after a few
> moments—(*pause*)—after a few moments she did, but the eyes
> just slits, because of the glare. I bent over her to get them in
> the shadow and they opened. (*Pause. Low.*) Let me in. (*Pause.*)
> We drifted in among the flags and stuck. The way they went
> down, sighing, before the stem! (*Pause.*) I lay down across her
> with my face in her breasts and my hand on her. We lay there
> without moving. But under us all moved, and moved us, gently,
> up and down, and from side to side.[14]

The dramatic opportunity here consists of Krapp's present reaction to the lines we have just heard with him, an opportunity, it should be noticed, that takes place in silence, in the enactment of gesture and movement rather than in words. As members of Beckett's audience we watch Krapp-on-stage build a dramatic confrontation in response to Krapp-on-tape. Time, what Beckett will later label "that time," has been electronically retrieved and can now be controlled by a mechanical device as simple to operate as any on-off switch. Proustian memory is literally made concrete, permanent, and concise in a series of recording sessions designed for future broadcast. A paragraph, a line, sometimes even an erotic phrase, can now contain what might have been, in other hands or at some other time, a whole story. A novel, one as expansive as the *Effi Briest* Krapp so much admires, is reduced on tape to the "last fancies" of a voice searching for some literary image: "The face she had! The eyes! Like . . . (*hesitates*) . . . chrysolite! (*Pause.*)" Only such a powerful simile can make time stand still for Krapp: *temps perdu* becomes *temps retrouvé* and stimulates, as does whiskey, additional image making:

> Sometimes wondered in the night if a last effort mightn't— (*Pause.*) Ah finish your booze now and get to your bed. Go on with this drivel in the morning. Or leave it at that. (*Pause.*) Leave it at that. (*Pause.*) Lie propped up in the dark—and wander. Be again in the dingle on a Christmas Eve, gathering holly, the red-berried. (*Pause.*) Be again on Croghan on a Sunday morning, in the haze, with the bitch, stop and listen to the bells. (*Pause.*) And so on. (*Pause.*) Be again, be again. (*Pause.*) All that old misery. (*Pause.*)
>
> —*Krapp's Last Tape*, p. 26

Images on tape, like Krapp's of a girl with green eyes, can be deceptive, however. What Beckett is really concerned with in this play is as much the image we see in the theater as the voiced images mechanically recorded. For time passes in the theater, too. It is our own temporality that is being manipulated here. We, too, leave the theater struggling with an intimate image, the solitary one Beckett has chosen to share with us:

> Pause. *Krapp's lips move.*
> No sound. *Past midnight. Never knew such silence. The earth might be uninhabited.*
> Pause.

Here I end this reel. Box—(*pause*)—three, spool—(*pause*)—
five. (*Pause*.) Perhaps my best years are gone. When there was
a chance of happiness. But I wouldn't want them back. Not
with the fire in me now. No, I wouldn't want them back.
Krapp motionless staring before him. The tape runs on in si-
lence.

CURTAIN

—*Krapp's Last Tape,* p. 28

Unlike Krapp's, Beckett's image is immediate and real and takes place
in a live dimension that goes beyond the poetic, in the mere literary
sense of the word. For, as demonstrated here, the private image turns
public in an instant of communion between actor and audience that
can only take place in the spontaneity that makes theater happen. A
private world is suddenly revealed, a veil is lifted, only to recede once
more into stage darkness. Beckett's image is "come and gone" in the
specific "no time" the stage space so palpably renders.[15] "That time,"
the time we spend in the theater watching Krapp prepare to make this
last of all tapes, takes place on *that space,* the very particular mise-
en-scène Beckett's stage directions carefully balance and control. And
just as Krapp's words on "spool . . . five" provide us with a romantic
story full of the visual potential a classical playwright would assign to
the messenger's speech, so too does Beckett's lonely image of an old
man cry out for identification, recognition, and empathy. "The end of
life," Beckett writes in *Malone Dies,* "is always vivifying"—particularly when its emotional complexity has been given the high definition, as it will later be in *Rockaby,* of an unsentimental theater image.

Beckett's early plays such as *Godot, Endgame,* and *Krapp's Last*
Tape demonstrate not so much the supremacy of theater art over language art, but rather their more proper coordination. In *Krapp's Last*
Tape Beckett's language actually comes into its own by the elimination
of the second actor. Krapp-on-tape plays "voice" and Krapp-on-stage
plays "listener," the special duet for one we associate more typically
with Beckett's later works such as *Footfalls, That Time,* and *Rockaby.*
In an ordinary play, and in some early Beckett (*Godot* and *Endgame*),
there are other actors who can feed the appropriate emotional level.
But in plays like these it is language itself that must create the conflict.
Beckett's concern is now with "the sound of the human voice and its
power to evoke an entire world."[16] No longer will it be possible for a
Gogo or a Didi to "return the ball, once in a way." Dialogue is there-
fore called upon to play a new role. Punctuation is liberated to the

flow of the spoken word as the actor is required to play the drama on the line. Pausing on commas and ellipses or lingering on incidental elements of phraseology, as Winnie must do in *Happy Days,* the actor is forced to keep going, thinking forward, for the dialogue of these plays, typically structured in the shape of a monologue, is hard to take to pieces in order to work on separate details. Each section produces another in the emotional life that goes into building a character through language. In *Krapp's Last Tape* this new approach to dialogue is still tentative, however, relying as it does on the naturalistic device of an old man alone in a room with a tape recorder. In the later plays Beckett will abandon such intrusive trappings of realism in order to explore in greater depth a new dimension of theater form for dialogue and stage language based on the recorded possibilities of the human voice.

Beckett's preoccupation with recorded sound can be traced back to his first radio play, *All That Fall,* which he wrote in 1956. His interest in preparing a script for broadcast should come as no surprise, for radio drama is an ideal medium for the transmission of the interior consciousness. All through Beckett's fiction characters claim to hear voices, and Hamm in *Endgame* is plagued by "Something dripping in my head, ever since the fontanelles . . . Splash, splash, always on the same spot . . . Perhaps it's a little vein" (pun intended). Winnie, whom the playwright called "a bird," another pun, "with oil on its wings,"[17] suffers a similar fate in *Happy Days:*

> . . . Sometimes I hear sounds. (*Listening expression. Normal voice.*) But not often. (*Pause.*) They are a boon, sounds are a boon, they help me . . . through the day. (*Smile.*) The old style! (*Smile off.*) Yes, those are happy days, when there are sounds. (*Pause.*) When I hear sounds. (*Pause.*) I used to think . . . (*pause*) . . . I say I used to think they were in my head. (*Smile.*) But no. (*Smile broader.*) No no. (*Smile off.*) That was just logic. (*Pause.*) Reason. (*Pause.*) I have not lost my reason. (*Pause.*) Not yet. (*Pause.*) Not all. (*Pause.*) Some remains. (*Pause.*) Sounds. (*Pause.*) Like little . . . sunderings, little falls . . . apart.[18]

Such unearthly sounds, materialized as voices onstage, become the hallmark of Beckett's late style, yet it is his work with the contingencies of radio drama that prepares us for their adaptation to the live theater. Beckett's experience with mechanically organized sound actually begins with the technical problems of taping *All That Fall* for the BBC.[19] He had originally insisted that the opening sounds of his play, the "sheep, birds, cow, cock, severally, then together,"[20] be real; he wanted to avoid the overtly artificial tones of the canned noises in stock in the ample BBC archives. Donald McWhinnie, who produced the show, persuaded him that this would be a mistake:

> The purpose of this prelude is not primarily to evoke a visual picture, and if it resolves itself into "farmyard noises" it will in fact be pointless, since it is not directly linked to the action, although echoes of it are heard during the course of the play, in various contexts. It is a stylized form of scene-setting, containing within itself a pointer to the convention of the play: a mixture of realism and poetry, frustration and farce. It also demands a strict rhythmic composition; a mere miscellany of animal sounds will not achieve the effect. The author specified four animals; this corresponds exactly to the four-in-a-bar metre of Mrs. Rooney's walk to the station and back, which is the percussive accompaniment to the play and which, in its later stages, becomes charged with emotional significance in itself. But in this case it is impossible to use real animal sounds, since the actual sound of a cow mooing, a cock crowing, a sheep bleating, a dog barking, are complex structures, varying in duration and melodic shape; to put these four sounds in succession would be to create a whole which is only too obviously composed of disparate elements. The way to deal with the problem seemed to be by complete stylization of each sound, that is to say, by having human beings to impersonate the exact sound required.[21]

McWhinnie commissioned Percy Edwards, the animal imitator, to record the sounds, and then had them changed electronically. Mechanical media were allowed to place their mark on the human voice, even when that voice was imitating barnyard sounds. Schubert, too, sounded strange in this work, as it later did in the television play, *Nacht und Träume,* once a magnetic recording tape had its inevitable say. Voices, music, and other noises came "out of the dark,"[22] in this instance with a purity of sound that is something uniquely recorded, an art, as the Italian futurist Marinetti predicted, that would imitate electricity.[23] Beckett was in Paris when *All That Fall* was broadcast on the Third Programme on January 13, 1957. Across the Channel, he could hear it only poorly. He then wrote to the BBC Radio Drama Division in London asking for a tape of the show. This was soon followed by another letter to Broadcasting House requesting an instruction manual on how to operate a tape recorder.[24] The rest is stage history: *Krapp's Last Tape* had its primary inspiration in a situation not so much romantic as technological.

   That Beckett is technology-minded can be seen in his handling of the sophisticated stage machinery that goes into making the apparent simplicity of his late theater images. It is essentially this involvement with complex theater technology that makes these Beckett plays *look* so very different. Beckett's concern is not only with the verbal language of drama, but with the enrichment of its inherent relationship to the other stage languages of movement and blocking, sound and silence, costume and set design, gesture, and, above all, lighting.[25] Even an early radio play like *All That Fall* demonstrates Beckett's involvement with the multidimensionality of a given performance medium. For despite the fact that this play is heard rather than seen—or more likely because of it—the work remains one of the playwright's most visually suggestive. In this work Beckett makes vivid pictures fly, literally, out of thin air "on the air": the radio drama changes its "set" more often than any other Beckett play and uses a cast of characters that is, by comparison to the playwright's other works, legion. Through sound a large cast of characters must be identified one from another. Here one figure must "sound" fat (Maddy Rooney), another must "sound" blind (her husband, Dan Rooney) and yet another must sound "very distray" ("the dark Miss Fitt"):

MRS. ROONEY: Oh there is that Fitt woman, I wonder will she bow to me. (*Sound of Miss Fitt approaching, humming a hymn. She starts climbing the steps.*) Miss Fitt! (*Miss Fitt halts, stops humming.*) Am I then invisible, Miss Fitt? Is this cretonne so becoming to me that I merge into the masonry? (*Miss Fitt descends a step.*) That is right, Miss Fitt, look closely and you will finally distinguish a once female shape.

MISS FITT: Mrs. Rooney! I saw you, but I did not know you.

MRS. ROONEY: Last Sunday we worshipped together. We knelt side by side at the same altar. We drank from the same chalice. Have I so changed since then?

MISS FITT: (*shocked*). Oh but in church, Mrs. Rooney, in church I am alone with my Maker. Are not you? (*Pause.*) Why, even the sexton himself, you know, when he takes up the collection, knows it is useless to pause before me. I simply do not see the plate, or bag, or whatever it is they use, how could I? (*Pause.*) Why even when all is over and I go out into the sweet fresh air, why even then for the first furlong or so I stumble in a kind of daze as you might say, oblivious to my coreligionists. And they are very kind, I must admit—the vast majority—very kind and understanding. They know me now and take no umbrage. There she goes, they say, there goes the dark Miss Fitt, alone with her Maker, take no notice of her. And they step down off the path to avoid my running into them. (*Pause.*) Ah yes, I am distray, very distray, even on week-days. Ask Mother, if you do not believe me. Hetty, she says, when I start eating my doily instead of the thin bread and butter, Hetty, how can you be so distray? (*Sighs.*) I suppose the truth is I am not there, Mrs. Rooney, just not really there at all. I see, hear, smell, and so on, I go through the usual motions, but my heart is not in it, Mrs. Rooney, but heart is in none of it. Left to myself, with no one to check me, I would soon be flown . . . home. (*Pause.*) So if you think I cut you just now, Mrs. Rooney, you do me an injustice. All I saw was a big pale blur, just another big pale blur. (*Pause.*) Is anything amiss, Mrs. Rooney, you do not look normal somehow. So bowed and bent.

MRS. ROONEY: (*ruefully*). Maddy Rooney, née Dunne, the big pale blur. (*Pause.*) You have piercing sight, Miss Fitt, if you only knew it, literally piercing.
Pause.

—*All That Fall,* pp. 54–56

In stage plays like *Footfalls* and *That Time* Beckett will provide his audience with a similar range of visual stimulation, sometimes based on the image-making potential of a recorded human voice, sometimes based on its "live" counterpart offering a narrative recital onstage, as May will do in the third movement of *Footfalls:*

Old Mrs. Winter, whom the reader will remember, old Mrs. Winter, one late autumn Sunday evening, on sitting down to supper with her daughter after worship, after a few half-hearted mouthfuls laid down her knife and fork and bowed her head. What is it, Mother, said the daughter, a most strange girl, though scarcely a girl any more . . . (*brokenly*) . . . dreadfully un— (*Pause. Normal voice.*) What is it, Mother, are you not feeling yourself? (*Pause.*) Mrs. W. did not at once reply. But finally, raising her head and fixing Amy—the daughter's given name, as the reader will remember—raising her head and fixing Amy full in the eye she said—(*pause*)—she murmured, fixing Amy full in the eye she murmured, Amy, did you observe anything . . . strange at Evensong? Amy: No, Mother, I did not. Mrs. W.: Perhaps it was just my fancy. Amy: Just what exactly, Mother, did you perhaps fancy it was? (*Pause.*) Just what ex- actly, Mother, did you perhaps fancy this . . . strange thing was you observed? (*Pause.*) Mrs. W.: You yourself observed nothing . . . strange? Amy: No, Mother, I myself did not, to put it mildly. Mrs. W.: What do you mean, Amy, to put it mildly, what can you possibly mean, Amy, to put it mildly? Amy: I mean, Mother, that to say I observed nothing . . . strange is indeed to put it mildly. For I observed nothing of any kind, strange or otherwise. I saw nothing, heard nothing, of any kind. I was not there. Mrs. W.: Not there? Amy: Not there. Mrs. W.: But I heard you respond. (*Pause.*) I heard you say Amen. (*Pause.*) How could you have responded if you were not there? (*Pause.*) How could you possibly have said Amen if, as you claim, you were not there? (*Pause.*) The love of God, and the fellowship of the Holy Ghost, be with us all, now, and for evermore. Amen. (*Pause.*) I heard you distinctly.

—*Footfalls,* pp. 47–48

In *Footfalls* the little that we see in this "all strange away" contrasts very sharply with the much that we hear, as Beckett makes us visualize through the mantic power of the two female voices a "total object, complete with missing parts."[26] There is, then, very much more to *see* in these plays than first—or directly—meets the human eye.

Even when Beckett makes us "see" in the theater an arresting visual image, as he does in *Footfalls,* our attention is before long being drawn "elsewhere" by the mystery of a human voice as it recites the story it so much wants to tell. "Something she had to tell," Mouth says in *Not I,* "could that be it?" Generic distinctions between radio drama and stage drama begin to break down, too. In *Waiting for Godot* Beckett must bring on Pozzo and Lucky as "reinforcements, at last!," but by the time of *Happy Days* he merely needs to have Winnie tell a story and a whole new set of characters begins to happen onstage:

Cooker, Willie, does Cooker strike a chord? (*Pause. Turns a little further. Louder.*) Cooker, Willie, does Cooker ring a bell, the name Cooker? . . . Well anyway—this man Shower—or Cooker—no matter—and the woman—hand in hand—in the other hands bags—kind of big brown grips—standing there gaping at me—and at last this man Shower—or Cooker—ends in er anyway—stake my life on that—What's she doing? he says—What's the idea he says—stuck up to her diddies in the bleeding ground—coarse fellow—What does it mean? he says—What's it meant to mean?—and so on—lot more stuff like that—usual drivel—Do you hear me? he says—I do, she says, God help me—What do you mean, he says, God help you? (*Stops filing, raises head, gazes front.*) And you, she says, what's the idea of you, she says, what are you meant to mean? It is because you're still on your two flat feet, with your old ditty full of tinned muck and changes of underwear, dragging me up and down this fornicating wilderness, coarse creature, fit mate— (*with sudden violence*)—let go of my hand and drop for God's

sake, she says, drop! (*Pause. Resumes filing.*) Why doesn't he
dig her out? he says—referring to you, my dear—What good
is she to him like that?—What good is he to her like that?—
and so on—usual tosh—Good! she says, have a heart for God's
sake—Dig her out, he says, dig her out, no sense in her like
that—Dig her out with what? she says—I'd dig her out with
my bare hands, he says—must have been man and—wife. (*Files
in silence.*) Next thing they're away—hand in hand—and the
bags—dim—then gone—last human kind—to stray this way.

—*Happy Days,* pp. 42–44

As in *Godot,* where Pozzo and Lucky are made to reappear in act 2,
Winnie's "Mr. Shower—or Cooker" returns in the second part of this
play, too, albeit within the linguistic confines of her monologue: "Getting on . . . in life. (*Pause.*) No longer young, not yet old. (*Pause.*)
Standing there, gaping at me. (*Pause.*) Can't have been a bad bosom,
he says, in its day." In performance *Happy Days* offers us less and
less physical action and more and more verbal action. To visualize the
point, Beckett buries Winnie up to her waist in a mound of earth in
the first act; in the second, we see her buried up to her neck as she is
literally "devoured by the earth."[27] But Winnie has language, Beckett's language, full of those "wonderful lines" of the past. Along the
way she creates some rather memorable ones of her own:

My first ball! (*Long pause.*) My second ball! (*Long pause. Closes eyes.*) My first kiss! (*Pause.* WILLIE turns page. WINNIE opens
eyes.) A Mr. Johnson, or Johnston, or perhaps I should say
John*stone.* Very bushy moustache, very tawny. (*Reverently.*)
Almost ginger! (*Pause.*) Within a toolshed, though whose I
cannot conceive. We had no toolshed and he most certainly had
no toolshed. (*Closed eyes.*) I see the piles of pots. (*Pause.*) The
tangles of bast. (*Pause.*) The shadows deepening among the
rafters.

—*Happy Days,* p. 16

Winnie's alternation from sex to sensibility is clear and hard and gen-
uinely poetic, though it is, as Peggy Ashcroft observed, "like climbing
Everest to perform."[28] Avoiding the overly lyrical, her unified style
of speaking directs the audience to the language of this play: so little
else competes for our attention. The set, for example, designed according to the stage directions for a "*maximum of simplicity and symmetry,*" is, relatively speaking, undecorated, as it had previously been
in *Waiting for Godot.* But unlike *Godot,* a play of enormous physical

movement which features what Beckett called the "perpetual separation and coming together of Estragon and Vladimir,"[29] *Happy Days* is a play of enormous physical restraint. Except for Willie's ultimate ascent that signals the play's closure, all the physical action must take place in or behind the mound. Even Winnie's many cues for limited body movement (in act 1) or rigorous eye contact (in act 2) exist primarily to provide her with a series of verbal opportunities which are, not coincidentally, dramatic opportunities as well. Beckett selected a woman for this role because the contents of a lady's handbag would provide such a character in such a crisis with more business to do onstage—and therefore much more to *say* about it.[30] Continuing to explore the possibilities of the actor's art, a play like *Happy Days* makes us see "how much could be done, not only while the performer's mobility was denied but even with a diminishing presence."[31]

What is at stake here, dramatically, is not so much the voice of the character, but rather the voice of the playwright. The role of the actor changes. Sometimes telling a story, sometimes reciting what sound like lines of verse, the actor here is always a vehicle for Beckett. The strongest actor in this drama is the playwright himself. Language becomes the center of action in these plays because, in an attempt to relyricize the genre, this is the only way the voice of the would-be poet can break open the constraints of a performing arts medium. This is not drama in the shape of poetry, but poetry in the shape of drama. The experience for the audience in the theater is like the experience of reading a poem, except that in this instance the poem has been staged. Language art and theater art draw together, progressively validating through stage time and our own time the purity of the writer's voice as he builds a sustained dramatic metaphor. In his late plays Beckett will pursue the limits and possibilities of such a unified dramatic form even further, challenging his audience to analyze and encounter with him the special effects on a stage situation when one genre breaks into another.

CHAPTER TWO

The Eye in Not I

It is difficult to tell if *Not I* is primarily spectacle or literature—"ill seen," or "ill said." Certainly in production one is all but overwhelmed by the sheer persuasiveness of the image: a mouth staring out at us from otherwise "empty" theater space. Disembodied, suspended in space, and throbbing with a constant pulsation of lips, teeth, tongue, and saliva, Mouth gives shape to words and phrases as segmented as itself. Never formulating any structure as unified or coherent as a sentence, Mouth opens this play with an unintelligible verbal onslaught, gets beaten into life as she rises toward an agonizing scream, then settles down once more into a dull, incomprehensible drone. At the other side of the stage is a silent, elongated, hooded figure, "*sex undeterminable,*" standing on an invisible podium four feet above stage level, covered from head to bottom of platform in the folds of a djellaba. This mysterious, towering figure interrupts the monologue at four strategic moments, raising its arms "in a gesture of helpless compassion," then slowly returns them to its sides. The repeated gesture lessens with each recurrence "till scarcely perceptible at third." Although Auditor is "*fully faintly lit,*" only a sharp spotlight illuminates Mouth, an isolated, unconnected, gabbling orifice furiously opening and shutting. The house lights go down as the "play" begins: the voice continues unintelligible behind the curtain, "*10 seconds,*" "*ad-libbing from text as required*" as spotlight and comprehensibility both gradually gain intensity. At the conclusion of the piece, spotlight and voice fade out in a simultaneity of diminishing perception. Sight and sound of Beckett's "mouth on fire" are slowly extinguished. Such diminution of light enlarges, iron-

ically, the illusion of movement, the same autokinetic phenomenon
created when concentrating on a bright object in a darkened room.
Mouth appears to swoop and hover like a monotonous butterfly, a
threatening, grotesque perversion of Dante's *angelica farfalla*. As Jessica Tandy remarked after she brought Mouth to life in New York in
1972, "You may find nothing in it, but I suspect you will never forget
it."[1]

Although *Not I* focuses our attention on Mouth, not eye (costar-
ring Auditor as ear), the piece is a far more ambitious exercise in
dramatic perception than this unruly trinity might seem to imply. Although Mouth speaks, Auditor hears, and audience *sees,* Beckett establishes for the viewer of his work a visual horizon as well as an aural
stimulus closely approximating the "matter" of the monologue itself.
The "buzzing" in the ear is in fact the strange buzzing in our ears; the
spotlight on Mouth becomes the "ray or beam" we ourselves see, for
exposed to us is a "bright" figure I and a "shrouded" figure II (and,
therefore, in one of the various possibilities for the title of this play,
not I, but II):

> . . . what? . . . the buzzing? . . . yes . . . all the time the
> buzzing . . . so-called . . . in the ears . . . though of course
> actually . . . not in the ears at all . . . in the skull . . . dull
> roar in the skull . . . and all the time this ray or beam . . .
> like moonbeam . . . but probably not . . . certainly not . . .
> always the same spot . . . now bright . . . now shrouded . . .
> —*Not I,* p. 16

Not I makes an oblique reference to Beckett's *Film,* whose own jet-
tisoned title was *The Eye,* and which elaborates on Bishop Berkeley's
premise that "to be is to be perceived."[2] The Mouth which "stares"
at us from the stage, crying out to us from the depths of darkness, is
horrifying, like Buster Keaton's "eye" alternately staring and blinking
at us in the film. We are frightened by Keaton's "eye," just as Keaton
himself recoils from the "eyes" of everything around him—dog, cat,
fish, bird, a picture on the wall, the clasps on a manila envelope, the
silhouette formed by his *Murphy*-like rocking chair. In *Film,* where in
the first frame an enormous eye fills the screen to introduce the theme,
Beckett uses the eye as the central mechanism of perception that it is.
The eye functions both as the perception of the camera-spectator in
pursuit of the protagonist and as the perception of the protagonist in
pursuit of himself.[3] Beckett explains in the filmscript that the protagonist is in flight while the viewer is in hot pursuit: E (eye or camera

lens) searches for O (object or full facial exposure). The quest in this case is a visual metaphor for the character's ambivalence about recognizing his own authentic "I," or as Beckett attempts to clarify, it is a search "of non-being in flight from extraneous perception breaking down in inescapability of self-perception."[4]

In *Not I* such "agony of perceivedness" is experienced directly by Beckett's audience. As Mouth talks about fixing something with her eye, "lest it elude her," this is precisely the audience's visual limitation in focusing the lenses of its own eyes on the minimal image of Mouth. Such steady concentration on a minute object calls attention, quite literally, to the cameralike lenses we carry about with us all the time and bring with us, inevitably, to the theater:

> . . . no part of her moving . . . that she could feel . . . just the eyelids . . . presumably . . . on and off . . . shut out the light . . . reflex they call it . . . no feeling of any kind . . . but the lids . . . even best of time . . . who feels them? . . . opening . . . shutting . . . all that moisture . . .
>
> —*Not I*, p. 17

Not I forces to the drama's surface our own sensory deprivation in seeing, in perceiving, for this is our annoying situation as members of Beckett's audience. Like the "she" of Mouth's monologue, we have no idea what position Mouth or "she" is in—whether standing, or sitting, or kneeling. We see merely "whole body like gone." In Beckett, concentration on eyes leads before long to concentration on tears: "palm upward . . . suddenly saw it wet . . . the palm . . . tears presumably . . . hers presumably . . . no one else for miles . . . no sound . . . just the tears . . . sat and watched them dry . . . all over in a second," which takes us all the way back to the conclusion of Watt's fictional whatnot relationship with the celebrated Mr. Knott:

. . . he was no sooner in the public road than he burst into tears. He stood there . . . with bowed head, and a bag in each hand, and his tears fell, a slow minute rain, to the ground, which had recently been repaired. He would not have believed such a thing possible, if he had not been there himself. The humidity thus lent to the road surface must, he reckoned, have survived his departure by as long as two minutes at least, if not three.[5]

As we have difficulty seeing Beckett's "goings on" onstage in *Not I,* so we are constantly "straining to hear" the words in this rapid-fire monologue—we want to "piece it together" so that we ourselves can hit upon "something that would tell . . . how it was . . . how she—

. . . what? . . . had been . . . yes . . . something that would tell
how it had been." Auditor is apparently in a much more advantageous
stage position. He seems to hear the telegraphic monologue more clearly
than we do and, like Nell nagging Nagg in *Endgame,* he even urges
Mouth to be a little more accurate in her choice of words, a suggestion
Mouth accommodates when she can. Yet as members of this audience
we wonder how their dialogue is carried on. Auditor is "practically
speechless," and Mouth is only lips, teeth, and tongue, not, as far as
we can see, eye or ear.

In *Not I,* then, Beckett makes a visual statement concerning the
heart of this play, one which bears, moreover, an uncanny resemblance
to the thematic considerations of his earlier fiction. His most elabo-
rately plotted examination of the "I" takes place in the trilogy, *Molloy,
Malone Dies,* and *The Unnamable.* The opening paragraph of each
novel is a veritable epidemic of the first person singular: *Molloy* displays forty-one "I"s in forty-three lines, *Malone Dies* forty-eight "I"s
in forty-five lines, while the first thirty lines of *The Unnamable* repeat
the personal pronoun twenty-one times, not-I-ing the narrative situation as "it" goes along: "It, say it, not knowing what. Perhaps I simply
assented at last to an old thing. But I did nothing. I seem to speak, it
is not I, about me, it is not about me. These few general remarks to
begin with."[6] For Malone, disinheritance of the first person singular
becomes equivalent with dissolution of self. The release he longs for
is a ceremony of death followed by burial, but in his case the funeral
is a grammarian's.

I am being given, if I may venture the expression, birth into death, such is
my impression. The feet are clear already, of the great cunt of existence.
Favorable presentation I trust. My head will be the last to die. Haul in your
hands. I can't. The render rent. My story ended I'll be living yet. Promising
lag. This is the end of me. I shall say I no more.

—*Malone Dies,* p. 283

By the time of *The Unnamable* this obsession with pronouns has become the distillation of the narrative adventure itself:

But enough of this cursed first-person, it is really too red a herring. I'll get
out of my depth if I'm not careful. But what then is the subject? Mahood?
No, not yet. Worm? Even less. Bah, any old pronoun will do provided one
sees through it. Matter of habit. To be adjusted later. Where was I? Ah yes,
the bliss of what is clear and simple.

—*The Unnamable,* p. 343

The intrigue of a proper pronoun becomes here a vain quest for a reliable voice through which the narrator can effectively speak. He had formerly wasted his time with all those "moribunds," those Murphys, Molloys, and Malones when, as he says, "I should have spoken of me and of me alone." The search for a new voice thus emerges as the essential "story" of *The Unnamable;* the tension within the novel is in the struggle of this new voice to be born. It never makes it. For it is in the nature of Godot never to arrive. "The essential is never to arrive anywhere, never to be anywhere," but simply to go on talking, filling up the silence with words: "In the meantime no sense in bickering about pronouns and other parts of blather. The subject doesn't matter, there is none. Worm being in the singular, as it turned out, they are in the plural, to avoid confusion, confusion is better avoided, pending the great confounding." The action of speaking, novelistically speaking, is thus a process of formulating a new voice, an authentic pronoun, which remains all the while relentlessly elusive. In *The Unnamable* the narrator retreats, necessarily, into his nasty fictional habits, his worn-out tools, his Mahoods, his Basils, his Worms.

Within the mechanics of a novel this frustrating search for the elusive "I" is rich with implications, metaphysical as well as downright funny. If one can never *speak* of one's self, one can never *be* oneself:

Oh I know, I know, attention please, this may mean something, I know, there's nothing new there, it's all part of the same old irresistible boloney, namely, But my dear man, come, be reasonable, look, this is you, look at this photograph, and here's your file, no convictions, I assure you, come now, make an effort, at your age, to have no identity, it's a scandal.

—*The Unnamable,* p. 377

Lacking "convictions" in both a legal and moral sense, the nameless protagonist faces a dilemma already predicted by his "vice exister" in *Malone Dies:* "I say my pots, as I say my bed, my window, as I say me." For nothing finally belongs to these fictional heroes, neither the stories they invent nor the pronouns they are desperate to seize upon: "what am I doing in Mahood's story, and in Worm's, or rather what are they doing in mine?" Beckett's characters in the trilogy are not only barred from formulating an inventory of their possessions, they are excluded from a sense of personal identity as well: "perhaps I'm a dying sperm, in the sheets of an innocent boy." They are compelled to speak through unfamiliar voices in bodies unrecognized as their own.

Dislocated and finally disembodied speakers, removed from any recognition of self, they end up depreciated and diminished in a circle of endless frustration. The question of pronouns, of voices, is thus a grammatical metaphor for what is in reality an ontological disaster.

In *Not I*, however, Mouth is no longer searching for a coexistence with its authentic first person singular but is instead frantically running away from such an encounter. For what it fears in the "I" is its own bête noire. Like the figure of O tearing up a series of old photographs of himself in Beckett's "comic and unreal" *Film*, Mouth is hell-bent on obliterating any relationship to a questionable past. The staging of the play suggests both a religious confessional—Auditor's attentive cowled figure, the mouth pouring out words while the rest of the face remains hidden in darkness—and also a literally dislocated personality: an old woman listening to herself, yet unable to accept that what she hears, what she says, refers to her. All she seems able to acknowledge as her own is a painful "roar in the skull." Mouth's repeated refusal to identify with the first-person singular demonstrates self-immolation in the process of self-recognition, not self-probing, but self-mutilation.[7]

In Beckett's theater, however, we are drawn to such considerations of plot only secondarily. It is the visual impact, not the priorities of theme and variation, which commands our attention. "I am not unduly concerned with intelligibility," the playwright told Jessica Tandy. "I hope the piece may work on the nerves of the audience, not its intellect."[8] Having said that, let us consider the element of time for this play in performance, a unit of dramatic action Beckett has himself specified. He did not attend the original New York production, but he did see Billie Whitelaw's Mouth in London the following January in the fifteen-minute production directed by Anthony Page at the Royal Court Theatre. Miss Tandy, who planned to take the show on tour, was disheartened to learn from Beckett that he was revising the script after seeing the work staged at Sloane Square. Having heard that his scripts "are carefully annotated, like a musical score," she feared she would be forced to memorize the verbal onslaught all over again. He changed "only a word or two," took out most of the exclamation points, and specified eighteen minutes for the whole.[9] Though the slower pace was a lucky break for the actress, giving her more time to build the "character" and recite the monologue without error, the extra three minutes yields little to the audience in terms of its ability to understand in any rational way just what is going on. The experience for the audience of *Not I* remains primarily visceral, the effect hypnotic.

Beckett's concern with the preeminence of the visual figure and ground, what one critic has called "a poetry of moving images,"[10] is everywhere apparent in the sources frequently cited as having given him the idea for this play.[11] In a letter to James Knowlson postmarked April 30, 1974, he wrote, "Image of *Not I* in part suggested by Caravaggio's *Decollation of St. John* in Valetta Cathedral," which Beckett had visited during his stay in Malta in the fall of 1971. He told Hume Cronyn and Jessica Tandy, on the other hand, that Auditor was the real inspiration for the play. Sitting in a cafe in North Africa, which Beckett visited in 1969 and again in February–March 1972, he observed a solitary figure, completely covered in a djellaba, leaning against a wall. It seemed to him that the figure was in a position of intense listening—what could that lonely figure be listening to? Only later did Beckett learn that this figure leaning against the wall was an Arab woman waiting there for her child who attended a nearby school. To Alan Schneider, Billie Whitelaw, and A. J. Leventhal, Beckett mentioned an even earlier source for the elemental figure of Mouth: "I knew that woman in Ireland . . . I knew who she was—not 'she' specifically, one single woman, but there were so many old crones, stumbling down the lanes, in the ditches, beside the hedgerows. Ireland is full of them. And I heard 'her' saying what I wrote in *Not I*. I actually heard it." S. E. Gontarski reports that Beckett was dealing with material similar to *Not I* as early as 1963. In a discarded piece entitled "Kilcool" he was already preoccupied with the image of a severed head and the theme of involuntary speech: "every word is mild torture I would give all I have to stop, but I have nothing, nothing left, or there are no takers." In the "Kilcool" manuscript Beckett gives, moreover, a description of the stage to accommodate the image of a speaking head: "Old woman's face, 4 ft. above stage level. Slightly off centre, lit by strong steady light. Body not visible. Stage in darkness. Nothing visible but face. Gray hair drawn slightly back from forehead. Shrill . . . voice, bad enunciation."[12]

Implicit in each of these possible sources for *Not I* is the need to pinpoint dramatically an arresting visual impression. The scenic effect and the playwright's care in its preparation offer us an uncluttered platform from which a voice communicates dislocation, threat, and unease. Astonishing and uncompromisingly plain, the "set," empty yet full of darkness, never dulls the eye. Its closest analogues can be found in painting and film rather than in earlier drama. Beckett's stage space in *Not I* looks very much like a surrealist painting come to life. One thinks in particular of René Magritte, who fills his canvas not only with the same sense of *insolite,* but also with a similar *dépaysement* of the perceptual field: an eye is at once human and celestial, red shoes are concurrently toes and things to wear, a painting resting on an easel is simultaneously a work in progress and a window to the world. In surrealist film, too, one finds images as visually haunting and disruptive. *Un chien andalou,* which Salvador Dali made in 1928 with Luis Buñuel, features an extremely gruesome close-up of an eyeball slit by a razor blade, followed by one of Beckett's favorite images, used not only in *Not I,* but in *Molloy* and *Footfalls* as well: "like moon through passing . . . rack."[13] Eyes are projected all over the frame in Dziga Vertov's experimental movie of 1928 entitled *Man with a Movie Camera,* as they will later be in Beckett's own *Film.* Closer to the particular image of disembodiment in *Not I,* however, is Jean Cocteau's *The Blood of a Poet* (1930), where mouths materialize everywhere to throb and stare out at us from a black, white, and gray screen.

Images of physical fragmentation, which we typically associate with the avant-garde in the visual arts, have been far more difficult to organize onstage. Roger Blin, working in close collaboration with Beckett, directed the premiere of *Fin de partie* in Paris on a skull-like set in which the two windows served as "eyes."[14] Yet in this directorial choice the approach is interpretive, rather than fundamental to the stage setting. A more pronounced use of this motif, however, belongs neither to Beckett nor to his French director, but to the dada poet-playwright Tristan Tzara. The dramatis personae of *The Gas Heart* (1920) include not only Mouth and Eye, but Ear, Nose, Neck, and Eyebrow as well. The characters speak without reference to their names and repeatedly confuse one sense with another. Ear's line: "The eye tells the mouth: Open your mouth for the comedy of the eye." The play presents an outrageous visual spectacle which Tzara coordinates with the peculiar verbal strategy of the dialogue. As if obsessed, the characters repeat simple proverbs or employ elementary verbal patterns. Each speaks without specific recognition of his own individual plight, though Ear seems capable of identifying his problem with fragmentation in someone else: "He is not a being because he consists of pieces." It is not clear, however, to whom Ear's remark is directed or about whom it is said. In *The Gas Heart* characters speak, but no one of them appears to be listening to anyone else. The result is a series of disturbing, though more often amusing, nonsequiturs. Tzara's Mouth shows some indication of its own lack of being, but the metaphysical overtones are never seriously pursued: "Everyone does not know me. I am alone here in my wardrobe and the mirror is blank when I look at myself." Act 3 ends with the Ubu-esque dance of a gentleman fallen from a funnel in the rafters onto a table, followed in the script by a series of alphabetical doodles, variations of the letters Y, R, and perhaps V, shown to be related forms. Here the dramatic genre seems to have broken down completely. The final act of the "play" ends with some additional textual designs: a pen and ink representation of a blossom or flower with an arrow pointed toward an italic-scripted version of *l'Amour*. Unlike *Not I*, *The Gas Heart* ends with a crisis vaguely mimed, never dramatically realized.

Another work of the twenties, the youthful frivolity *Humulus the Mute* (1929), a sophomoric confection in four scenes by Jean Anouilh and Jean Aurenche, makes use of a Mouth-Auditor dualism to structure "a bitterly silly, pointless joke, in the purest Dadaist tradition."[15] Humulus, like Beckett's "she" before the "something" that happened to her in the field, has minimal verbal capacity: he can speak only one word per diem, a sugarplum generally reserved for the Duchess, his doting grandmother. And then he falls in love—he is silent for the eternity of a month, saving his word-hoard for an avalanche declaration. The moment arrives; Humulus, like Beckett's "she," suddenly breaks his silence. In a steady, unbroken flow of words, Humulus the mute makes his thirty-word proposal. But the fair Hélène, his Auditor, is, sadly, hard of hearing. The deaf demoiselle in distress takes a large ear trumpet out of the little black box on the handlebars of her bicycle as the curtain falls.

The Gas Heart and *Humulus the Mute* are, however, like the "Cornelian nightmare" called *Le Kid* that Beckett wrote while still a student at Trinity College, Dublin,[16] parodies of theatrical conventions rather than significant breakthroughs in the development of a new dramatic form. They hardly prepare us for the shock value of the disembodied vision so carefully fostered by Beckett in *Not I*. For the origins of this new theatrical mood we must turn to the work of directors rather than playwrights. In 1921, for example, Max Reinhardt produced his celebrated performances of Strindberg's *A Dream Play,* in which the scene in the Lawyer's office was acted against a background wall of real human faces, white, distorted, and staring. By using "black light" and "white faces," Reinhardt's revolutionary concept is now easily manageable onstage, though pictures of the original productions show that it was then necessary to direct the scene against dark curtains, the pale faces of suffering clients enshrouded in djellaba-like robes. Antonin Artaud's visual concept for the same play in the 1927–28 season at the Théâtre Alfred Jarry attempted to create a similar illusion of dismemberment. Artaud produced the play under the title *Le songe, ou Jeu des rêves,* adding some unusual details to the blocking: at one point the Lawyer, like Clov in *Endgame,* brought a ladder onstage and climbed to the top of it in order to get his overcoat from a hanger attached to a makeshift ceiling.[17] In 1949 Roger Blin, Artaud's friend, directed *The Ghost Sonata,* another Strindberg play of dreams and obsessions, a production Beckett saw twice, but only *after* and *because* Suzanne Beckett brought Blin the *Godot* typescript. (*En attendant Godot* became the director's fifth production.)[18] It is the tone suggested by the stagecraft of Max Reinhardt, Antonin Artaud, and Roger Blin, rather than the lighthearted exuberance of the dada/surrealist Paris playwrights of the twenties, that is at the core of Beckett's vision in *Not I* and the works that follow.

Unlike Tristan Tzara, who gives us virtually no clues concerning how his anatomical "characters" are to be brought to life onstage except to remind his actors "to give this play the attention due a masterpiece such as *Macbeth* or *Chantecler,*" and to treat the author "with no respect and . . . note the levity of the script which brings no technical innovation to the theatre," Beckett has been fastidious in providing information about how his work should be presented. The stage directions and the "Note" appearing in the printed version of *Not I* are an integral part of what constitutes the multidimensionality of a Beckett text. Concerned with translating an idea for a dramatic image into scenic space and patterns of speech and sound, the stage directions provide the proper cues to widen the resonances of the play:

NOTE

Movement: this consists in simple sideways raising of arms from sides and their falling back, in a gesture of helpless compassion. It lessens with each recurrence till scarcely perceptible at third. There is just enough pause to contain it as MOUTH recovers from vehement refusal to relinquish third person.

Stage in darkness but for MOUTH, upstage audience right, about 8' above stage level, faintly lit from close-up and below, rest of face in shadow. Invisible microphone. AUDITOR, downstage audience left, tall standing figure, sex undeterminable, enveloped from head to foot in loose black djellaba, with hood, fully faintly lit, standing on invisible podium about 4' high, shown by attitude alone to be facing diagonally across stage intent on MOUTH, dead still throughout but for four brief movements where indicated. See NOTE.

> As house lights down MOUTH's voice unintelligible behind
> curtain. House lights out. Voice continues unintelligible behind
> curtain, 10 seconds. With rise of curtain ad-libbing from text
> as required leading when curtain fully up and attention suffi-
> cient into [dialogue].
>
> —Not I, p. 14

Beckett's preoccupation with the making of his stage image has grown
steadily, and even in an earlier work such as *Happy Days* there seem
to be as many stage directions as there are lines to be recited. In *Play*,
where three characters involved in a sordid love triangle are literally
"potted" in large urns on a darkened set, Beckett seems as much concerned with the movement of his spotlight as he is with anything else.
Technology with a stage personality is the real hero of this dramatic
rendition, making *Play* a quartet rather than a trio. The privileged spotlight initiates the action, and controls it as well. Players recite their
lines only when their privacy has been invaded by this luminous source
of energy. Light, specifically stage light, is welcomed by the characters, each of whom exhibits Pozzo-like self-preoccupation: "Are you
listening to me? Is anyone listening to me? Is anyone bothering about
me at all?" One character even goes as far as to acknowledge, ironically, his own stage position: "Silence and darkness are all I craved.
Well, I get a certain amount of both. They being one." What the spot
discovers onstage has also been carefully considered:

> *Front centre, touching one another, three identical grey urns
> . . . about one yard high. From each a head protrudes, the
> neck held fast in the urn's mouth. The heads are those, from
> left to right as seen from auditorium, of* w2 [*Second Woman*],
> M [*Man*], *and* w1 [*First Woman*]. *They face undeviatingly front
> throughout the play. Faces so lost to age and aspect as to seem
> almost part of urns. But no masks.*
>
> *Their speech is provoked by a spotlight projected on faces
> alone . . .*
>
> *The transfer of light from one face to another is immediate.
> No blackout, i.e., return to almost complete darkness of open-
> ing, except where indicated.*
>
> *The response to light is not quite immediate. At every solic-
> itation a pause of about one second before utterance is achieved,
> except where a longer delay is indicated.*
>
> *Faces impassive throughout. Voices toneless except where an
> expression is indicated.*
>
> *Rapid tempo throughout.*

> *The curtain rises on a stage in almost complete darkness.*
> *Urns just discernible. Five seconds.*
> *Faint spots simultaneously on three faces. Three seconds.*
> *Voices faint, largely unintelligible.*[19]

At the end of the script Beckett will address himself to such practical stage matters as lighting, sound, and stage props:

> The source of light is single and must not be situated outside ideal space (stage) occupied by its victims.
>
> The optimum position for the spot is at the centre of the footlights, the faces being thus lit at close quarters and from below.
>
> When exceptionally three spots are required to light the three faces simultaneously, they should be as a single spot branching into three.
>
> Apart from these moments a single mobile spot should be used, swivelling at maximum speed from one face to another as required.
>
> The method consisting in assigning to each face a separate fixed spot is unsatisfactory in that it is less expressive of a unique inquisitor than the single mobile spot. . . .
>
> In order for the urns to be only one yard high, it is necessary either that traps be used, enabling the actors to stand below stage level, or that they kneel throughout play, the urns being open at the back.
>
> The sitting posture results in urns of unacceptable bulk and is not to be considered.
>
> —*Play,* pp. 62–63

In the first three manuscripts of *Play,* there is a separate spotlight for each character; following illumination, a five-second pause is indicated before each victim is required to respond.[20] The peculiar staging of placing his actors in urns (originally white boxes in earlier manuscripts of the piece) is considered only in the eighth of the ten typescript versions, where Beckett gives an indication of just how the actors might be able to fit themselves into the urns. In the French translation of this work, *Comédie,* players are given the option of repeating the entire action, which is indicated as a must in the English version. The explanation for the option is that the light, not the actors, may be growing tired.[21] In *Not I* Beckett reduces his stage image in *Play* one degree further: instead of a spotlight discovering a character planted in an urn, a "novel" situation already familiar to us from *The Unnamable,* the "character" discovered by the spotlight is now merely a disembodied mouth.

Beckett's concentration on the details of staging calls into question how far a playwright and a script can legitimately control production. In 1984 Beckett said, with specific reference to *Endgame,* that "any production which ignores my stage directions is completely unacceptable to me." Barney Rosset took the playwright's statement one step further: "In Beckett's plays the set, the movements of the actors, the silences specified in the text, the lighting and the costumes are as important as the words spoken by the actors."[22] As the occasional director of his own works, Beckett has filled each detailed notebook for production with possibilities and constraints "practically Cartesian" in their "organisation of information and insight."[23] Yet it is not so much each production of his work that Beckett seeks to control as it is the formal integrity of his private vision, what Billie Whitelaw said was, in the case of *Not I,* like "a piece of Schoenberg in his head."[24] In *Not I* Beckett's stage directions must be seen as a mandate for realization consistent with his visual image, rather than a call for any "authorized" staging. The New York production, for example, remained faithful to the script while developing totally original solutions to problems of mounting the show.

Jessica Tandy remembers her own "tremendous challenge" in portraying Mouth, "because it's so hard to do. I don't enjoy it—I don't enjoy having so much taken away." When she took this production on tour in October–November, 1973, her eyes onstage were covered by a black crepe blindfold in order to prevent them from reflecting any glare from the beam on her mouth: "There isn't another actor I can respond to—there isn't an audience I can see."[25] The actress, given limited visibility, can speak words and she can hear—that is all. She cannot even move head or body, for if she does so, the beam of light will shift its steady stream off her mouth and upset the consistent visual image designed for the audience. In this production Miss Tandy was therefore placed in a modified pillory, specially arranged to hold her head in place; she was also attached to a metal back brace to prevent any possible shift of position. Her teeth were then coated with a substance that would exaggerate their brightness and her lips were polished to attract the glare.[26]

Beckett specifies in his script that Mouth is "*about 8' above stage level,*" so it is necessary for the player to be elevated on an invisible box. The one used in New York was actually a rather complicated affair; covered with black velour, it was large enough to hold two people in its base: one held a spotlight focused sharply on Miss Tandy's mouth (a necessary contrivance since any spots originating from

the rafters would have resulted in extensive shadowing), while the other
held large cue cards from which Miss Tandy could, if necessary, con-
sult the text through her crepe blindfold (the prompter held a flashlight
to the cards, hence the black velour surrounding the box to absorb the
light). The "*invisible microphone*" in Beckett's stage directions calls
for amplification of the steady flow of words; this metallic prop had
to be as close to the actress as possible, not reflecting any light and
never in the spectator's view. For this production Beckett even specified the running time (eighteen minutes): so fast was the original speed
of the verbal frenzy that Miss Tandy's understudy could not get through
the monologue without some help. One night in Miss Tandy's absence
she performed the play by reading the text through her black crepe
blindfold from a teletape machine invisible to the audience. Billie
Whitelaw has similarly expressed the difficulty of performing in *Not
I*. Beckett advised her that she should "just say it"; he wanted it "flat,
no emotion, no color." "What happened to me," she told Mel Gussow,
"was a terrible inner scream, like falling backwards into hell." She
did two demanding seasons of *Not I* at the Royal Court and then taped
the play for television. "I will never do the play again," she said. "If
I did, I think I would lose my sanity."[27]

"*Downstage audience left*," the actor portraying Auditor has his
own problems. He is "*standing on invisible podium about 4' high,*"
enveloped "*from head to foot in a loose djellaba, with hood.*" At Lincoln Center Henderson Forsythe, elevated on a box, steadied himself
against a specially constructed railing to maintain a consistently even
balance; the djellaba was draped over the railing to reach the floor of
the stage itself. Cold stage lighting exaggerated his threatening verti-
calization. The resulting image for the audience was thus a larger-than-
life Auditor, a wordless giant who stood in mute contrast to the minimal image of a panting orifice. The dramatic conflict between the two
figures creates an extraordinarily rudimentary eye movement for the
theater audience. As Auditor makes his four gestures of raising arms
as specified in the script, forming a cruciform pattern, we shift our
own eyes from Mouth to Auditor, then back to Mouth again. Such
refocusing proves to be essential, for if we concentrate too steadily on
Mouth, we begin to discern in the stage darkness the actress behind
the mouth. By focusing and refocusing at least four times during the
course of the developing action, the audience's attention is absorbed
exclusively by images I and II; no interference of "extras" such as face
or body interrupts the stark antagonism between Mouth and Auditor,
that shadowy figure fully but faintly lit.

The visual relationship between Mouth and Auditor therefore makes out of what would otherwise be a one-woman show an unforgettable dramatic confrontation. Is Mouth the "she" of her own story, or is that "she" her menacing projection of Auditor? Neither situation accounts for the possibility that the "buzzing" in the head (". . . but the brain . . .") Mouth mentions might be a "stream of words" running through Auditor's own hooded head, nor the possibility that the silent figure of Auditor is as consistently wordless as the "she" of Mouth's story before the whatever-it-was that took place in the field. Mouth mixes memory with desire, reflecting her own ambivalence about the sudden change which she says has taken place in the field. With her "face in the grass," perhaps "she" has been raped: "just at that odd time . . . in her life . . . when clearly intended to be having pleasure . . . she was in fact . . . having none . . . not the slightest." When Alan Schneider asked whether or not "she" had been raped in the field, Beckett said he was surprised by the question; however, he didn't say yes and he didn't say no.[28] The Mouth-Auditor duality is susceptible to a variety of explanations, not the least of which would see Auditor as goad for "the words . . . the brain . . . flickering away like mad." Mouth keeps checking with Auditor to make sure she's got it right:

> . . . April morning . . . face in the grass . . . nothing but the larks . . . pick it up there . . . get on with it from there . . . another few—. . . what? . . . not that? . . . nothing to do with that? . . . nothing she could tell? . . . all right . . . nothing she could tell . . . try something else . . . think of something else . . . oh long after . . . sudden flash . . . not that either . . . all right . . . something else again . . . so on . . . hit on it in the end . . . think everything keep on long enough . . . then forgiven . . . back in the— . . . what? . . . not that either? . . . nothing to do with that either? . . . nothing she could think? . . . all right . . . nothing she could tell . . . nothing she could think . . . nothing she—what? . . . who? . . . no! . . . she! . . .
>
> *—Not I*, p. 22

Like an actress trying to remember her lines, Mouth checks back with the prompter in a desperate attempt to remember her cues. Sometimes she even reads the stage directions out loud, thinking that might help: "screams . . . (*screams*) . . . then listen . . . (*silence*) . . . scream again . . . (*screams again*) . . . then listen again . . . (*silence*)." Auditor, the goad, the prompter, raising its arms and letting them fall back, responds with a gesture of helpless compassion. Mouth, who has "some flaw in her make-up," never gets it "all right." In *Not I* the rehearsal goes on indefinitely.

It is, in fact, this peculiar convolution of possible explanations, backtracking on one another as surely as the words and phrases of Mouth's story itself, that contributes to the particular fascination of *Not I*. As we are forced to focus and refocus on figures I and II, so we are forced to focus and refocus on the series of overlapping explanations, encountering each time in a new light the same stubborn visual stimulus. Like a lens focusing on the same image from a multiplicity of camera angles, so Beckett makes us do with our eyes the work that is usually accomplished in cinema by what is called in this play "the whole machine." As it is with the multiplicity of possible interpretations of this work, so it is with the drama of the pronoun "I" itself. For *Not I* is also "not aye," what Beckett has called elsewhere "the screaming silence of no's knife in yes's wound."[29] Unlike Joyce's reverence for "the saying yes" of Molly Bloom, Mouth's monologue consists of negations, "no matter," "no love," "no moon," "no screaming," "no part," "no idea," "no speech," "no stopping," "no sound," "no response," "no feeling," not to mention the endless litany of "nots," "nevers," and "nothings." Parents are either "unknown" or "unheard of," and prayers go "unanswered." An individual is "speechless" and "powerless" and the situation is "painless." Human beings, those encountered in a courtroom, a supermart, or a public lavatory, are "incapable" of feeling or simply "insentient." Life on earth ("Christ, what a planet!" moans Mrs. Rooney) is reduced to Beckett's disconnected knot.

Mouth, another Beckett hero whose name begins with *M*, is hard of hearing, which accounts in part for the pattern of "what"s running through her monologue. But what exactly does Auditor do to elicit Mouth's reactive "what?" And is this "what?" reactive after all? Is the monologue perhaps a soliloquy, and the respondent yet another fiction in the story Mouth unfolds? We never know for sure. The dimly lit figure is so enshrouded in the folds of its stage costume that no gesture can be discerned apart from the four movements locking it into its life in the script. How can Mouth, a disembodied voice, hear or see? Onstage this is not a woman at all, only lips, teeth, and tongue, not eyes or ears. Can a mouth, "coming up to sixty . . . what? . . . seventy? . . . good God! . . . coming up to seventy," go for a walk in a field, looking "aimlessly" for cowslips one morning in Croker's Acres, a real place near Beckett's childhood home? Why "April," the month in which Nell and Nagg claim to have spent a romantic interlude on

Lake Como? Exposition is delayed indefinitely as Beckett, as usual, spares us the art and craft of denouement.

Within Mouth's story, nevertheless, we are bound to ask several questions. What really happened to the woman in the field, resulting in her uncontrollable talking? Did she suffer a "stroke," a seizure Beckett mentions in *The Unnamable*? Did this hypothetical stroke result in the strange "buzzing" she now hears in her head? When Jessica Tandy, attempting to build the character she was to portray, asked Beckett these questions, he responded by raising his arms, like his own Auditor, in a gesture of helpless compassion.[30] What happened in the courtroom and what happened to her in the supermart? Why are there several references to a child born before its time, then deserted by its parents ("so no love . . . spared that")? Why does she have "no idea what she's saying . . . imagine! . . . no idea what she's saying!"? Why did "she" get "half the vowels wrong" when she made a desperate attempt to blurt out some statement in the public loo? And why is God the punch line of some private little joke ("that notion of punishment . . . which had first occurred to her . . . brought up as she had been to believe . . . with the other waifs . . . in a merciful . . . [*brief laugh*] . . . God . . . [*good laugh*]")? "For God's sake!" the Director will lament in *Catastrophe*. "This craze for explicitation! Every i dotted to death! Little gag! For God's sake!"

Like Pozzo and Lucky, Hamm and Clov, Winnie and Willie, Krapp and his tape, urn and spotlight, Mouth and Auditor are tied down, and to one another—antagonism, *pure* and *simple,* and "in the ancient sense no doubt."[31] Remove Auditor from the stage, as was done in *Pas moi* when originally performed in Paris by Madeleine Renaud in 1975, and the dramatic conflict is gone. Beckett reluctantly agreed to this excision only because the Paris company ran into technical problems in staging the play. In April 1978, however, when he redirected *Pas moi,* he not only restored the towering presence, but gave it greater prominence at the end, where Auditor now covered his head with his hands "in a gesture of increased helplessness and despair, as if unable to bear any longer the torrent of sound." In the French version, moreover, Auditor adds a "gesture of blame" to his stance of helpless compassion.[32] The presence of Auditor onstage thus makes firm theater sense, providing those other auditors in Beckett's audience not only with a human witness to Mouth's suffering, but also an indispensable focal point from which to "see" the action of the play unfold. It is the eye, therefore, the rich itineraries of the audience's eye, which makes the full text of *Not I* emerge in performance.

The filming of *Not I* for television validates, not surprisingly, the appeal of this piece as a work for live theater. When, in 1976, the BBC received Beckett's permission to screen the play for home viewing, the technical problems of television adaptation were quickly apparent. The small screen simply could not accommodate the expanses of darkness integral to proscenium effect. In the first run-through, Mouth and Auditor were reduced and cramped on the television screen; it became obvious that this approach was not going to work at all.[33] A more effective adaptation, one more in tune with the limits and possibilities of a quite different visual medium, was clearly needed. The BBC asked Beckett if it would be possible for the camera to zero in on Mouth alone, omitting any picture of Auditor. Intrigued by the idea of a close-up, the playwright, always open to the adventure of exploring what a given medium can be made to do, agreed. What resulted from this decision was a stunning performance by Billie Whitelaw in what emerged as an entirely different play. On screen the actress' teeth, as in T. S. Eliot's "Hysteria," "were only accidental stars with a talent for squad drill." Like the persona of the same prose-poem, the viewer is inevitably "drawn in by short gasps, inhaled at each momentary recovery, lost finally in the dark caverns of her throat, bruised by the ripple of unseen muscles."[34] In close-up color Beckett's protagonist looked more like a vagina than a mouth. So obscene and frightening was the visual image, so horrifying and insistent was the verbal onslaught, that the play, originally shot in color, had to be neutralized by broadcast in black and white. Even then, *Not I* as a television play is so entirely shocking, so sensational in its effect on the viewer, that its merits as a work of dramatic literature seem to pass its audience by completely. On television *Not I* is, nevertheless, spectacular, though reports that Beckett prefers this version to the original have been largely exaggerated.[35]

In the theater Beckett makes us desperately conscious of the agonizing limitations of seeing, hearing, and speaking. Yet before *Not I* such constraints never seemed so theatrically enticing. Beckett's "drama stripped for inaction"[36] thus implies, ironically, an extraordinary amount of tension radiating from the stage, simultaneously visual, verbal, and aural. The "I" in Beckett's *Not I* is the most minimal dramatic character in Beckett's repertory, the ingenue who, like Godot, fails to make an appearance on the boards before the curtain comes down. But while waiting for this first person singular to arrive, Beckett sets into motion a multidimensional, multimedia extravaganza in which each sensory stimulus has the kinetic potential to stimulate all three sensory organs activated in this play. "Next to this," the Canadian actor Donald Davis said, "*Godot* looks like an MGM musical."[37] Balancing the spectacular with the literary, *Not I* opens up Beckett's theater to the evocation of a new kind of dramatic image, one he will explore with ever-increasing purity in the next play "of the *Not I* family,"[38] *That Time*.

CHAPTER THREE

That Time *on That Space*

In *That Time* drama and poetry come together in the urgency of an image which matches the urgency of the subject matter. Time, that time we spend in Beckett's theater, is rendered economically in terms of stage space. A severed head with "*long flaring white hair as if seen from above outspread*" is simultaneously character, stage prop, and stage set. The rest—and in this play Beckett will show it to be the far greater part—is silence. In *Not I,* as the playwright said, "she talks"; in *That Time,* "he listens."[1] Beckett told the actor Patrick Magee, who played Listener at the Royal Court Theatre in the spring of 1976, during a season mounted to mark the author's seventieth birthday, that he would never allow the two plays to run together on a double bill. *That Time,* he explained, was too self-consciously "cut out of the same texture as *Not I.*"[2] Exquisite visual compositions with a sense of spontaneous life, both works display a maximum of emotional intensity with a minimum of definition. "Less is more," reads Beckett's marginal note to his own copy of *That Time.*[3] Each play lasts a short time, a few minutes, yet each is timeless. Translating an obstinate proscenium into a small-scale performance space, Beckett creates in these works intimate chamber plays in which stage decor unveils interior consciousness. Remarkable for their use of light, the works restrict stage space and concentrate attention so that the audience's vision of the play is as controllable as the lens of a camera, constantly switching from wide angle to close focus. Holding the stage with confidence, *Not I* and *That Time* release to the full the latent power of a small playing space on an otherwise large set. The interaction of light and language, as carefully controlled as the blocking is confined, holds in fine balance a tiny cosmos in which private emotions have apocalyptic consequences. What each piece lacks in physical scale is replaced by intensity: what we watch in the theater is a play of the tortured mind, as vivid as a hallucination.

That Time is, however, something more than a replay of the same preoccupation with fragmentation and theatrical form so ferociously energetic in *Not I*.[4] In this case poetic language convincingly supports the scenic language of the drama. Responding to the difficulties Billie Whitelaw was having in rehearsing another late play, *Footfalls,* the playwright, concerned with the immediacy of the visual impact, once dismissed the dialogue as nothing more than a wrapper for a medicinal prescription: "What matters is the rhythm of the piece—the words are merely what pharmacists call the excipient."[5] In *That Time,* however, he depends on a tightly "scripted" language of concentrated poetic power for a somber reconciliation of sight and sound. The curtain rises on stage darkness which slowly fades up to unveil the immaculate clarity of a modernist's John the Baptist, a head without a body *"about ten feet above stage level midstage off center."* The device heightens the sense that one is watching a theatrical performance: this is a staged world, where script, direction, and design place props and characters at will. Like the desolation of a disembodied Dali head, the image we confront here is at once sensational and intimate, empty but filled with suggestion, deserted, yet full of mysterious panic, an apparition that is never explained and that never ceases to pall. Simultaneously subdued and monstrous, the presence cannot be easily rationalized. Yet onstage it is agonizingly real. As in the case of *Not I,* here too is a dramatic "text" that is not really accessible without performance. *That Time* is, as the author wryly notes in an early manuscript of the piece, like "something out of Beckett."[6] The audience looks out, staring and blinking ("all that moisture," Mouth jokes in *Not I*), and as it does so the lighting seems to shift its focus to work subtle changes of tone and angularity on the solitary head. But this is (mere) optical illusion. The spectral flesh becomes, nevertheless, as shifting and changing as the subject of our dreams—yet there is a nightmare hidden in this dream. Although the laws of optics do not normally permit such fragmented perspectives and sight lines onstage, Beckett makes us enter a new world instead of remaining within the theatrical modifications of this one: "This one is enough for you?" Gogo taunts Didi in *Waiting for Godot.* The style is antirealistic, but it is so primarily because it takes off from where realism comes to an end. For in *That Time* Beck-

ett gives visual existence to inner experience. Despite the morbidity
and sheer sensationalism of this unattended and unexplained figure,
the vision is surrounded by a sense of melancholy as well as mystery.

Beckett's *"old white face"* is, as stage directions make clear, a
"Listener," and what we watch him listen to is as literally and con-
cretely fragmented as the visual presence we see. Listener hears three
voices, *"coming to him from both sides and above,"* each taunting him
with parts of stories based on times gone by, a past recycled rather
than recaptured. This Listener cannot sleep, he cannot rest in peace,
for the fragments he hears awaken emotions he is forced to recollect
by no means in tranquility. Voices A, B, and C *"modulate back and
forth without any break in general flow"*; the play which begins and
ends with the eloquence of silence is abruptly violated, twice, by an
intermediate and artificial stage silence of *"10 seconds."* During each
"playing" silence Listener's breath, *"audible, slow, and regular,"* is
amplified to engulf the entire theater; after *"3 seconds"* the eyes suddenly open on us in desperate supplication, as if trying to remember
something, some image, some emotion, some sign of life that might
have once been lived, at least in the imagination. "It is not decided,"
Beckett commented, "whether he opens his eyes and the voice stops
for that reason or whether the voice stops and therefore he opens his
eyes."[7]

Like the woman in a chair in *Rockaby,* this listener's eyes appeal
for "More." The monologues of memory resume, but the helpless eyes
are still searching, still staring pathetically into the darkness—and at
us—until weary with weariness they, too, close out what little light
the fragments from the past have made them—and us—envision. We
are, once again in Beckett, inside a head, for the voices we hear, the
persistent dream and the continual delirium, are, as the stage directions
tell us, Listener's own. There is no release, no relief, no ritual puri-
fication, no denouement. What remains of the past is only the remnant
of a threnody, the tattered shreds of what might once have been a
coherent memory or a unified past. Nothing, literally nothing—certainly not the excesses of Wordsworthian lyricism—can bring back the
passing hour, for Listener finds no splendor in the grass and no glory
in the flower. His unenviable situation is, as we read in *Murphy,* "less
Wordsworthy." It is theater "spots," not "spots of time," that illuminate Listener here. "What remains of all that misery?" to quote the
voice from years gone by which Krapp, another listener, hears as he
prepares to make his last tape. Only a lonely trinity of isolated fragments offering no mediation and no resolution.

Fragments, however, come in different shapes and sizes, and those offered to us in *That Time* by voices A, B, and C evoke distinct though inconclusive vignettes of three separate moments chiseled from what Beckett calls in *Proust* "the poisonous ingenuity of time." Voice A presents a vivid picture of a grown man's return to see once again, for the last time perhaps, a setting sacred to youth, a ruin where he hid all alone as a child. B conjures from the ruins of the past an image of innocent young lovers sitting still "on the stone together in the sun on the stone at the edge of the little wood," vowing every now and then that they love each other—"just a murmur not touching or anything of that nature." And C sets his pentimento in a portrait gallery where a man, taking refuge from cold winter rain, sits all alone. It would be tempting to view the three scenes as in some way representative of three ages of man—youth, maturity, and old age—but the "unfacts," to quote Joyce, "did we possess them, are too imprecisely few to warrant our certitude."[8] All we have here are three pieces of what seems to be a much larger and a much more complicated puzzle. Our attempts to order the bits and pieces, to place them in a hierarchy, a chronology, and a progression, lead nowhere but back to the images themselves. As each voice returns again and again to amplify the scene it has already outlined, "like a car drawing up," Beckett said, "a machine,"[9] the images assume a reality and a plasticity of their own. Repeated, recycled, redistributed, rearranged, recombined, but never synthesized, the scenes impose themselves on every listener not so much as true but as real. In rehearsal Beckett defined the function of the three loudspeakers:

They are supposed to make the transition from one story to another clear. It is the same voice but the stories are taking place at different levels of time. The voices flow without serious interruption into one another and are only differentiated by the position of the loudspeakers on the left, in the middle and on the right of the 8 foot high platform on which the man is sitting. The B story has to do with the young man, the C story is the story of the old man and the A story that of the man in middle age. From a great distance he hears the voice he has today. . . .[10]

Conditioned by the limitations of perception as well as by the need to locate a semblance of order in the flux of fragmentary phenomena, the memories shaped by the voices from the past may be merely unfolding still another inescapable fiction: "In the frenzy of utterance," states a very different voice in the trilogy, "the concern with truth."[11] And as each voice moves forward, curiously, by turning inward and backward upon itself, it is not the possible fictivity of the process which ensnares our attention, but its overwhelming and outrageous authenticity. Echoes from the past, firm, compact, elegiac, melodic, and above all haunting, hover over us in the theater in much the same way as we see them threaten the security and serenity of Beckett's disembodied Listener. The tables have abruptly turned, and what we have taken as inhuman abstraction has suddenly, horribly become in this performance space the substance of our own nightmare. Trying to fit the fragments together into some concrete, coherent whole, we find that "that time" has disingenuously invaded "our time."

In order to accomplish this effect on his audience, Beckett relies very heavily in this play on the use of recording tape to stabilize his human voices. "It should be spoken quite quickly," Beckett told Klaus Herm when he directed him for the German premiere of *That Time* at the Schiller-Theater Werkstatt in West Berlin. "Since [the actor] can't physically manage to speak it without pauses, he should make pauses where it is necessary, which would then be cut out by the sound engineer."[12] The "Note" to the English text makes Beckett's intention clear:

> Moments of one and the same voice A B C relay one another without solution of continuity—apart from the two 10-second breaks. Yet the switch from one to another must be clearly faintly perceptible. If threefold source and context prove insufficient to produce this effect it should be assisted mechanically (e.g., threefold pitch).
>
> —*That Time*, p. 28

Like Beckett's work in radio drama, *That Time* features voices which quite literally "come out of the dark."[13] In this medium, however, it is "live" stage darkness that most convincingly renders A, B, and C the voices of Listener's interior consciousness. Unlike *Krapp's Last Tape*, where the source of broadcast is localized as a tape recorder, a central stage prop, in *That Time* the mechanism controlling the projection of voices is as disembodied onstage as Beckett's lonely head. Voices appear to come from nowhere in an offstage action whose only theatrical existence will be in sound. "On all sides megaphones possible technique something wrong there," we remember reading in *How It Is*, "recordings on ebonite or suchlike a whole life generations on ebonite one can imagine it nothing to prevent one mix it all up change the natural order play about with that."[14]

Language in *That Time* therefore offers us a new scenic space. Arranging the place of secondary scenes, it is language that not only underlines and follows the psychological journey of the character, but also precedes and creates it through an unveiling of the body by the words. Listener's eyes are open until he hears them; when the words come, *"eyes close."* There is no need to look for stage action when all the conflict is in language. As voice B asserts, it is the function of words, and ultimately of the memory comprising them, to try and fill the void. Despite the author's disclaimer, *That Time* thus represents a considerable advance over the dramatic structure of *Not I*. For here Beckett's technical solution allows his language to occupy center stage. His words need no longer be "mouthed" at breakneck speed by the spectacle of some gaping "hole" furiously opening and shutting. There is now enough time on "that space" to listen as the distinctive sound of Beckett's language rhythmically unfolds:

> B: . . . that time alone on your back in the sand and no vows to
> break the peace when was that an earlier time a later time before
> she came after she went or both before she came after she was
> gone and you back in the old scene wherever it might be might
> have been the same old scene before as then then as after with
> the rat or the wheat the yellowing ears or that time in the sand
> the glider passing over that time you went back soon after long
> after . . .
>
>   —*That Time*, p. 35

B's story is, as Beckett said, "the most emotional,"[15] and though it is not specifically printed in the script as traditional verse, the language here might be more immediately credited as such if we were to think about it, arranged spatially on the page, in the following way:

> . . . that time
> alone on your back in the sand
> and no vows to break the peace
> when was that
> an earlier time
> a later time
> before she came
> after she went
> or both
> before she came
> after she was gone
> and you back in the old scene
> wherever it might be
> might have been
> the same old scene

> before as then
> then as after
> with the rat
> or the wheat
> the yellowing ears
> or that time in the sand
> the glider passing over
> that time
> you went back soon after
> long after . . .

Rendered lyrically, Beckett's "dialogue" in *That Time* adds texture to his set, refines and intensifies it, and gives it the full illusionary power it demands. Stimulating the imagination of the audience, words introduce an illusion of force that emanates from emptiness. Less is more, but only if that less is in the right place. It is Beckett's poetic language that transforms the stage "lessness" that we see in *That Time* into something palpable and alive. The lesson is not only one in economy, but in functionalism: how to make an open, empty space, the stage, into an arena of dramatic tension.

"The purpose of the verse," T. S. Eliot wrote in his famous essay, "Poetry and Drama," "should be to operate upon the auditor unconsciously so that he will think and feel in the rhythm imposed by the poet." Such a rhythm needed to be developed in modern drama, Eliot argued, "until the audience feels, not that the actors are speaking verse, but that the characters of the play have been lifted into poetry."[16] Beckett's language in *That Time* instantly sets the tone of all that is to follow, just as his minimalist decor presents a distillation of the play. Such a well-crafted organization of stage space not only lifts his character into poetry, but his audience as well. The poetry in language corresponds to the poetry in gesture. In order to create through sound the clarity and symmetry that must ultimately result in visual realization, Beckett makes the facets of his stimuli, poetry and drama, into a unity of expression that gives his audience a sense of inevitability. In *That Time* stage technology wears a human face, the face, if not of tragedy, then of dramatic poetry.

Let us look more closely at how language works in this play. First and foremost, the three recorded voices appear in systematic repetition, each emanating from its distinct position offstage.

ACB	ACB	ACB	CAB
CBA	CBA	CBA	BCA
BAC	BAC	BAC	BAC

Quite literally here, individual units of "time" become actual in terms of stage space: language will "move" on this set from right to left and from left to right. Every sequential combination occurs except the logical one: ABC.[17] The play itself is divided into three "acts" separated by two intervals of silence. And though each act has twelve voiced units, only the final one fails to permute its established sequence, thus giving the impression, mathematically at least, of going on forever. Act 3, however, substitutes an inscrutable smile, "toothless for preference," for what has become in the course of this action the standard and expected deviation, thereby bringing definitive closure to the piece in a visual "curtain line."

But is Beckett's audience aware that such a tight system operates in the precise repetition? Probably not, yet what the audience does hear, what it slowly becomes conscious of in the course of performance, is what the playwright himself called the "desired legato" in the threefold source and the threefold pitch. "Between A, B, C there must be a transition without interruption," Beckett states, "as for example in music from A minor to C major. . . . A flow without beginning and end, without very much being emphasized or pointed up." Here Beckett employs theater technology to help his performer act as an exclusive medium for his words, which are to be recited "flat, inaudibly breathing, murmuring, dreamy, without any noticeable interruption." And yet the tone here is not so exclusively mechanical as Beckett's directions might imply. The end of each speech should be "somewhat slower," he admitted, "at the end of the twelfth speech slowest of all."[18] Beckett calls our attention to the various elements of sound as it exists in space, heightening the mood and forcing us to listen intensely. The structure of his play is dense, yet the narrative is swift. Huge events have been telescoped into a series of three tight scenes which define and enhance a fourth scene, the privileged one we see in the theater. The stark interplay of space, sound, and light therefore makes us sensitive to language and its repetition, which controls the flow of this work. In performance a pattern emerges, perceived subliminally, even though Beckett's audience may be at a loss to describe precisely how it has been formulated. As in *Not I*, this piece, too, must work on the nerves of the audience, not its intellect.

In *That Time* Beckett's rhythmic simplicity has therefore been responsible for a variety of interactions between time and space, some of the most important of which take place on the repetitive level of language itself. The vocabulary of this play is as rich in its use of relative time ("before," "after," "come," "gone," "now," "then," "earlier," "later," "soon," "still," "till," "when," "next," "first," "last") as it will be in the configuration of relative space ("there," "back," "in," "out," "among," "down," "up," "on," "off," "far," "near," "high," "low," "behind," "away"). Not only does Beckett make time actual in terms of stage space through the stationing of loudspeakers, but he also more fundamentally makes us see time in terms of space and space in terms of time once the recording process begins. Every memory of "that time" is tied to a memory of "that space," a ruin where a child hides, two lovers sitting together at the edge of a little wood, or an old man seated on a marble slab in a portrait gallery. Framing all of this, moreover, is Beckett's use of "stage time" and "stage space," the running time of the show and the finite dimensions of a given proscenium. For theater, unlike literature, is a medium of physical space as well as imaginative time. Stories and poems do not need to be staged.

The sound of human voices in this play is perceived as time is passing in the theater. Beckett's visual image, the face of his Listener, is the perceivable mask the character wears to perform an objective reality, a stage reality that exists outside of the time of the viewer's own experience. As time passes in performance, articulated sounds mark time. Verbal images resist time. And it is exactly by virtue of their relation to time that the verbal elements represent the process of decay. In the poetic language of this piece everything exists to appear and fade away. We move from "that time" to "no time." The verbal text therefore reenacts the plot. Beckett writes specific objects into the narration which will connect the three voices to each other as well as the Listener to the past. The images have been selected, moreover, to reflect and define the ruined, old white face that we see. The most foregrounded of these is a rock that appears, in various forms, in the three different memories recited by A, B, and C. At the ruins which A describes, the child sat on "a stone among the nettles" in order to look at his picture book. C details another incident in which "you" ducked into an art museum to get out of the rain and "found a seat marble slab and sat down to rest and dry off." B refers to "you" and a woman "on a stone together . . . you one end of the stone she the other long low stone like millstone." The three voices trigger memories that have therefore stimulated one another: A's rock evokes C's rock evokes B's rock. Memories are inextricably linked together by a plurality of images, as Beckett has previously shown in *Krapp's Last Tape:*

> I was there when—(*Krapp switches off, broods, switches on again*)—the blind went down, one of those dirty brown roller affairs, throwing a ball for a little white dog, as chance would

have it. I happened to look up and there it was. All over and
done with, at last. I sat on for a few moments with the ball in
my hand and the dog yelping and pawing at me. (*Pause.*) Moments. Her moments, my moments. (*Pause.*) The dog's moments. (*Pause.*) In the end I held it out to him and he took it
in his mouth, gently, gently. A small, old, black, hard, solid
rubber ball. (*Pause.*) I shall feel it, in my hand, until my dying
day. (*Pause.*) I might have kept it. (*Pause.*) But I gave it to
the dog.
Pause.
Ah well . . .

—*Krapp's Last Tape,* pp. 19–20

In *That Time* A's rock is set among ruins, and this evocation clearly
connects with the fragmented figure onstage. This rock is set near
"Foley's Folly bit of a tower still standing all the rest rubble." In the
theater it is now Listener's face which towers above the audience. The
marble bench in C's narration is a stone seat in a picture gallery, but
it is also a stone slab to mark a grave. C reminds Listener that he
thought of his mother lying in her grave when he huddled on the cold
slab trying to get warm.

The rock on which the lovers sit in B's narration has overtones
equally ominous. While it would not be unusual to find a millstone
near a field of wheat, we do not hear that this is a millstone; rather,
it is a "stone like millstone." Three out of the four apostles who wrote
the Gospels quote some pretty grim words by Jesus with regard to
millstones: "And whosoever shall offend one of these little ones that
believe in me, it is better for him that a millstone were hanged about
his neck, and he were cast into the sea." When A remembers sitting
on yet another stone, "down on a step in the pale sun a doorstep say
someone's doorstep," he makes a similarly forbidding biblical allusion: "the passers pausing to gape at you quick gape then pass pass
on pass by the other side." "That is a story of depersonalization,"
Beckett commented, "seeing oneself as an object." Klaus Herm spot-
ted the reference during rehearsal, even though Beckett said, "I looked
it up, but I didn't find it, aha, Luke . . ."[19] What Beckett did not tell
Herm, however, was that the allusion came to him by way of Apol-
linaire: "Passons, passons, puisque tout qui passe." Death and fragmentation hover beneath the surface of such allusions, darkening the
tone of the recurrent imagery and the verbal motifs: the lovers never
touch and their hard bed is "like millstone," the agent of destruction
and damnation.

The symmetrical structure of language in *That Time* will evoke still other images equally time-bound. In this play the child is not only father to the man, but to the corpse as well. In the "flotsam" voice B memorializes the image of a drowned rat, C remembers the Doric "colonnade," another stone marker, on the terminus of the Great Southern and Eastern, "all closed down" and "crumbling away," while A uses a figure of speech which brings us all the way back to Adam, whose loss of innocence first made man conscious (so the story goes) of his own frail mortality. Voice B invokes an image so strikingly reminiscent of Listener as not to be overlooked: "suddenly there in whatever thoughts you might be having scenes perhaps way back in childhood or the womb worst of all that old Chinaman long before Christ born with long hair." The allusion to Lao-Tze, the "extreme eastern sage" of *How It Is,* connects the child of the ruins to the old, white-haired man whose face appears onstage, for this ancient Chinese philosopher (so *this* story goes) was born with the hair of an old man.

Seasonal imagery as well as the frequent reference to the time of day will also make us conscious of things passing on and closing in, increasing the atmosphere of claustrophobia inherent to this play. It will not be surprising to hear the voice of old age attach itself "always" to "endless winter"; his persona stares "there alone with the portraits of the dead black with dirt and antiquity" while late afternoon approaches "closing time." The memories of childhood and youth, however, develop a more complex strategy in their relationship to temporality. The young lovers appear "no better than shades" in B's evocation, a description more suitable to an impressionistic canvas in C's portrait gallery than to naturalistic detail:

> no sight of the face or any other part never turned to her nor she to you always parallel like on an axle-tree never turned to each other just blurs on the fringes of the field no touching or anything of that nature always space between if only an inch no pawing in the manner of flesh and blood no better than shades if it wasn't for the vows . . .
>
> —*That Time,* pp. 32–33

B's mournful lovers sit beneath a blue sky, but their sun is "sinking" as they face "downstream." There are "no signs of life" and the wheat is "turning yellow." Childhood, like youth, takes place in daytime, but among rubble and nettles, the same prickers mentioned in *The Lost Ones:* "there was childhood for you." In these ruins only a "pale morning sun" brings "light coming in where the wall had crumbled away."

This reclusive child, however, hides from the sun as he pores over his book "well on into the night . . . and they all out on the roads looking for him." It is late, "eleven or twelve in the ruin"; "moonlight" replaces this "pale sun" as the boy sits alone "making up talk breaking up two or more talking to himself being together that way where none ever came." Old age comes much too soon: this particular description of the child is abruptly cut off and replaced by C's "always winter then endless winter year after year as if it couldn't end the old year never end like time could go no further." Seasons change and daylight changes, yet time within this landscape, bringing with it mutability in place of transcendence, is always "the same." As in *Waiting for Godot,* "the light gleams an instant, then it's night once more."

The community of images in *That Time* makes not only time collapse, but space as well. C, for example, moves swiftly from a scene in a portrait gallery, to a scene in a public library, to yet another scene in a post office:

> always winter then always raining always slipping in somewhere when no one would be looking in off the street out of the cold and rain in the old green holeproof coat your father left you places you hadn't to pay to get in like the Public Library that was another great thing free culture far from home or the Post Office that was another another place another time . . .
>
> —*That Time,* p. 34

Though it might be in the National Portrait Gallery "far from home" in London where C remembers seeing "a vast oil black with age and dirt someone famous in his time some famous man or woman or even child such as a young prince or princess some young prince or princess of the blood black with age behind the glass," the Post Office, so memorable in *Murphy,* evokes memories of Beckett's Dublin. The kaleidoscope of a possible English time followed by an Irish space links C's story more securely to A's settings at Foley's Folly, the ferry in Dublin's harbor, and the Doric terminus of the Great Southern and Eastern, not to mention the geography of the repressed lovers in B's Gaelic pastoral. In this play space, like time, has been patterned to create an illusion of free association, making connections among images rather than among Anglo-Irish urban landmarks. In this sense, its fluid existence is no different from the pronoun "you." Clearly the "you" and the "you" and the "you" in voices A, B, and C are distinct from one another in that each owes its existence, its shape, its desires, its very loneliness, to a different moment in time. But the child is "you"; the one who returns is "you"; the old man is "you"; Listener is "you"; the audience is "you." Every object, every space, every memory exists in time: you are different, but you are the same.

In its literary borrowings, as we have already seen in the case of specific biblical material, *That Time* will be as free in its use of time as it is condensed in its use of space. Its obsessive referentiality to other works by the same author make it unabashedly like "something out of Beckett." The ruins here resemble the "ruins true refuge" in the "false time" Beckett weaves for us in *Lessness;* the "always winter" repeats the "always winter some strange reason" of Mouth's seasonal solstice in *Not I;* the stones recycle the subject of a projected story Malone never has time to tell, the hilarious episode of Molloy's sucking stones, as well as "the earth abode of stones" of Lucky's speech in *Godot;* the "old green holeproof coat," inherited from a father, has been worn by several other heroes in a variety of shades and altered sizes; the figures "just blurs on the fringes of the field" reactivate "Maddy Rooney, née Dunne, the big pale blur" of *All That Fall;* "stock still always stock still" animates once again the static and immobile attitude of the seated figure in *Still;* and the toothless smile of Listener at the play's curtain resurrects the specifically dental emptiness of Molloy as well as the orthodontial virtuosity of Sucky Moll's "bare canine" shaped like a Cross to represent "the celebrated sacrifice" in *Malone Dies.* There will be other echoes as well: the "did you ever say I to yourself in your life come on now" of *Not I;* Krapp's "turning-point that was a great word with you"; the dead rat from *Watt;* the blue eyes of *Lessness;* the pale morning sun of *Murphy* and *Still;* the "passers pausing to gape" of *Film;* the "glider passing over" from *Malone Dies* and later from *Company;* the "eyes passing over you and through you like so much thin air" of Miss Fitt's distress in *All That Fall* and Mr. Endon's in *Murphy;* the "come and gone" of the blocking in *Come and Go;* the "voice without quaqua on all sides then in me" of *How It Is,* which shares with this piece a topography of "slime"; and the long white hair that will later feature so prominently in *Ohio Impromptu.*

Close readers will uncover still other Beckett shards, but in the process of unearthing the remnants of the playwright's uncanny self-reference, one must not neglect the "Shakespeherian Rag"[20] bubbling to the surface of this particular text. Although *That Time* is hardly the same baroque composition Shakespeare had been able to make in "That time of year thou mayst in me behold," the play shares with Sonnet 73 the atmosphere of "yellow leaves," "sunset," "twilight," and "Death's second self, that seals up all in rest." Shakespeare's "birds" from the same sonnet may be only a drowned rat floating downstream as Beckett renders it here, but a vague recollection of the "bare ruin'd choirs where late the sweet birds sang," ominously confused with the deathly foray of a rodent, still floats like flotsam and jetsam on the murky surface of *That Time*. The rhythmic incantation of "that time" ("was that another time all that another time was there any other time was there any other time but that time"), a poignant refrain that appears at least twenty-one times in the few pages of the playscript, parallels Sonnet 49 as well ("Against that time, if ever that time come"), where the same fretful phrase repeats itself three times in the narrow room of the poem's fourteen lines. "Devouring Time," "swift-footed Time," is the classic theme Beckett shares with the Bard. But whereas Shakespeare as sonneteer triumphs over time in the immortality of verse, Beckett as playwright mirrors "only dust and not a sound . . . something like that come and gone come and gone no one come and gone in no time gone in no time." The light slowly fades and the curtain slowly falls. Only fragments remain, Yeats' "Old kettles, old bottles, and a broken can, / Old iron, old bones, old rags." There are no more sugared sonnets; Hamm's supply of "sugarplums" has run out long ago. We are in the same situation as Listener, isolated and alone: "We cannot know and we cannot be known."[21] Riveted in our seats in the theater, like Beckett's frozen figure sitting at an empty window in *Still*, we too are still, still "listening for a sound." As stage darkness erases Beckett's disembodied image, silence envelops Beckett's listeners. In *That Time* voices come and go, but their time onstage is all too brief a fugue. They disintegrate, dry as dust, into silence and darkness, into "something to do with dust something the dust said." Even breathing stops. There is, finally and brutally, nothing: only the vague reveries, the blurred image, the faint voices we have heard, like Hamm, "dripping" in our head during that time we have spent listening to a new kind of choral poetry emerge in Beckett's theater.

The time spent watching this play therefore involves us in a theatrical enterprise whose form is simple only by deception. The play seems longer than it actually is, perhaps the longest fifteen or twenty minutes in theater history, because in condensing so much, Beckett reverses our normal expectations for how stage time functions. Unlike most plays, which use theater space to make real time pass more quickly within the confines of a scene, Beckett stretches out dramatic time. An instant on this new stage has never seemed quite so long before; and in no sense can *That Time* be considered a "dramaticule," an interlude, or a short. "All of Mr. Beckett's plays are full-length; some of them are longer than others, that's all, but they're all full-length," replied Alan Schneider to a question concerning *Rockaby* as a one-acter.[22] "Gradually of all things a face appeared," and as it does so in the climactic moment of C's experience when he stares at a *portrait d'un inconnu* under glass, it does so onstage in *That Time,* where the playwright gives voice to that which is normally mute, shifting our attention from recounted tale to spoken mental processes and dissolving boundaries between the naturalistic and the supernatural. In this play time and space are made "perceptible to the heart"[23] in a "text" for live performance that is both boldly personal and stylistically innovative. In *Waiting for Godot* "all the dead voices" make a noise— or rather they "rustle"—in Estragon's simile, "like leaves." In *That Time* Beckett develops a poetic metaphor several steps further, lifting it into a concise and compelling dramatic image. The playwright's use of stage space, his insistence not on time but on *that time,* and his coordination of all that is poetic in the visual and the verbal, semi-human and semimanufactured, will provide *Footfalls* with the unity of a formal design to shape and contain the chaos of character.

CHAPTER FOUR

Footfalls to Infinity

As the curtain rises in *Footfalls* we are relieved to find a human being onstage who is, as far as the eye can see, of "the same species as Pozzo," made "in God's image." In this play Beckett discards abstraction for the simplicity of a surprisingly realistic image, the stark figure of an isolated woman treading a premeditated path from right to left, back and forth, like one of "Dante's damned."[1] Rigid, bent, restless, tense, frightened, and pitiful, she is fated to a stage existence that makes us "hear the feet, however faint they fall." The seeming abandonment of physical fragmentation in this play, however, does not so much signal a retreat from the dramatic material of *Not I* and *That Time* as it does a further development of the minimalism central to the impact of Beckett's late works in performance. Any trace of naturalism in the stage apparatus for *Footfalls* is quickly and quietly disposed of, and, as we have come to expect in Beckett's theater, it is lighting which serves as realism's principal agent of destruction. The atmosphere of this play is established by light that "should be as weak as possible without becoming unbearably dark. . . . A great coldness and tautness without sentiment."[2] "*Dim, strongest at floor level, less on body, least on head,*" stage lights confine the acting area and concentrate attention on the "*clearly audible rhythmic pad*" of nine steps on a strip downstage, parallel with front, "*width one metre, a little off centre audience right,*" but growing progressively shorter and narrower after each fade-out.[3] No feet can be discerned; May is shrouded in a "*worn grey wrap hiding feet*" which trails behind her. As in the radio play *All That Fall,* it is the sound of footsteps, not the sight of

52

any fractured part of the human anatomy, which determines the endless time, the boundaries of space, and the rhapsodic pacing of the "Faint, though by no means invisible" subject of this play: "the motion alone is not enough."

> Footfalls echo in the memory
> Down the passage which we did not take
> Toward the door we never opened
> Into the rose-garden. My words echo
> Thus, in your mind.
> > —T. S. Eliot, "Burnt Norton"[4]

Footfalls, which alert Celia to the butler's existence in *Murphy*, and which remind Voice C of a museum guard shuffling behind him in *That Time*, accompany other sounds: in addition to two voices, one onstage and one off, a faint chime each time growing fainter divides the play into three acts and provides its dark, empty closure of diminishing space, diminishing light, and diminishing sound. Like so many Beckett characters before her, May, another lead with an *M*, walks, talks, and hears voices; she cannot stop revolving "it all" in her "poor mind."[5] "Who he," we ask like one of Beckett's more inquisitive heads in *Play*, "and what it?" We never know for certain; every element of this play's exposition will be rendered partial and fragmentary. Knowledge is nowhere categorical, everywhere conditional. Besides footfalls and chimes, all we hear is May's voice and another low female voice *"from dark upstage."* In the preproduction version of the script, published as a separate volume by Faber, V (Voice) candidly admits, "My voice is in her mind." Beckett omitted this in revision, thereby understating a crucial plot line of the dramatic situation and widening its complexity. He added, however, a critical prefix. In May's monologue, "Dreadfully—" is changed to the suggestive "Dreadfully un—," a mysterious negation which further enhances the range of narrative possibility.[6] "It all. . . . It all," like the carafe of water tempting the protagonist in *Act Without Words I*, forever eludes our fingertips. In *Footfalls* there are "limits," as Beckett writes in his much quoted addendum to *Watt*, "to part's equality with whole." Trapped, like May, in some unnamable net, the title of Lucky's dance in *Godot*, fact and interpretation are potential rather than resolved. We retrace the same steps, back and forth, right to left, powerless to stop the flow this drama carefully sets in motion. It is Beckett's audience that can never cease "revolving it all."

In *Footfalls* Beckett provides us with a compensatory formal coherence to replace any easy apprehension of plot summary. What haunts us in the separate sections of this work is the curious disconnection of similitudes composing the tension between the acts. The play opens with May's anguished apostrophe to her dying mother, an appeal for contact which the faraway maternal voice answers from Beckett's radiant void: "There is no sleep so deep I would not hear you there." M (May) and V (Voice) establish a dialogue which is simultaneously time present and time past. Although the mother's voice is an echo from a remembered past, May speaks to her in the stage presence dramatized before our eyes. In this act Beckett liberates his unity of time from the limited frame of past and present and replaces it with a perspective more appropriate to the interior space of human consciousness. Onstage it can only be "that time," May's endless moment of purgatory in which she relives the past in her "poor" mind. "Words are as food for this poor girl," the playwright said. "They are her best friends." Here time neither progresses nor stands still; like a "metronome," a word Beckett used to describe the walking in this play, time merely continues its rhythmic pacing.[7] This is stage time plotted on stage space, and though both may at first appear empty to the spectator's view, the possibility of their being filled fills them. Time past, time present, and "that time" recaptured in drama are subject to a dimension even more puzzling than this. We never know for sure whether the scenes we witness are lifted from personal history or are part of some fictional work in progress, truth or mere illusion. "You are composing," Beckett advised Hildegard Schmahl at the Schiller-Theater Werkstatt. "It is not a story, but an improvisation. You are looking for the words, you correct yourself constantly. You are in the church with the girl. The voice is the voice of an epilogue. At the end it can't go any farther. It is just at an end."[8] As we seek to impose limits on Beckett's fugitive pacing of "that time," all footsteps lead us in the wrong direction. Act 1 closes in a slow fade-out; the audience, like May, is left "revolving it all" as the chime rings "*a little fainter,*" announcing that our time for this act is up.

Act 2 of *Footfalls* is a solo, a piece of monologue for the same offstage Voice to the accompaniment of May's silent but nevertheless startlingly reactive stage blocking. In this scene May is a steady listener on a slightly smaller strip as several tempting narrative details accumulate. "She" has "not been out since girlhood" and "she" is now in "the old home . . . the same where she began. . . . Where it began. . . . It all began." Voice develops her story by creating a "semblance" of dialogue within her monologue, a two-character exchange between protagonists identified as "the mother" and "May." There is, then, within her own singular register a simulation of two additional voices, one of which may be her own. Voice's play-within-a-play is a drama in the making, for her script contains stage directions and background information marked by tentativeness and subject to revision. "The same where she—(*Pause.*) The same where she began" soon becomes "Where it began" and a word searched for is eventually found: "When other girls of her age were out at . . . lacrosse she was already here." Other narrative elements are temporarily suspended, to be more appropriately incorporated later on for a better fit in the story or until more inspiration comes:

> The floor here, now bare, once was— (M *begins pacing. Steps a little slower.*) But let us watch her move, in silence. (M *paces. Towards end of second length.*) Watch how feat she wheels. (M *turns, paces. Synchronous with steps third length.*) Seven eight nine wheel. (M *turns at L, paces one more length, halts facing front at R.*) I say the floor here, now bare, this strip of floor, once was carpeted, a deep pile.
>
> —*Footfalls*, p. 45

Voice anticipates some of our own questions and, as she does so, she directs our attention to May's wordless motion on the stage before us, fleshing out the action and urging us to attend to it more closely. Her words fall on waiting ears: in this play lighting is minimal and movement is repetitive, so the audience appreciates any interpretative focus it can get, "strange or otherwise." When Voice urges us to "see how still she stands," May stands still, *"facing front at R."* "Stark, with her face to the wall," May "fancies she is alone." But the wall May stares at is the imaginary fourth wall of the proscenium. Voice reminds us that we are in the theater: this floor, now bare, once was carpeted with "a deep pile," perhaps for some other scene in some other play.

> Does she still sleep, it may be asked? Yes, some nights she does, in snatches, bows her poor head against the wall and snatches a little sleep. (*Pause.*) Still speak? Yes, some nights she does, when she fancies none can hear.
>
> —*Footfalls*, p. 46

Voice has an odd sense of humor and a Beckettian addiction to puns: on your feet night and day causes another sort of "deep pile" from the one we recall in a Kidderminster carpet from *Mercier and Camier*.

When she asks us to note "how feat she wheels," echoing Polixenes' observation about Perdita in *The Winter's Tale* ("she dances featly"), we watch May's neat, smart, and dexterous shift of course. Her feet now pace in the opposite direction, this time from stage left to stage right. There are, therefore, two Mays, the May of Voice's story and the "semblance" we see in the theater wearing, as the playwright said, "the costume of a ghost . . . worked like a cobweb."[9] What is each May thinking when she speaks aloud, believing she is all alone but all the while reciting her lines before a paying clientele, the audience? Voice maintains that her configuration of May is trying to tell not how it is, the subject of another Beckett narrative, but "how it was": "It all. . . . It all." Fade-out and darkness once more, the chimes *"a little fainter still."*

The third act in *Footfalls* presents us with a second monologue, but this time of a more conventional sort: this extended speech belongs to the May we can see and therefore constitutes an "outward bound soliloquy."[10] Now it is Voice's turn to maintain a discreet offstage silence, though in doing so her absent "presence" lurks in the wings. May introduces her big scene by heralding it as a "sequel" ("Seek well"), thus setting us up for the next installment to continue the discourse of some narrative preceding this one.[11] This is in no case to be a sui generis undertaking.

May's soliloquy, however, displays its relationship to Voice's monologue more in technique than in substance. She, too, is telling a story whose end she doesn't know, this one about Amy, anagram for May, and Amy's mother, old Mrs. Winter, "whom," we are told, "the reader will remember." "One must sense the similarities of both narratives," Beckett observed. "Not so much from the text as from the style, from the way the text is spoken."[12] May, too, displays the writer's self-correcting craft, the "prolonged creative effort" Hamm complained of long ago: "A little later, when she was quite forgotten, she began to—(*Pause.*) A little later, when as though she had never been, it never been, she began to walk." A little later in structuring her story May will replace the prosaic "she said" with the infinitely more effective "she murmured," conveying with this substitution the right emotional mood to the scene she seeks to portray. For the narrative style May uses is something more impressive than a parody of the elements she might have picked up while listening to Voice. Her poetic vein runs deeper: onstage we watch her construct an elaborate verbal image, one which, moreover, defines more precisely than anything Voice could come up with the visual image we see in the theater:

> The semblance. (*Pause. Resumes pacing. Steps a little slower still. After two lengths halts facing front at R.*) The semblance. Faint, though by no means invisible, in a certain light. (*Pause.*) Given the right light. (*Pause.*) Grey rather than white, a pale shade of grey. (*Pause.*) Tattered. (*Pause.*) A tangle of tatters. (*Pause.*) A faint tangle of pale grey tatters. (*Pause.*) Watch it pass—(*pause*) watch her pass before the candelabrum how it flames, their light . . . like moon through passing . . . rack. (*Pause.*)
>
> —*Footfalls,* p. 47

In telling her tale imagistically May will not shy away from using arcane vocabulary. Her use of ellipsis indicates that she considers words carefully and pauses in order to give them their full dramatic effect. Her "rack," a wind-driven mass of high, often broken clouds, shows us that she has learned a thing or two from Voice after all. The mentor's use of "feat" had been not merely recondite, but archaic as well. "I use only the words you taught me," Clov tells Hamm. "If they don't mean anything any more, teach me others. Or let me be silent." May's image of the moon condenses a number of new meanings: as a representation of the goddess Diana, the moon symbolizes virginity, thus extending the implications in V's speech of a young girl who never played at "lacrosse." Shades of what Malone calls "the celebrated sacrifice" aside for the moment, "lacrosse" means transition, a commitment to maturity this ageless shadow never seems to have made. Billie Whitelaw recalls a joke Beckett shared with her when he decided to insert the word "lacrosse" into the script of *Footfalls,* "just because he liked the sound of it and because it conjured up the image of the cross." "Oh, God," said Beckett as he scribbled it in, "tomes are going to be written about this."[13]

May, like Voice, will also set about to create a "semblance" of dialogue in her long speech which comprises the third act of this play. Here the two characters in *Footfalls* follow a pattern we can identify in Beckett's earlier plays. In *Endgame* Nagg, an accomplished raconteur, uses this technique when he tells his joke about the tailor and a pair of pants. "I tell this story," he interjects, "worse and worse." Hamm picks up the same motif in working out his own "chronicle," though in this case the names of his characters remain undetermined at this early—but endless—stage of composition:

> It was then he took the plunge. It's my little one, he said. Tsstss, a little one, that's bad. My little boy, he said, as if the sex

mattered. Where did he come from? He named the hole. A
good half-day, on horse. What are you insinuating? That the
place is still inhabited? No, no, not a soul, except himself and
the child—assuming he existed. Good. I enquired about the
situation at Kov, beyond the gulf. Not a sinner. Good. And you
expect me to believe you have left your little one back there,
all alone, and alive into the bargain? Come now! . . . Gradually I cooled down, sufficiently at least to ask him how long
he had taken on the way. Three whole days. Good. In what
condition had he left the child. Deep in sleep.
(*Forcibly.*)
But deep in what sleep, deep in what sleep already?
                                             —*Endgame,* pp. 52–53

The line Hamm assigns to his fictional hero, "Deep in sleep," will be
repeated by Voice in the opening lines of *Footfalls* as a variation on
the same parent-child theme:

> M: Mother. (*Pause. No louder.*) Mother. (*Pause.*)
> V: Yes, May.
> M: Were you asleep?
> V: Deep asleep. (*Pause.*) I heard you in my deep sleep. (*Pause.*)
>   There is no sleep so deep I would not hear you there.
>   —*Footfalls,* pp. 42–43

Krapp has been a writer of dialogue too, not only on the tape he listens
to ("Let me in") but as we see him speak this "*late evening in the
future*" into his machine:

> Fanny came in a couple of times. Bony old ghost of a whore.
> Couldn't do much, but I suppose better than a kick in the crutch.
> The last time wasn't so bad. How do you manage it, she said,
> at your age? I told her I'd been saving up for her all my life.
>   —*Krapp's Last Tape,* pp. 25–26

May can be similarly irreverent in the development of dialogue: "What
is it, Mother, said the daughter, a most strange girl, though scarcely
a girl any more. . . . What is it, Mother, are you not feeling yourself?" As Amy may have done in May's story, Krapp remembers attending an evening church service, though his "deep" slumber there
has been abruptly terminated: "Went to Vespers once, like when I was
in short trousers. . . . Went to sleep and fell off the pew." Winnie,

too, counts on the creation of dialogue to get her through her long
monologue on another happy day. Her elaborate speech about Cooker
or Shower ("ends in er anyway") displays the same narrative technique
Beckett's two characters will use with much greater concision in *Footfalls*.

May and Voice are, however, primarily actresses. Much of the
editing that connects their dual monologues may not be the manifes-
tation of their roles as storytellers so much as it is the occupational
hazard of their life's work as bit players. Like Mouth in *Not I*, their
search is for cues to remember their lines. "Not been out since girlhood" is Voice's correction for "She has not been out since girlhood,"
and May will soon be stumped by "No sound. . . . None at least to
be heard. . . . The semblance. . . . The semblance." As the actress
playing Winnie must do with the text of *Happy Days*, May tries to
connect her lines with specific movements onstage, in this case the
measured cadence of her nine steps, her pauses, and her turnabouts.
"Dreadfully un—," delivered "*brokenly,*" is the ultimate embarrass-
ment of a professional actress forgetting an author's, in this case Beckett's, line. May has this problem even in the first section of the play.
V repeats her lines "And I? (*Pause. No louder.*) And I?" and "Forgive
me . . . again (*Pause. No louder.*) Forgive me . . . again" in a last
attempt to jog May's flagging memory. Such self-conscious theatricality links *Footfalls* not only to *Not I* but to earlier works like *Godot*
and especially *Endgame*, where Hamm and Clov more directly employ
the technical language of theater ("audition," "speech," "revels,"
"technique," "no forcing," "soliloquy," "aside," "silence," "under-
plot," "play") to reassure us that their roles must be played out on the
boards.

Within their own life in the theater, there are several haunting
parallels between what Voice says, what May does, and what May
ultimately murmurs. The "snatch a little sleep" of Voice's monologue
returns us to the opening "deep sleep" of the play. The "poor mind"
of act 1 becomes the "poor head" of act 2 and finally "His poor arm"
and "that poor arm" of May's sequel. Who is Amy and who, indeed,
is old Mrs. Winter? Does "old Mrs. Winter" have any relationship to
the head of Old Man Winter we see in *That Time*? Is Amy May? Is
Mrs. Winter Voice? What are we to make of the "certain seasons" of
May, Mrs. Winter, and the "one late autumn"? Why did May's mother
have her so "late"? When did May's mother die? How old is May
now? Why do May and Voice invent stories? Is May's story autobiographical? Why does Mrs. Winter remember a scene at evensong that

Amy cannot or will not recall? Why does the illuminated space grow
smaller after each fade-out? Are the chimes of this play "necessarily"
the sounds of a bell at evensong? Are we watching Amy/May pacing
at vespers, the capital H in "His poor arm" (a change Beckett made
in the text[14]) suggesting the figure of Christ on the cross and therefore
the cruciform pattern of a church? If so, how did Amy/May get in?
The "north door," so the story goes, is supposed to be "always locked
at this hour." What's it mean, to paraphrase Winnie in *Happy Days*?
What's it all meant to mean?—a sentiment May has Mrs. Winter echo
in her improvisation about her own "semblance": "What do you mean,
Amy, to put it mildly, what can you possibly mean, Amy, to put it
mildly?" What, indeed, is this very "strange thing" we have "observed" in the theater as we watch *Footfalls* take its course? The image
onstage is come and gone before we have had time to answer any of
the questions it inevitably gives rise to. The chime is now "*even a
little fainter still,*" the stage lights "*fade up to even a little less still
on the strip,*" but there is suddenly "*no trace of May.*" "*Hold fifteen
seconds, fade out,* and *curtain.*" Is May dead? Like the Amy in her
story, she is simply "not there" at all by the time we encounter the
emptiness of act 4. "Strange or otherwise," we hear nothing, we see
nothing. Beckett has finally succeeded in making absence a palpable
stage presence: one cannot be more minimalist than that and still write
a play. "This is what we call," Clov remarks, "making an exit."

Footfalls is, then, "a very small play" with "a lot of problems
concerning precision." "Am I dead?" Billie Whitelaw asked Beckett
when he directed her as May in London. "Let's just say," he responded, "you're not really there." During rehearsals for the Berlin
production he directed in 1976, Beckett emphasized the importance of
May's footsteps: "The walking up and down is the central image."
The script for the play, he continued, was "built up around this picture."[15] Observed from our seats in the theater, May's tracked movement is "*parallel with front*" and appears to be singularly linear. Met-
aphorically circular, her motion, from where we sit, seems to be strictly
limited to one horizontal plane. But movement in Beckett's world is
often a complicated business. Coordinates of right and left are not always to be trusted. "What ruined me at bottom was athletics," an un-
identifiable narrator puns in one of the prose pieces called *Fizzles*.[16]
Long before this, as far back as *Watt*, we have been literally overwhelmed by the variety of "funambulistic" staggers encountered in
Beckett's work. In the abandoned "J. M. Mime," sketched on two
pages from a *Herakles* notebook, two players begin their "progres-

sion" at a central point onstage. The entire action consists of the great-
est number of permutations and combinations within the framework of
a large square blocked on the same stage floor.[17] Beckett will develop
this strategy of movement further in *Quad I* and *Quad II,* the plays
first shown on German television. "That's not moving," we read in
"Whoroscope," "that's *moving.*" Maddy Rooney in *All That Fall,*
Winnie in *Happy Days* ("What a curse, mobility!") and Hamm and
Clov in *Endgame* have run (usually in slow motion or in no motion at
all) into similar difficulties with space, for the direction of movement
on Beckett's stage depends not necessarily on east, west, north, or
south, left or right (or their opposites from where we sit, stage left or
stage right), but on the particular vantage point from which "it all" is
being perceived. Even "the north door" in May's story in *Footfalls*
has a circuitous evolution. The first English edition read "south door."
"That is a correction," says Beckett. "South Door is too warm, North
Door is colder. You feel cold," he told Hildegard Schmahl. "The whole
time, in the way you hold your body too. Everything is frost and night."[18]

 Direction and motion in Beckett are therefore subject to a "poetics
of indeterminacy" where every vector is relative.[19] Human perception,
as Maurice Merleau-Ponty reminds us, will not allow us to see everything in its totality all at once. We cannot, to use one of his most
graphic examples, see a cube: we can only imagine it. We intuit the
completeness of its six surfaces from the three that show themselves
to our restricted visual horizon.[20] The rest we must take on blind faith
or, for the less spiritually inclined, on epistemological evidence. This
is also true of May's blocking on Beckett's stage. The movement we
perceive along a horizontal plane will look quite different, for instance,
when seen from above. From this lofty perspective we would see the
tracing on the stage floor of a tremendously elongated variation of the
figure 8 turned on its side, the mathematician's symbol for infinity:

Beckett's theater has long been interested in the significance of numbers. Clov romanticizes his offstage kitchen for its "nice dimensions,
nice proportions" of "ten feet by ten feet by ten feet" and Dan Rooney

anxiously laments a threatened dismissal of arithmetic: "Not count! One of the few satisfactions in life?" The figure 8 in *Footfalls* similarly demands our consideration, for, as rendered here, Beckett has used it before. Commenting in 1938 on the poetic value of Denis Devlin's "Communication from the Eiffel Tower," Beckett wrote in the pages of *Transition*:

If only the 8 in the last line had been left on its side. So: ∞[21]

In 1981 Beckett provided the editors of *College Literature* with a typescript for publication which uses not only the same symbol for infinity, but the symbol for indefinite number as well. Several lines in this two-paragraph prose piece detail the crossways that bear a close resemblance to May's movement in *Footfalls*:

8

The way wound up from foot to top and thence on down another way. On back down. The ways crossed midway more and less. A little more and less than midway up and down. The ways were one-way. No retracing the way up back down nor back up the way down. Neither in whole from top or foot nor in part from on the way. The one way back was on and on was always back. Freedom once at foot and top to pause or not. Before on back up and down. Briefly once at the extremes the will set free. Gait down as up same plod always. A foot a second or mile and hour and more. So from foot and top to crossways could the seconds have been numbered then height known and depth. Could but those seconds have been numbered. Thorns hemmed the way. The ways. Same mist always. Same half-light. As were the earth at rest. Loose sand underfoot. So no sign of remains no sign that none before. No one ever before so—

∞

Forth and back across a barren same winding one-way way. Low in the west or east the sun standstill. As if the earth at rest. Long shadows before and after. Same pace and countless time. Same ignorance of how far. Same leisure once at either end to pause or not. At either groundless end. Before back forth or back. Through emptiness the beaten ways as fixed as if enclosed. Were the eye to look unending void. In unending ending or beginning light. Bedrock underfoot. So no sign of remains a sign that none before. No one ever before so—[22]

Patterns of infinity can be found in several other Beckett works, from the intersecting arcs inevitably traced in space by the trajectory of a rocking chair as it sways in *Rockaby* to the more explicit journey whose route circumscribes a figure 8 in an unpublished short piece entitled "The Way." At the Humanities Research Center of the University of Texas in Austin there are seven consecutive versions of "The Way"; the first page has Beckett's diagram and accompanying calculations related to the journey that traces the contour of a figure 8 lying on its side.[23] Such formulaic patterns of infinity pay homage to the self-exegetical schema for Joyce's Penelope chapter in *Ulysses*. In contrast to the numbered hours that clock all the other episodes in that novel, the "Time" marked for this ultimate episode is infinity (∞) in one schema, "Hour none" in the other.[24] Even in *Endgame* Beckett plays with the concept of infinity in his allusion to the pre-Socratic philosopher Zeno. The "little heap, the impossible heap" refers to Zeno's paradox of the pile of millet: if you halve it, then divide "one of the resulting two piles in half and add it to the other, then divide the smaller pile in half again and add one half to the larger pile, and so on, you can never complete the operation (that is, remove the smaller, diminishing heap completely) because you are operating in space-time; only in infinity would the operation be completed."[25] Mrs. Lambert's two piles of lentils in *Malone Dies* is a parody of this same paradoxical notion:

She set down the lamp on the table and the outer world went out. She sat down, emptied out the lentils on the table and began to sort them. So that soon there were two heaps on the table, one big heap getting smaller and one small heap getting bigger. But suddenly with a furious gesture she swept the two together, annihilating thus in less than a second the work of two or three minutes. Then she went away and came back with a saucepan. It won't kill them, she said, and with the heel of her hand she brought the lentils to the edge of the table and over the edge into the saucepan, as if all that mattered was not to be killed, but so clumsily and with such nervous haste that a great number fell wide of the pan to the ground. Then she took up the lamp and went out, to fetch wood perhaps, or a lump of fat bacon.

—*Malone Dies*, pp. 213–14

What makes the figure 8 turned on its side functional in *Footfalls* is the recognition that this mathematical symbol effectively represents May's condition, and our own, as we set about "revolving it all":

Amy. (*Pause. No louder.*) Amy. (*Pause.*) Yes, Mother. (*Pause.*) Will you never have done? (*Pause.*) Will you never have done . . . revolving it all? (*Pause.*) It? (*Pause.*) It all. (*Pause.*) In your poor mind. (*Pause.*) It all. (*Pause.*) It all.

—*Footfalls*, p. 48

In *Footfalls* the "insistence with which the ground invades the surface," as Beckett wrote about the work of Denis Devlin, is everywhere quite extraordinary." And for this tribute to his compatriot he added the very Irish-sounding "Extraaudenary." For in *Footfalls* the seemingly infinite implications of the "stiff interexclusiveness" will not put themselves to rest.[26] Even the simple "Yes, Mother" of May's story in act 3 echoes the "Yes, May" of V's response to May in the dialogue which opens the play. May's pacing on this platform therefore sustains a miniaturized grandeur in which mathematical symbol, allusive content, and emotional effect coincide and even mutually support each other. At the end of the piece May disappears from the set; all that remains is the faint trace of an ever smaller circle of light. Infinity can only be approached, never reached. May's absence serves as both a sharp reminder and a stark contrast: she is human and therefore finite in her sudden unity-of-no-place. Staged darkness, staged silence, and staged emptiness frame the only real eternity on Beckett's tiny plane.

Footfalls, however, may not really set out to expose this troubling conflict between human limitation and the ineffability of some infinite sphere. May may not really be human after all: the three parts of this play may be only another variation of some other "ghost trio." In performance May is everywhere trying to convince the audience that she exists. Even her name, "May" rather than "Bea," implies potentiality of being rather than being itself. Beckett suggested to his German actors that May herself has not been properly born. The voice of the offstage mother interrupts itself in the sentence, "in the old home, the same where she—(*Pause.*)," and then continues, "The same where she began." Beckett explained the pause as well as the subsequent emendation in the following way: originally the mother's voice was going to say, ". . . the same where she was born." But that would have been wrong. May is "ageless" because she has not been born. She just began. "It began," Beckett told his company. "There is a difference. She was never born." The dramatic situation therefore concerns a life which didn't begin as a life, but which was just there, as a thing. Beckett said that in the thirties he attended a lecture in London in which the psychologist Jung spoke about a young patient he was unable to help even after fifteen years of therapy. She existed, but she did not actually live. "But, of course," Jung expostulated, "she was never born," a conclusion Beckett paraphrases in the "never been properly born" of *Watt*.[27] Maddy Rooney refers to the same lecture in the following exchange with her husband from *All That Fall*:

MRS. ROONEY: I remember once attending a lecture by one of these new mind
doctors, I forget what you call them. He spoke—

MR. ROONEY: A lunatic specialist?

MRS. ROONEY: No no, just the troubled mind, I was hoping he might shed a
little light on my lifelong preoccupation with horses' buttocks.

MR. ROONEY: A neurologist.

MRS. ROONEY: No no, just mental distress, the name will come back to me in
the night. I remember his telling us the story of a little girl,
very strange and unhappy in her ways, and how he treated her
unsuccessfully over a period of years and was finally obliged
to give up the case. He could find nothing wrong with her, he
said. The only thing wrong with her as far as he could see was
that she was dying. And she did in fact die, shortly after he
washed his hands of her.

MR. ROONEY: Well? What is there so wonderful about that?

MRS. ROONEY: No, it was just something he said, and the way he said it, that
have haunted me ever since.

MR. ROONEY: You lie awake at night, tossing to and fro and brooding on it.

MRS. ROONEY: On it and other . . . wretchedness. (*Pause.*) When he had done
with the little girl he stood there motionless for some time, quite
two minutes I should say, looking down at his table. Then he
suddenly raised his head and exclaimed, as if he had had a
revelation, The trouble with her was she had never been really
born! (*Pause.*) He spoke throughout without notes. (*Pause.*) I
left before the end.

—*All That Fall,* pp. 82–84

Like the young girl in Maddy Rooney's story, and like "mad" Maddy
herself, May is a presence, not a person—certainly not a person who
has ever been properly born outside of the dramatist's imagination.
Her existence is neither more nor less substantial than that of any other
stage character. The play, then, to paraphrase Beckett's famous statement about *Finnegans Wake,* cannot really be "about" something; it
must, instead, be that something itself,[28] a theatricalized enigma rendered timeless as an image.

In *Footfalls,* perhaps more graphically than anywhere else in the
Beckett canon, intellectual dilemma and physical staging coincide in
an "absolute absence of the Absolute."[29] The title of Beckett's French
translation for this piece, *Pas,* neatly accommodates the problem: French
pas is both "steps" and "not." Our questions about this drama will
prove to be as endless as the path May treads, just as the figure 8
turned on its side emblematizes our experience as we confront this

strange work. A combination of completion and continuity, the dramatic image assaults us with its own uneasy presentness. As members of the audience we find that Beckett's obsession becomes, at least for the few minutes of performance, our own. What we watch is a precise illusion, its menace, and its progressive validation. Central to the integrity of the image is not symbolism, but consistency. There is no authorization to construct any subtext from the "text" that unfolds in production. The drama is primarily concerned with linking its own absolute qualities, its own inner vitality and definiteness, within the limits of its own narrow space. Making no appeal to any reality outside of itself, *Footfalls* is, instead, a synthesis of those visual and verbal harmonics we see and hear in the theater as performance takes place.

May's footsteps are therefore gigantic. Into their singular compactness Beckett places an enormous range of intention and suggestion: infinity is always there before us in the continuous actuality of the continuous pacing that is this play. *Footfalls* is a constant becoming because, as drama, its essence lies in the process of its being staged. Indexification is refined out of existence, a gratuitous intrusion. Objects, motivations, exposition, and even explanation, the paraphernalia of a once realistic theater, have been cancelled and omitted. What remains is an immense landscape of potentiality, infinite possibility on the finite dimensions of a stage. No two encounters with this play, like no two stagings of this play, can ever be exactly the same, for the multiplicity and simultaneity of interpretations forever compete for our attention. The adventure of experiencing this play, then, is a continual temptation. The actuality of the staged image, May's endless pacing and the haunting reverie of her footsteps, therefore subjects us to the most infinite of all dramatic options, spartan simplicity.

Within this simplicity, however, Beckett is concerned with sustaining a neo-realistic illusion based on the communicative possibilities of a draped human form reacting to sound in motion. Emphasizing the function of sound in motion as well as the function of sound in emotion, the stage offers us an unlimited palette of grays, in May's image "a faint tangle of pale grey tatters," to present the subjective world of its principal and solitary character. The dynamic relationship between scenic language and textual language turns the actor's body into an expressive instrument that stimulates the imagination of the audience. Lighting organizes stage space with a minimum of detail and a maximum of geometric symmetry. Costume design highlights the figure and serves as a further revelation of character. But it is sound that will be featured in this requiem: the sound of a chime, the sound of an echo, the sound of feet shuffling and of a costume trailing on the boards, and the sound of a human voice as, *"low and slow throughout,"* it accents the rhythmic sequence of Beckett's dramatic lyricism. In *Footfalls* "to be is to be perceived" through sound: to be is to be heard.

It is appropriate for existence through sound to make its imprint through a radio play, but such an existence is expanded and clarified when brought to a visual medium like theater.

> . . . one night, while still little more than a child, she called her mother and said, Mother, this is not enough. The mother: Not enough? May—the child's given name—May: Not enough. The mother: What do you mean, May, not enough, what can you possibly mean, May, not enough? May: I mean, Mother, that I must hear the feet, however faint they fall. The mother: The motion alone is not enough? May: No, Mother, the motion alone is not enough, I must hear the feet, however faint they fall.
>
> —*Footfalls*, pp. 45–46

In *Footfalls* Beckett's landscape is dominated by sound, so much so that the speaker of the lines quoted above is reduced to a spectral voice whose only presence is in electronic amplification. What makes this play dramatic is the conflict that engulfs the words recited into a microphone by the offstage voice, the dialogue recited by the figure pacing onstage, and the way in which both prefigure the scenic situation we encounter. The agon here is language, theater language: how lines are heard by a character, how they are meant to be spoken onstage, how they may be listened to by an audience:

> VLADIMIR: Listen!
> *They listen, grotesquely rigid.*
> ESTRAGON: I hear nothing.
> VLADIMIR: Hsst! (*They listen. Estragon loses his balance, almost falls. He clutches the arm of Vladimir who totters. They listen, huddled together.*) Nor I. *Sighs of relief. They relax and separate.*
> ESTRAGON: You gave me a fright.
> VLADIMIR: I thought it was he.
> ESTRAGON: Who?
> VLADIMIR: Godot.
> ESTRAGON: Pah! The wind in the reeds.
>
> —*Waiting for Godot*, p. 13

The structure of listening, however, always assumes special liabilities in Beckett's theater. "Just to know that in theory you can hear me even though in fact you don't is all I need," says Winnie to Willie, "just to feel you there within earshot and conceivably on the qui vive is all I ask." And later: "just to know you are there within hearing and conceivably on the semi-alert is . . . er . . . paradise enow." Unlike *That Time,* where a silent listener hears three movements of his interior consciousness which have been prerecorded by his own voice, the listener we meet in *Footfalls* has the additional faculty of talking. In the first part of this play, moreover, there is not only one listener, but two. This is after all a dialogue encounter between two separate characters, even though one is invisible and, more properly speaking, imagined. The performance calls for two actresses, the interplay of two different, though related, voices in order to establish contrast and nuance. Mechanical manipulation of a single vocal register will not do the trick here. "The daughter only knows the voice of the mother," Beckett said in pointing out the relationship that brings them close together:

One can recognize the similarity between the two from the sentences in their narratives, from the expression. The strange voice of the daughter comes from the mother. The "Not enough?" in the mother's story must sound just like the "Not there?" of Mrs. W in Amy's story, for example. These parallelisms are extremely important for the understanding of the play. . . .[30]

May reacts verbally to her mother's voice in act 1 and physically to her mother's voice in act 2. By the time of act 3 her response has been so total that we watch her literally become her mother's voice as she intones not only similar patterns of speech, but some crucial lines as well: "It all. . . . It all." In production the audience hears the transformation take place in sound. Plot development therefore exists in the audience's act of listening, listening to May listen and listening to May speak. In *Footfalls* Beckett tries to regulate on the live stage the technical sound proficiency of a radio play, but in this case to achieve the visual impact of a sound. Beckett sets the scene minimally and dresses his figure economically so that we will listen more fully to the sound of his language echoing through a rectangular box, the stage space. Sound structures sight, sight structures sound.

The most important sounds we hear in *Footfalls* are those that contain the tight composition of Beckett's language. In this play plot as a progression of events growing out of each other is submerged in favor of plot as pattern and, on its most elementary level, as the pattern of sounds making up language. When May says, in Voice's story, that "I must hear the feet, however faint they fall," no secret, no message is revealed in any narrative way. All we learn is that one night a girl called May told her mother that the motion alone was not enough, that she had to hear the footfall as well. We cannot be sure, in view of May's following soliloquy, if the mother and the May described here are the same women we will meet in other sections of the play. Though no explanations are delivered, a pattern begins to form. V's monologue loops back on itself. As "not enough" is repeated several times in the monologue's progression, each phrase is integrated into the last: "What do you mean May, not enough, what can you possibly mean May, not enough?" May's soliloquy will work in the same way: "Mrs. W: You yourself observed nothing . . . strange? Amy: No, Mother, I myself did not, to put it mildly. Mrs. W: What do you mean, Amy, to put it mildly, what can you possibly mean, Amy, to put it mildly? Amy: I mean, Mother, that to say I observed nothing . . . strange is indeed to put it mildly." The plot is not advanced, but the pattern is. Puns, for example, such as the one on feet/feat, are a play on voiced units of speech, where language serves as the most advanced structuring of the sound patterns we hear. May adds "as the reader will remember" to V's "the daughter's given name," for Amy (A-M-Y) is not only a repatterning of the letters that comprise the name May (M-A-Y) but also another opportunity for the actress to voice and emphasize the same $\bar{a}$ sound. "Try saying the word Amy as quietly as you can," Beckett told Billie Whitelaw in rehearsal for this play.[31] In the play it will be sound relations such as these which recall a word or phrase to mind. Repetition evaporates meaning and emphasizes rhythm instead:

> M: Would you like me to inject you . . . again?
> V: Yes, but it is too soon.
> *Pause.*
> M: Would you like me to change your position . . . again?
> V: Yes, but it is too soon.
> —*Footfalls,* p. 43

Beckett's lyrical language, however, comes from more than just word repetition. In *Footfalls,* primarily, it comes from the rhythmic pattern of sounds:

Straighten your pillows?	ˋ ˘ ˘ ˋ ˘
Change your drawsheet?	ˋ ˘ ˋ ˘
Pass you the bed pan?	ˋ ˘ ˘ ˋ ˘
The warming-pan?	˘ ˋ ˘ ˋ
Dress your sores?	ˋ ˘ ˋ
Sponge you down?	ˋ ˘ ˋ

As recited in performance, the rhythm of the lines can be felt by the audience. Yet the sound pattern we hear does more to reinstate itself than to clarify meaning. May's prosaic questions turn into a poetic structure as Beckett renders them in this scene. The occasion calls for naturalistic speech, but Beckett uses it instead as an opportunity for a lyrical interlude. Lines of dialogue become lines of poetry. "I must hear the feet, however faint they fall" therefore demands to be read in still another way. For what Beckett is talking about here is poetic feet, the iambs, trochees, and spondees we use to mark the measured cadence of a rhythmic line. "The motion alone is not enough": dramatic action requires an appropriate dramatic language, what Hamm calls, as he warms to the occasion of his final soliloquy, "a little poetry." "I must hear the feet," the specifically poetic feet, "however faint they fall."

Integrating the sound and visual patterns in *Footfalls* is time, for we do not hear or see in the theater but over a period of time. "O time!" cries out Viola toward the end of her first scene in *Twelfth Night*, "Thou must untangle this, not I; / It is too hard a knot for me t'untie." The language of *Footfalls* presents us with a formal vocabulary of temporality marking, as does the sounding of a chime, the passing of an hour: "autumn," "sequel," "Evensong," "Vespers," the names May and Winter.

> M: What age am I now?
> V: And I? (*Pause. No louder.*) And I?
> M: Ninety.
> V: So much?
> M: Eighty-nine, ninety.
> V: I had you late. (*Pause.*) In life. (*Pause.*) Forgive me . . . again. (*Pause. No louder.*) Forgive me . . . again.
>   *Pause.*
> M: What age am I now?
> V: In your forties.
> M: So little?
> V: I'm afraid so. (*Pause.* M *resumes pacing . . .*)
> —*Footfalls*, p. 44

The frequent pauses in the play prepare us for the final pause, when light fades up for the fourth and last time on the now empty strip. The last words of the play, uttered in act 3, gain their power and intensity through the repetition of the same pattern we have heard before at the conclusions of acts 1 and 2. But the final line of the play is silence, thus reinstating the overall pattern with which the dramatic episode began, a pattern we also recognize in Beckett's poem "neither":

> to and fro in shadow from inner to outer shadow
>
> from impenetrable self to impenetrable unself
> by way of neither
>
> as between two lit refuges whose doors once
> gently close, once turned away from
> gently part again
>
> beckoned back and forth and turned away
>
> heedless of the way, intent on the one gleam
> or the other
>
> unheard footfalls only sound
>
> till at last halt for good, absent for good
> from self and other
>
> then no sound
>
> then gently light unfading on that unheeded
> neither
>
> unspeakable home[32]

Unlike a lyric poem, however, the merged surface of sight and sound in *Footfalls* cannot be fully perceived as an integrated image until the time of the play is over. Time encapsulates the cycle; the title of the play contains the whole idea. While Mouth complains of a "dull roar like falls" and Winnie mentions "little . . . sunderings, little falls . . . apart," what is a footfall but the sound of a foot falling through space in time?

Partly choreographic, partly musical, *Footfalls* displays a rhythmic system in its structure that is essentially poetic. Employing onomatopoeia, anaphora, and epistrophe, Beckett's language in this play is calculated on sound in relation to movement. In his production notebooks and in notes taken during rehearsals, Beckett even specifies which words and which sounds should accompany which footsteps:

The walking should be like a metronome, one length must be measured in exactly nine seconds. The fade-out at the end of Part I begins with the third step from the left, so that it is dark after the ninth step, i.e., in seven seconds. The mother speaks her text at the end of Part I on certain definite steps of May's. The first "May" comes on the fourth step while May is walking from right to left, the second "May" on the eighth step. May says her "Yes, Mother" on the fourth step when she is walking from left to right and on the sixth step of the same stretch, the mother begins with "Will you never have done?" The sentence ends immediately before the turn. During the next length (from right to left) the mother begins on the second step with "Will you never have done revolving it all?" and ends before the turn on the left.[33]

The spacing of sound and movement indicated here resulted when Beckett increased May's footsteps from seven to nine during rehearsals at the Royal Court Theatre. Seven paces looked too small on the strip, so Beckett, aware of the practical contingencies of translating script to stage, expanded the authorized blocking by two measures.[34] In this play even phonic units have the same length as May's footsteps. Based on such a strict principle, *Footfalls* reveals Beckett at his most classical: the drama depends on the interplay of strophic and antistrophic elements. May's footsteps, signaling "the absolute encapsulation of the figure in itself,"[35] imitate the movement of the classical Greek chorus while turning from one side to the other of the orchestra. Voice's monologue is the strophe, May's the antistrophe, exactly paralleling through return movement the speech that comes before through the repetition of words and phrases at the end of successive clauses. The second actor is reduced to a mere voice, yet the function here is that of an "answerer," the *hypokritēs* who plays his part in the classical Greek theater. The rhythm of movement and the balance of sound create May's dance of death, but it is the three elements of drama, poetry, and narrative that make this highly theatrical piece come to life in performance. Here is the language of theater, which Beckett borrows from his dramatic heritage.

Echoes of Shakespeare, which reverberate so lyrically in *That Time,* reappear in *Footfalls.* In this work Beckett relies on our memory of another theater language, the language of Shakespeare's *Macbeth*: the "Macbeth doth murder sleep" of May; the endless pacing of Lady Macbeth's sleepwalking; the never having been properly born of Macduff; the south door later changed to the north; and the amen stuck in Amy's throat. Even the technique of creating a "semblance" of dialogue in monologue is a Shakespearean legacy. The Nurse uses it, for example, in remembering her young charge in *Romeo and Juliet*:

> Yea, quoth my husband, "falls't upon thy face?
> Thou wilt fall backward when thou comest to age;
> Wilt thou not, Jule?" It stinted and said, "Ay."
> —act 1, scene 3

In paying tribute to the dramatic past, Beckett takes from it fragments still capable of being made luminous in the present. Beckett therefore uses his inheritance to develop a dramatic style whose characters may be shades, but whose language is nevertheless "visionary." On his stage he will build "an image which develops gradually,"[36] an image, like May's, which returns his theater to the essential humanity of *Waiting for Godot*.

CHAPTER FIVE

Shades for Film and Video

I

Moving from one medium to another, Beckett extends his search for theatrical metaphors. In radio, television, and in one instance film, Beckett clarifies the sight-sound relationships which leave their mark on his late stage plays through their technical precision. The rigid patterning of voices on tape and images in film and video brings to his work a stability and a measure of control normally absent from the arena of live performance. Recording pictures that are permanent and unearthly sounds that never change, technology establishes a truly "concrete" poetry, one that not only imitates electricity, but also lasts forever.[1] In radio, a medium of sound, Beckett makes us visualize a world made up of private time and public space. *All That Fall* exposes us to an exterior reality, Maddy Rooney on the road, as well as to the intimacy of memory, the sad recollection of a daughter long dead: "Minnie! Little Minnie! . . . In her forties now she'd be, I don't know, fifty," she sobs in an aside, "girding up her lovely little loins, getting ready for the change. . . ." In *Embers* we move even deeper inside a character's head: there is no reality outside the "white world, not a sound" of Henry's consciousness.[2] We hear his words, the voices, music, and miscellaneous noises he summons with "great trouble" from the past, and the break of a wave on the shore, the obsessive sound of the sea which plagues him when language, invented or remembered, fails to materialize. Through sound Beckett conjures up the fading pictures of commemoration, but it is the sound of the sea that finally extinguishes the embers. Film and video offer Beckett the chance to chronicle visually as well as aurally the iconography of a mind in dialogue with itself. Working in collaboration with sound or with its absence, silence, the camera establishes a totally compressed environment in which visual imagery forms a tacit pact with idea.

Film, presenting Buster Keaton in his last screen role, was written for a composite work planned by Grove Press under a title inscribed "Project I, Three Original Motion Picture Scripts by Samuel Beckett, Eugène Ionesco, Harold Pinter." Beckett's *Film* was the only one of the pieces completed under this rubric. The filming of Ionesco's *Hard-Boiled Egg* was postponed indefinitely, and Pinter adapted *The Compartment* into a 1967 television play broadcast on the BBC as *The Basement.*[3] Produced in 1964 by Barney Rosset's Evergreen Theatre, *Film* was shot in 35mm black and white under the direction of Alan Schneider, with Boris Kaufman as cinematographer and Sidney Meyers as editor. Beckett made his only trip to the United States to participate in the shooting of this film, which took place on the then rundown Manhattan side of the Brooklyn Bridge.[4]

Perhaps the most distinctive feature of *Film* is its period quality. Unlike the timeless, boundless, seemingly endless atmosphere we associate with most of Beckett's novels and plays, *Film* is specifically set "about 1929." Only *Murphy,* which centers its narrative on the peculiar arrivals and departures of a zany set of characters between February and October 1935,[5] is similarly time-bound. Temporal location is crucial to *Film,* for Beckett sets out not only to re-create the ambience of the late twenties but to incorporate the cinematic techniques in use at that time. The result is a latter-day cultural artifact, with some surprising visual anachronisms. Besides the abject poverty and dated costumes which make only a mild gesture toward historical accuracy, very little tells us it is 1929 except the manner in which *Film* has been shot: a silent movie (except for that one fateful "sssh!"); the use of black-and-white film; a hero resurrected from twenties comedy (Beckett had originally wanted Chaplin, but he was unavailable); slapstick comedy in the large cat/small dog business (what Robert Desnos called in "Mack Sennett libérateur du cinéma" the "most disconcerting form of lyricism");[6] a series of tracking shots; the surrealist habit of juxtaposing unexpected visual perspectives (E's point of view colliding in montage with O's); a twenty-two-minute running time, like the experimental shorts of the dada-surrealist filmmakers. Beckett's *Film* displays a fascination with the technology of the camera lens linking it very closely to the more ambitious films of the twenties.

"One day," Philippe Soupault noted very simply in the magazine *Sic,* "man was endowed with a new eye."[7] In *Film* Beckett goes back in time to encounter this "new eye." In the process he evokes both the mood and substance of a highly experimental film, circa 1929.

The camera lens is, in fact, the true hero in *Film.* The original title for Beckett's version of man-with-a-movie-camera was *The Eye,* and he tells us in his notes to the scenario that the work is based on Bishop Berkeley's dictum that *esse est percipi.* It is the eye, therefore, and more specifically the eye of the camera, which gives life to the characters in *Film.* Under the careful scrutiny of a mechanical lens, Keaton repeatedly checks his pulse to remind himself that he is still among the living. The close-up shot of Keaton's eye, introducing the theme in the first frame, is an oblique reference to Luis Buñuel's seventeen-minute *Un chien andalou,* first shown in Paris in 1928, the silent movie[8] in which a young man (Buñuel himself) slits the eyeball of a young woman with a razor blade in one of the most chilling and therefore most memorable close-ups in film history. Beckett's opening shot resembles as well René Magritte's *False Mirror* of 1928, a surrealist close-up oil on canvas: we stare into an eye in which the ball is a dark sphere floating in an orbit composed of sky and clouds. Like Magritte's false mirror on canvas and the supposed eyeball of the young woman in *Un chien andalou* (which was in fact the lifeless eye of a dead donkey),[9] Keaton's reptilian eye, though blinking, is not dilating, not focusing. Not until the end of *Film,* when we finally achieve the full facial exposure we have been searching for, do we make the subtle connection: the close-up has been of Keaton's "blind" eye, the one hidden all the while by that forbidding dark patch. The opening frame is thus an extended shot of a defective eye, a lens which does not see at all.

Beckett's pattern of cinematic allusions is one of the rich centers of metaphor in his work. He owes a special debt to Buñuel. Both contributed to the special surrealist number of Edward Titus's *This Quarter* (September 1932), where the filmscript of *Un chien andalou,* Buñuel's collaboration with Salvador Dali, appeared along with Beckett's translations into English of works by René Crevel, Paul Eluard, and André Breton. Winnie stuck up to her "diddies" and then up to her neck in a mound of earth in *Happy Days* resembles the figures similarly planted in the final moments of *Un chien andalou.* Beckett also draws on this scenario for two important scenes in *Molloy.* The Buñuel filmscript notes the angry, rancorous gesture of a young woman who has just watched from her window as a man passing in the street below falls from his bicycle into the mud of the gutter,[10] resembling Molloy's first encounter with the wily Lousse: he falls from his own bicycle after running over her pomeranian, a dog also mentioned in *Endgame*. Buñuel's script notes as well a man looking at the sky through window panes and seeing a light cloud advancing toward a full moon, paralleling Molloy's own visual horizon as he lies awake in bed in Lousse's house speculating on the moon passing across the window panes: "like moon through passing . . . rack" is how May imagines this in *Footfalls*. In other places Beckett makes similar allusions to Buñuel's *L'Age d'or* of 1930; this scenario contains a brief footnote which declares: "You see . . . in this film . . . a blind man ill-treated, a dog run over, a son almost killed for no reason at all by his father." The first situation describes Pozzo in act 2 of *Godot;* the second, the fate of Lousse's pomeranian in *Molloy* mentioned above; the third, the father-son conflict between Jacques Moran and his constipated *fils* in the second part of the same novel. *L'Age d'or* also shows two lovers in sexual embrace rolling on the ground in the mud, a famous cinematic encounter Beckett parodies in the sadomasochistic relationships in the mud of *How It Is*. In Buñuel the lovers are separated and the man is beaten; in Beckett jabs are administered by a can opener up the anus.

But Beckett's cinematic reference points are by no means limited to Buñuel. His first piece for the stage, written with Georges Pelorson in 1931, was called *Le Kid;*[11] the name is both a burlesque of the French classicism of *Le Cid* and a tongue-in-cheek homage to Charlie Chaplin and Jackie Coogan in *The Kid,* the popular silent film of 1921. Various critics have noticed that "Godot" sounds suspiciously like "Charlot," the French nickname for Charlie Chaplin. In *Watt* Beckett has some fun with a "hardy laurel," the delightful exchange of hats in *Godot* is straight out of *Duck Soup,* and the "rosebud" highlighted in *Mercier and Camier* recalls the childhood name for a sled in *Citizen Kane*. Even in *Murphy,* the hero, a strict nonreader, has a penchant for cinematic allusions: awakening from a deep sleep, he sees Ticklepenny "as though thrown on the silent screen by Griffith in midshot soft-focus."[12] In *Not I* Beckett again displays his preference for the cinema of the twenties: Mouth's gradual fade-in/fade-out resembles the famous fade-outs in an experimental short like *Entr'acte* (1924) by René Clair and Francis Picabia, where in the final moments the characters literally disintegrate on the screen before our very eyes.

Despite its abstract Berkeleyan orientation, *Film* emphasizes image rather than word, feeling rather than thought. Beckett presents us with a series of pictorial equivalents of the conflicting inner-outer worlds of man, in this case represented by Keaton as object (O) and Keaton as eye (E). But it is not made clear until the final frames that the two perspectives involve an identical source: E = O. Throughout the film we are exposed to two distinct points of view, following Buñuel's pre-scription that a good film must have "the ambivalence of two opposed and related things."[13] Here Keaton is sundered into object and eye, the former in flight, the latter in pursuit, what Beckett defines as the ag-onizing tyranny of "self-perception."[14] Realized cinematographically, *Film* records itineraries of the eye in which ideas have been translated into verbs: moving, falling, balancing, straining, sifting, stumbling, hiding, intensifying, recurring, resisting, focusing, self-isolating. The dynamic conception for this piece resembles Paul Klee's "Creative Credo": "The work of art arose out of movement, is itself congealed movement, and is perceived by movement."[15] As film, Beckett's work is not congealed, but fluid—line, plane, and depth are in a constant rhythm of change. The camera's eye becomes the thinking eye; con-nections are made by an organ other than the mind. Following Artaud's demand for the exclusive attention owed to film images, we watch rather than elucidate.

The intensely visual story about Beckett's thinking eye is ex-tremely simple: O's attempt to remove all perception ultimately fails because he cannot escape self-perception. The shooting therefore re-quired not merely a subjective camera and an objective camera but two different perspectives of cinematic reality: that of the perceiving eye (E) constantly surveying the object, and that of the object (O) observing his environment. O is sometimes aware of being perceived by E and makes the necessary adjustments by attempting to escape from E's line of vision, as he does from all other perceptions, real or imagined. "The trouble," as Alan Schneider pointed out in his essay "On Directing *Film*," "was that because of the rigid dichotomy of the two visions we couldn't cut anywhere and splice parts of two takes together. Each take had to go on till the end of the shot."[16] Beckett predicted that this would be the chief difficulty in filming: how to establish unique points of view for E and O which would be imme-diately recognized as such by the audience. He discarded the possi-bility of dividing the screen in two to expose the opposing images simultaneously, a device he had earlier considered using onstage in the unpublished play of 1947, *Eleuthéria*, where to one side the audience sees Victor Krap alone in bed in his garret, to the other side his con-cerned family in domestic crisis. This problem was solved by the use of a lens gauze for the filming of O's perceptions, making a visual distinction between the two series of images; the diffusion lens carefully separated O's eyes from E's. This device in fact intensified the distinction; the lens gauze makes O's point of view distorted and hazy. There is a steady "film," a cataract over his eyes, making his perceptions forever out of focus, precisely what we might expect from a seedy individual blind in one eye and seeing only partially through the other. The self-perception O achieves in spite of himself at the conclusion of the movie is, therefore, a very shaky one indeed: blurred, distorted, heavily out of focus. The final confrontation with self becomes the ultimate "film" itself.

But *Film* is something more than a battle royal between E and O ending in a cathartic "agony of perceivedness." For the struggle between E and O is by no means self-contained. The perceptions of both E and O have been dutifully recorded by the all-seeing eyes of the camera. "The cinema," wrote Philippe Soupault, "is a superhuman eye, much richer than the human eye, which is of doubtful fidelity."[17] The real privilege in *Film* belongs neither to E nor to O—and certainly not to us—but to the cinematographic eye. It makes connections that completely elude us: the close-up of Keaton's creased eye is followed by the camera's lingering on the similarly contoured texture of the about-to-be-knocked-down wall, foreshadowing the barrier between E and O that breaks down at the conclusion of the film. After the shot of the wall, the camera moves swiftly to record the facade of an old building, where glacial windows stare down at us in a frozen symmetry of glance and gaze. All those eyes in *Film*—including those wondrous eyes of the rocking chair—have really been looking not at Keaton, but at us. *Film* is thus a movie about the experience of our eyes watching other eyes watching us, the overexposure neatly accomplished by the superhuman eye of the camera. This thought is captured in its entirety by the meticulously coordinated spatial and temporal arrangements within the piece: all eyes on us. *Film* thus demands a new visual responsiveness, in the tradition of Man Ray's close-up of his favorite model, Kiki, in which we are shown artificial eyes painted on her eyelids which disappear when she opens her own eyes. *Film* is, then, about the process of film watching, what happens to each of us when, in darkness, we are exposed to a series of larger-than-life images staring out at us from an oversized screen. Far from distancing us, Beckett has his eyes on us, carefully drawing us into the action and making us the protagonists.

To accomplish these goals, a great deal of image breaking becomes necessary. Rather than disguise eyes, making us forget that we are being exposed to visual manipulation, Beckett consistently unveils them. Concentration on eyes makes us conscious of that phenomenon which cinema usually wants us to forget: the fact that we are seeing through the lens of a camera. Our cliché impression of film is fractured in the first frame. Beckett then dispenses with the talkie, magnifying the visual, discarding the verbal. His single inconsistency is a sound track which offers us a mere "sssh!"—reminding his actors and his audience that this is indeed a silent film. That one sound makes the remaining silence fall oppressively, deafeningly, on our ears. It also makes us apprehensive about the intrusion of other unwelcome sounds. Beckett then continues to short-circuit other preconceptions about this medium. Keaton, of course, carries with him a number of associations for the motion picture audience—harmonious spills, crazy falls, outlandish pratfalls on staircases, the vaudeville confrontation with malevolent objects, the pantomime with animals, above all the "great stone face" with its porkpie hat.[18] Beckett and his film crew give us all of these but transfigured in such a way that they become unsettling, evoking that visual, mental, and emotional dislocation of film which André Breton summed up in the word *dépaysement:* "I think what we valued most in it, to the point of taking no interest in anything else, was its *power to disorient (son pouvoir de dépaysement).*"[19] In *Film* Keaton's face eludes us until the last few frames; and when we finally see it, it is as disfigured as Duchamp's celebrated portrait of the Mona Lisa with a mustache. Beckett has made the familiar unfamiliar: Keaton has substituted his deadpan expression for "that look" of shock and dismay so different from his frozen public face. This betrayal of images transforms Keaton into a living sign, an old object seen in a new light. The trompe l'oeil sabotages Keaton's role as Buster and makes him the true "object" of *Film,* forever at the mercy of the cold logic of a candid camera's eye. The routines Beckett incorporates in *Film* parody the precision and timing of Keaton's successful athletic comedy. The chase-and-escape gags resemble a crisis mimed in *Sherlock Junior* (1924), where the hero studies a book called *How to Be a Detective.* In *Film* the projector, not the projectionist, is the indefatigable inspector-general, for Beckett makes his camera play sleuth to Keaton's O-like trajectories. Enticed by farce and vaudeville, the audience gets a phenomenology of visual perception instead.

The continuous eye contacts in *Film* accomplish a great deal of cinematic demystification. The couple and the old flower woman look at Keaton, staring at the famous face we long to see: instead of expressing delight at their sighting, the camera eye registers their sudden gaze of "intentness" represented in "that look." Such privilege is not easily achieved; in the special lens of the camera, the couple stares through special lenses of its own: she looks through a lorgnon, he peers through a pince-nez. Privileged sighting also carries a penalty: after seeing Keaton, the old woman falls to the ground with her face scattered in flowers. When the couple and the old woman are about to scream or sigh involuntarily, the thinking eye of the camera becomes disgusted with them and cuts them off—no one, we are relieved to discover, is permitted to violate the silence. The woman with the lorgnon reminds her thoughtless partner with the pince-nez about this prohibition when he is about to commit the unpardonable sin of saying something. The more conscientious of the two, she diplomatically saves him from his wayward ways with a sibilant, never uttering a word. In these scenes Beckett inverts the usual progression of montage. Rather than show us through film splicing the Keaton whom the couple and the old woman capture with their eyes, Beckett keeps the image they see from us. In its place he gives us Keaton's view of them. This substitution quickly establishes through use of the diffusion lens the distinct perspective of O in sharp contrast to the more clearly focused perspectives of the other characters. The old flower woman, like the couple before her, catches sight not only of Keaton, but of the superhuman eye of the camera as well as the audience looking at her. Her own eyes therefore register her own agony of "perceivedness" and her own triple horror. In the series of medium shots of the couple and the old woman, Beckett cleverly undercuts our preoccupation with the object and focuses it on the perceivers instead. At these crucial moments in *Film,* E effectively becomes O for the audience.

In the first part of *Film,* the devilish eye of the camera brutally chases Keaton into an illusory sanctuary. Thinking that he has escaped from the threat of being perceived when the camera forgets about him and is momentarily diverted by the old woman cascading with her flowers down the vestibule staircase, Keaton seizes upon this unexpected opportunity to make a sudden dash for freedom up the staircase. Here the scenario helps us identify O with earlier Beckett heroes like Malone and Molloy and later ones like the figures we will meet in *Ghost Trio,* . . . *but the clouds* . . . , and *Nacht und Träume.*

This obviously cannot be O's room. It may be supposed it is his mother's room, which he has not visited for many years and is now to occupy momentarily, to look after the pets, until she comes out of hospital. This has no bearing on the film and need not be elucidated.

—*Film,* p. 59

Keaton seeks relief from the camera in the maternal womb: a close-up of his hands touching the lock on the door visualizes his thanksgiving. But Keaton underestimates his opponent. This cyclopean antagonist is not so easily subdued, for the superhuman eye of the camera is not subject to humiliating limitations like time and space. It is there to greet him even in the maternal shelter. In this room Keaton faces other voyeurs as well: as the window exposes him to the outside world, the mirror seduces him with self-perception. Both must be covered up as quickly as possible. The mirror, like the framed looking glass Philippe Soupault once exhibited at a show of surrealist art, is an especially malevolent character: throwing off its dark cloak, this evil eye comes after Keaton yet again. The crucifying picture of God the Father, strategically located near a nail, must similarly be taken down from its position on high. Most annoying of all are those live animals and the bird and fish. The close-up of the goldfish is in fact the most deadly image we have seen thus far; its "nondilating" quality is the result of its having given up the ghost during the filming process, making this image an uncanny parallel to Buñuel's dead donkey eye in *Un chien andalou*.

Still photography presents yet another visual dimension to Keaton's most dangerous endgame. Even the folder containing the pictures presents a crisis: to avert the "eyes" of the folder, it must be shifted ninety degrees. Its seven photos represent the "eyes of the past" and become therefore the pictures within the picture:[20] the last one gives us our first full view of Keaton with a patch over his eye, foreshadowing the ultimate "investment." In the photograph Keaton maintains his porkpie nonchalance. Though we look over his shoulder to see with him the seven ages of man he sees, we still cannot see him directly. These photographs, even the one with the pretty little girl he strokes lovingly with his forefinger (the chair slowly rocking to emotionalize the setting), are, however, the dead representations of a younger O captured lifelessly in still photography. As he has already done with that awful picture of God the Father, Keaton tears up one by one the photographs of a past and a self he no longer wishes to acknowledge as his own. Like the captain in Strindberg's *Dance of Death,* he sweeps them away as they become quite literally out of sight. The interpolation of still photography into the fluid cinematic medium brings an additional eye medium to be reckoned with; yet the pictures snared by these mechanical lenses can be controlled, ripped apart, even rubbed into the ground. The thinking eye of the camera has, by contrast, an autonomy of its own, merciless, endless, never pausing even to blink. The photographs whet our appetite all the more for a taste of that mobile, lively Keaton on film. A Keaton frozen in photography is a paltry substitute.

The exposure is not long delayed. After violating that forty-five-degree angle of immunity, E enters enemy territory. But there is rest before battle. E discovers O asleep, and although the superhuman eye of the camera needs no rest, only more celluloid, O's fragile humanity requires a brief respite. E is big enough to indulge him. This quiet, almost pastoral scene, Keaton gently rocking and dozing in his mother's chair, provides the environment for the swift juxtaposition of perspectives which follows. E makes eye contact with O, O makes eye contact with E, one target on the rocking chair, the other next to the crucifying nail and literally up against the wall. Investment takes place; we see that E = O; the movie ends with those rapid-fire shots lingering in our mind's eye. Keaton as O covers his eyes with his hands; but the images, coming too fast and too unexpectedly, have caught us by surprise, and we have had no time to take cover. "That look" is turned on us, and it is Keaton's face which delivers the coup de grace. All through *Film* we have been looking for Keaton; in revenge for this gross invasion of privacy, Keaton nails us. But the quick-thinking eye of the camera is becoming impatient with this artificial darkness of the movie house. In one fatal blow it cuts off Keaton, dispatching us as well, refusing to record any further. Keaton is not cooperating. He, too, looks as though he now must say something, and at this late date in the game the eye is not going to play second fiddle to rhetoric.

Film thus tells its graphic story through a "literature of the un-word," a phrase Beckett used as far back as 1937 in a letter to his German friend Axel Kaun. "Grammar and Style!" he complained, "They appear to me to have become just as obsolete as a Biedermeier bathing suit or the imperturbability of a gentleman. A mask."[21] In the same letter he speculates on how a new literary genre might be able to nurture the "tonal surface" of the "large black pauses" in Beethoven's Seventh Symphony, "connecting unfathomable abysses of silence." To Lawrence E. Harvey he confided that

Joyce believed in words. All you had to do was rearrange them and they would express what you wanted. . . . If you really get down to the disaster, the slightest eloquence becomes unbearable. Whatever is said is so far from experience. . . . (There is a danger of rising up into rhetoric. Speak it even and pride comes. Words are a form of complacency.)[22]

Beckett's attraction to film therefore lies in the medium's ability to evoke the "said" by the "unsaid," quite the opposite of the "extraordinary evocation of the unsaid by the said" he admired so much in Denis Devlin's poetry of the thirties.[23] The manipulation of cinematic spatiality and temporality might be able to accomplish what words sometimes fail to do. "Comic and unreal," *Film* allows Beckett the opportunity to explore the presence of words by the disturbing dynamism of their conspicuous absence. To make an almost silent film in 1964 is, then, to do something more than pay homage to the past: it is to make the cinema "unreel," to make us listen carefully to the manufactured stillness of an artificially rich "literature of the un-word."

II

In his television plays Beckett brings the sound back into the picture. Words and music are revitalized once they are contained by the black-and-white geometry of camera movements designed for a small box, a more congenial metaphor for being inside someone's head. Beckett's disappointment at *Film*'s poor distribution was only part of the reason he turned his attention to television.[24] His work in each medium takes advantage of some fundamental differences, not the least of which is access to television's larger audience. The movie theater isolates and enlarges the film; we watch oversized images in the dark, with other people, removed from our everyday concerns. When the lights go up, however, reality intrudes: the silver screen has offered us release, an escape after all. The television set, on the other hand, brings audio-visual imagery into the living room, shortening the distance between the audience and the less than life-size object under scrutiny. The "grey rectangle" brings the strange into the comfortable room of the viewer, alongside the dirty dishes and the personal computer. Intruding its presence into the safety and security of a world we like to think we control, Beckett's television image invades our reality and makes it part of his own. "Knowing all this," we hear as we see *Ghost Trio*, "Look again": look again at your own "familiar chamber."[25]

As a writer for television, Beckett explores its shadowy potential to disrupt and transfigure any preconceptions we may have about the aesthetics of the medium. O doesn't hear voices in *Film;* it is sight rather than sound that he fears. In this case it is the audience's turn to yearn for absent words. In *Eh Joe*, a television play Beckett wrote in 1967 for Jack MacGowran, the figure both fears and craves the broadcast of a woman's voice "throttling the dead in his head."[26] We hear what Joe hears, but what we see on the screen after Joe settles down from his brief survey of the room is the result of a skillfully engineered choreography of nine camera movements, *"say four inches each time."* The close-up image of Joe's "mental thuggee" varies with every dolly-in, as though moving closer each time inside a head. What the camera records is an impassive face *"except in so far as it reflects mounting tension of listening."* Words subordinate the visual image. What Joe listens to is language, a language which not surprisingly creates a story in which he is the protagonist. We watch Joe listen, and we listen with him: "Look up, Joe, look up, we're watching you." The nine shots of Joe mark the tempo of our own rising tension as we struggle to hear the denouement of what this voice has to say for itself. Every pause, every second brings a delay that is unbearable. Sound cauterizes sight, sight skewers sound, but language has now become accusatory and malicious. In this television play Beckett turns our eyes once again toward the provenance of his words.

> This all new to you, Joe? . . . Eh Joe? . . . Gets the tablets and back down the garden and under the viaduct . . . Takes a few on the way . . . Unconscionable hour by now . . . Moon going off the shore behind the hill . . . Stands a bit looking at the beaten silver . . . Then starts along the edge to a place further down near the Rock . . . Imagine what in her mind to make her do that . . . Imagine . . . Trailing her feet in the water like a child . . . Takes a few more on the way . . . Will I go on, Joe? . . . Eh Joe? . . . Lies down in the end with her face a few feet from the tide . . . Clawing at the shingle now . . . Has it all worked out this time . . . Finishes the tube . . . There's love for you . . . Eh Joe? . . . Scoops a little cup for her face in the stones . . . The green one . . . The narrow one . . . Always pale . . . The pale eyes . . . The look they shed before . . . The way they opened after . . . Spirit made light . . . Wasn't that your description, Joe? . . . (*Voice drops to whisper, almost inaudible except words in italics.*) All right . . . You've had the best . . . Now *imagine* . . . Before she goes . . . Face in the cup . . . Lips on a *stone* . . . Taking Joe with her . . . Light gone . . . *"Joe Joe"* . . . No sound . . . To the *stones* . . . Say it now, no one'll hear you . . . Say "Joe" it parts the *lips* . . . *Imagine* the hands . . . The *solitaire* . . . Against a *stone* . . . Imagine the *eyes* . . . Spiritlight . . . Month of June . . . What year of your Lord? . . . *Breasts* in the stone . . . And the *hands* . . . Before they go . . . *Imagine* the hands . . . What are they at? . . . In the *stones* . . . (*Image fades, voice as*

before.) What are they fondling? . . . Till they go . . . *There's love for you* . . . Isn't it, Joe? . . . Wasn't it, Joe? . . . *Eh Joe?* . . . Wouldn't you say? . . . Compared to us . . . Compared to Him . . . *Eh Joe?* (*Voice and image out.*)

—*Eh Joe*, p. 41

Voice fades and image fades, but in this disappearing light hovers the living memory of those who are absent and yet still present. Sustained by "that time," a voice was there to accompany and confirm the existence of the lonely figure who remains. Joe, resigned, submits to the inevitable as he too begins to decay. Solitude, so sacred, now appears in its fully televised perspective: in this monochromatic frame the rhythms of the whispered fragments absorbed by Joe's eyes make it even more bleak and desolate. Converting technology into an experience of feeling, voice and image have together produced a new kind of telecast poetry.

Despite the lyricism that invigorates and ultimately consumes the passion of Beckett's figure in *Eh Joe,* the piece, like *Film,* nevertheless remains anchored in an identifiable sort of realism. Joe's world may be a strange world, but it is one that still retains the props and paraphernalia of our own. Beckett poeticizes the story of a mind turned inward upon itself by giving it a verbal language to match the progress of its visual statement. Although in this play we watch how the arrival and departure of sound animates the central figure, Joe's retreat from the real world presupposes how much he remains part of it. The piece looks abstract, as does *Play,* but a woman's voice personalizes this through the counterpoint of a dramatic narrative complete with sex, attempted suicide, and remorse. Centering an image on a television screen, and holding it, Beckett relies on his actor's face to express physically what his dialogue gives clues to. It is the sound of the story that matters, for it will be sound that arranges the psychological space of the videotaped image. As the television set is transformed for a few minutes into a talking box, a voice is not only saying lines, but conveying life. This is Joe's life, a life once lived in the real world but now only in the fading images of memory designed for public broadcast.

Since writing *Eh Joe* for television, Beckett has used studio geometry not so much to temper any sentimentality that might undermine his drama, but rather to evoke an emotional response from the interplay of the geometric pattern itself. The move toward a more advanced form of abstraction invites a greater reliance on specific musical, mathematical, and poetic motifs without the mediation of any documentation to explain their being there. Plot has been suppressed; the past leading up to it is, if anything, even more mysterious than the event performed in the present. The character of voice changes completely: no longer stationed inside a character's subconscious, the voice we hear no longer aims to be personally involved with the video image in any capacity other than as master of ceremonies. Voice has become as seemingly objective as the camera. Directing our attention to movement, sight lines, volume, light, and "shades of the colour grey," voice transposes the visual to the aural by controlling the television image and guiding our way of seeing it. Isolating the image from its purely visual context, voice appears to offer us a truthful depiction of some unnatural reality. The great emphasis placed on repeated images allows us to discover the hidden poetry in the poorest objects and the simplest movements. Seeing these elements better and more profoundly, voice works with camera to harmonize the previously imperceptible but highly acute relationships of shapes, spaces, and masses. Its concern with relief, tone, chiaroscuro, a sense of composition, and placement on the television screen forces us, ironically, to overlook the geometry which makes all of this possible and respond intead to the human quality located in the images themselves. Pushing everything to the point of abstraction, Beckett offers us a poetry of form and structure which, in the process of eroding the obvious identity of his characters, restores them, curiously enough, to dramatic life.

Beckett's breakthrough in television drama comes in 1976 with the writing of *Ghost Trio* and . . . *but the clouds* . . . , two plays transmitted the following spring (April 17, 1977) by the BBC along with the adaptation of *Not I* as a three-part program called "Shades." *Ghost Trio* is more involved with the evocative nature of its musical structure than with the communicative possibility of any "semblance" of dramatic narrative. "Good evening," a female voice tells us twice. "Mine is a faint voice. Kindly tune accordingly." Such an indistinct narrator forces us to listen more attentively and prepare ourselves for what will be a highly unpredictable video demonstration. Directed in its original English version by Donald McWhinnie and starring Billie Whitelaw as V and Ronald Pickup as F (male figure), the show was taped again as *Die Geister Trio* by the Süddeutscher Rundfunk in May 1977, directed by Beckett himself, this time with Klaus Herm as F. The play opens with a fade-up to a room with a decidedly rectilinear view. Within this gray domain every rectangle looks the same, either 0.70m × 2m or 0.70m × 1.50m: so much for floor, wall, door, window, and pallet with *"grey rectangular pillow at window end."* Voice offers us some sound advice: "Having seen that specimen of floor you have seen it all." What this particular "it all" reveals is "dust," yet one more encounter with a shade of gray. Soon the camera will display other rectangles: cassette (*"small grey rectangle on larger rectangle of seat"*), mirror (small gray rectangle *"same dimensions as cassette"* against *"larger rectangle of wall"*), and the corridor seen from the rectangular space formed by the door jamb.[27] A deviation from what Clov would appreciate as the singular pattern of such "nice dimensions, nice proportions" occurs in the witty downpour of those mini-rectangles called raindrops we hear recorded on the sound track and see *"falling in dim light"* through yet another rectangle, the open window. Props suggest further variations of rectangular framings: the cassette and the disembodied music, the gray pillow and the dreams beyond the waking world. As he has previously done with Ada in *Embers,* Beckett makes geometry our strong point here, "First plane, then solid."[28] We see every rectangle, and then every rectangle on a larger rectangle, inside the frame of the largest rectangle of all, the television screen placed in the rectangular living space of our own "familiar chamber."

The trio of rectangles is only one configuration in the structural principle at work here. The play contains commands numbered and written in list format and further separated by three progressively longer acts labeled Pre-action, Action, and Re-action. The first part is, in a sense, Voice's scene. Though the voice "will not be raised, nor lowered, whatever happens," it calls the shots and emphasizes the mechanical precision of the camera angles. The abrupt cuts to close-ups of floor, wall, door, window, and pallet, accompanied by the symmetry of five-second pauses, compels the viewer's eyes to acknowledge the visual exposition presented by the camera and given a name by the voice-over. The Pre-action is therefore an orientation to both the setting of the play and the mood which highlights grayness, sameness, and repetition. The Pre-action also serves as a prologue, a formal introduction to the silent male figure and to the female voice, as well as to the music (the "largo" from Beethoven's fifth piano trio), the dolly-in and dolly-out motion, the three camera angles A, B, and C (general view, medium shot, and near shot), and the three positions of the figure (5, 6, and 7): F seated by door, F at window, F at head of pallet. Though V tells us that the "seated figure" is the sole "sign of life," music serves as an additional character element in its own right rather than as mere background accompaniment. As the animated camera gets nearer, the music gets louder, and vice versa. The music can be raised or lowered, unlike the voice, which claims it cannot be. This quality of music is clearly not coming from the cassette. F makes no movement to manipulate the controls, and in any case such fine tuning could certainly not be produced by a micro-tape subject to battery-induced amplification.[29] The Pre-action therefore makes clear that this play features three autonomous offstage ghosts, each with a different role in the repertory: voice, camera, and music.

Who is Voice and where is it coming from? Its function in *Ghost Trio* is strangely imperative as it commands us to "Look," "look closer," "Look again," and "keep that sound down." Later it will call upon the action itself to "Repeat." Its opening monologue gives us the stage directions we need to localize the scene. And though it sounds authoritarian, it is not without a wry sense of humor. With its observation on the setting, light, and absence of color, it is only describing what the viewer should be able to see for himself: "Forgive my stating the obvious." V's imperative personality is extended in the first act to the camera, as cuts from close-up to close-up of floor, wall, door, and so forth, follow the naming of these objects. During most of the first act the camera just sees, offering us no reflection, no interpretation, and above all "no shadow," for true ghosts are not supposed to cast any. But a filmic cliché closes the Pre-action. The camera moves in, slowly, to a near shot of F, accompanied by the first fade-in of the music, building a melodramatic effect and creating a sense of suspense. Nothing happens. We move from A to B to C and back again to give the audience a tantalizing close-up of the "Sole sign of life" only to have it withdrawn. The camera retreats, timidly, to a less threatening general view. Music fades out, lending an air of completion to the Pre-action, which has been essentially comic: F has not responded at all and nothing has occurred to justify the camera's movement. Motionless for the entire first act, F still remains only part of the emerging composition, a gray stage prop no different from window, pallet, or door. He is merely there to give the camera something else to focus on.

In the second act the human figure comes to life. Voice gives him a bigger role, though it still saves the best part for itself. Continuing to monopolize all the lines, it now uses them to anticipate and interpret F's actions to the viewer. V announces at the start that, "He will now think he hears her," as F begins his series of motions, each one punctuated by V's commentary on what he sees or where he plans to go next. The actual moves are F's, but he does so only as instructed by the loudspeaker. V's omniscience is soon challenged, however, when

F momentarily makes an unprecendented dash for independence: "*F turns to wall at head of pallet, goes to wall, invisible from A.*" Voice, "*surprised,*" cries out, "Ah!" V is startled because it has given F no mandate to go to the wall and look in the mirror. Perhaps Voice expects F to return to the window after examining the pallet, as the camera does in act 1. Or perhaps it sees in act 2 what we see only in act 3, the mirror that catches nothing, the reflection of a ghost. In any case, its expectations are upset, along with the promise it made in the opening speech, never to vary the tone of voice. Any confidence we may have had in the omniscient power of this narrator is upset too. Unlike the others we have encountered in our video experiences, this narrative voice-over does not always seem to know everything that will happen next. Voice, however, quickly reasserts its hold on things after F's sudden improvisation: the mischievous actor is once again performing only on verbal cues. When F returns to his stool, the dolly-in, dolly-out exactly duplicates its earlier movement in the Pre-action in tandem with the music. V then says: "He will now again think he hears her." But despite the repetition of a line heard only moments before, the play is not going to backtrack on itself at this point. F now goes to the door, opens it, and looks out in one continuous motion, where before there were pauses of five seconds between separate actions. And after closing the door, F settles back into his opening position instead of going again to window and pallet. Music is then heard for the first time during the general view, a further deviation from part 2, where it was heard only during the dolly.

In the second part of *Ghost Trio* all of the "action" is seen from A, the general view. The camera moves in only once, when F resumes his motionless pose on the stool. As no close-up is called for during F's motion itself, the wide view reduces the figure and effectively increases the distance between his journey around the room and the spectator. F, moreover, has his back to us, further distancing his face from our view, as in *Film*. The voice returns for two simple imperatives after music is heard at A, first to order the chords to stop, then to signal "Repeat" in quick transition to the finale.

The third act does in fact repeat the action of part 2, but this time without voiced interpolation. Though in the Re-action the figure makes his moves without benefit of voice, he is, nevertheless, not acting independently this time. F is acting instead upon his last voiced command, "Repeat." Scene 3 is Re-action and exactly that, a repeat of the actions of 2, not a reaction of response. While Voice's presence is audibly diminished, other elements in the composition are all the while building up. First of all, the image is enlarged, the action is brought nearer to the viewer, and F's presence on the screen is increased by the positioning of the camera for a near shot at C, with occasional close-ups of F added for emphasis. Scenes 1 and 2 use mostly camera A, the general view. But in 3 the whole scene except for the last few moments is shot with close-up camera C. The Re-action thus allows us to see the same sequence of events, but from a closer viewpoint. The action also seems to expand in this part, as the number of cutaways from F to what he is looking at elongates the time span in which the action occurs. Sound also becomes more frequent and much more dominant in part 3, both in the use of music, which is now audible on the very first shot, and in the use of sound effects, such as the crescendo and decrescendo creaks of window and door, the sound of the cassette placed on the chair, the sound of rain, and the sound of the boy's footsteps and knocks. The various crescendo movements combine to build toward the climax of the play.

The climax that occurs in the Re-action is, in keeping with this medium, a visual one. Though F has apparently been waiting for some unspecified "her," a small boy appears in her place, shaking his head and repeating the movement of an unexpected messenger that brings closure to each act of *Waiting for Godot*. In a black oilskin with contrasting white face, wet with rain, the boy stands in complete opposition not only to the dry dust, but to the rest of the set for *Ghost Trio*, which is entirely pictured in "shades of the colour grey." The climax is not exclusively visual either, for music plays a fateful part in the making of this portentous denouement. Beckett has used music for dramatic emphasis before: Winnie begins her day in preparation for singing the waltz duet from *The Merry Widow*; in *All That Fall* Maddy Rooney hears the music of Schubert's *Death and the Maiden* Quartet; in *Embers* Henry hears little Addie bang out a choppy rendition of Chopin's Fifth Waltz in A Flat Major ("Santa Cecilia!" the master cries out in an Italian accent, evoking the name of melody's patron saint); and *Cascando* and *Words and Music* rely on original scores, respectively, by Marcel Mihalovici and John Beckett. The sudden appearance of the boy in *Ghost Trio* has been anticipated by the sound of Beethoven's Fifth Piano Trio, op. 70, the one, in fact, known as the *Ghost* Trio. The music we hear in this play is the haunting theme from the "largo," although in his script Beckett does not call for use of the famous "ghost chords." The two silent images of the boy's face and the long shot of him receding into empty space down the corridor are in a sense the real "ghost chords" in this play, the "unfathomable abysses of silence" Beckett mentioned long ago in his letter to Axel Kaun. Throughout *Ghost Trio* Beckett has equated silence with the "large black pauses" in Beethoven's piano trio, as he had done earlier with the "tonal surface" of Beethoven's Seventh Symphony.

In *Die Geister Trio* the appearance and disappearance of the boy are even more ghostlike: as the boy retreats, he does so without turning around, moving backwards down the hall as his face, reduced to a mask, gradually fades out. In both screenings of the play the sound track is carefully controlled and works in harmony with the action. Beckett frequently has a five-second camera hold on the action, just as an examination of the music finds that each bar lasts almost exactly five seconds. Important changes in the action coincide with changes in the music. As ghostly steps approach in the dark corridor and F stands by the door thinking he hears the long-awaited "her," the music seems somber and melancholy. But when the boy is finally seen, the music climaxes and changes to evoke surprise and mystery, reinforcing the shock we and the male figure undergo at the sight of such an unheralded visitor. Beckett grants as much dramatic importance to music as he does to action. Beethoven's *Ghost* Trio, with its slow, lingering passages surging quietly up and down, thus becomes a major protagonist in the unfolding conflict. The largo movement complements the grayness and emptiness of the room, foreshadows the irresoluteness of F's actions, and predicts the slow building of dramatic suspense.

Beckett, however, has chosen to use only selected passages from Beethoven's key "largo" movement. As in the structural principle for *Krapp's Last Tape,* these fade in and fade out, backing up to earlier parts of the movement, repeating bars we have already heard, just as Voice reintroduces phrases and the action repeats itself. Throughout the play music portrays dramatic significance. Elements lifted from the "largo" augment our vision of the door and the cassette, foregrounding them as the two indispensable props. This is, after all, a "largo assai ed espressivo." We cannot help but wonder what's behind the door or what's recorded on the cassette, the *what* and the *where* of this show. Perhaps the music has been taped on this machine after all. The volume increases as the camera zeroes in toward the cassette and decreases when the camera moves back. But this is manufactured illusion. Without the mysterious source of music, door and cassette would play no bigger role than wall or window. The music stimulates our perception and suggests their deeper significance. By act 3 we receive a view down the corridor that lies beyond the wall and the little boy appears at the door. We have been sensitized to this gateway by both the deliberation of the camera shots and the music. Our reaction is heightened as a result of the Pre-action. F has been waiting for someone to arrive: an earlier title for this play was, in fact, *Tryst,* the Anglo-Saxon word for rendezvous.[30] Beckett has made sight and sound collaborate to achieve his dramatic effect. The music evoked here is, however, really a silent music. This is a music without the tumult of sound which Mallarmé intended to transpose into poetry, a silence in which the real sound having been spent, a remembered sound takes its place and the music itself finds its ideal fulfillment. Music, like voice and camera, is a ghost.

There are, of course, some additional ghosts in this play, specifically the theater ghosts that haunt the studio in which the show has been taped. The actor, reduced for the most part to a stage prop, is the ghost of an actor. The small boy in the corridor drama is a ghostly apparition condemned, like the ghost of Hamlet's father, to walk this passageway through all eternity. A surprise visitor, he appears at the threshold of this chamber like a guest as unbidden as the ghost of Banquo in the banquet scene in *Macbeth,* giving this play an ancestry common to *That Time* as well. It should also be noted here that Beckett chose for *Ghost Trio* a piece of music that was, more than likely, inspired by *Macbeth.* Beethoven wrote his trio in 1808 as he considered writing the music for a projected opera based on Shakespeare's play. Beethoven's notebooks include a sketch for the largo movement of the trio on the same page as a sketch for the uncompleted opera to be based on *Macbeth.* Both pieces are in D minor. Alan Tyson observes that "it is not improbable that Beethoven had the weird sisters in mind when he first conceived his music."[31]

In *Ghost Trio,* however, Beckett draws upon other sources besides Shakespeare. The boy's footsteps, for example, echo those of that other ghost in Beckett's repertory, May in *Footfalls.* In act 3 we, too, hear his feet, "however faint they fall." The ghostly chamber is also familiar: we have seen its "semblance" before in *Film* and *Eh Joe,* and we have read about it even earlier in *Molloy.* Strindberg has brought us yet another ghost, his in the form of a sonata rather than a trio. And *The Ghost Sonata* is not the only Strindberg analogue; *A Dream Play* is present, too. Beckett incorporates from it the waiting for an actress by the stage door, the lonely corridor, the expressionistic use of music, as well as the pervasive atmosphere of a dream. Ibsen's *Ghosts* also lurks somewhere in the wings. Not to be overlooked is one more ghostlike character, John Gabriel Borkman, whose offstage footsteps resound through the theater to build suspense in the first scene of Ibsen's play. Indeed, *Ghost Trio* condenses an entire range of the ghosts of theater past, from the Eumenides of the Greek drama to Eliot's attempt to make them functional on the modern stage in *The Family Reunion*. Beckett's drama also relies on our recollection of Yeats' poetic story of an encounter between a boy and an old man in *Purgatory*, the verse drama which opens with a very different "Half-door, hall door." "What is a ghost?" Stephen Dedalus asks with "tingling energy" in *Ulysses*. "One who has faded into impalpability through death, through absence, through change of manners." "Who is the ghost from *limbo patrum*," Joyce's hero continues, "returning to the world that has forgotten him?"[32]

Rich with a suggestiveness that reminds Beckett's audience of its earlier theater experiences, *Ghost Trio* emphasizes its own staginess and its own theatricality. The camera work, the voice-over, and the sound effects point out its nature as a made-for-television thing, a manufactured drama which urges us to consider what video technology has to contribute to the conventions of live theater as we know them. The "familiar chamber" is a stage, in this instance the rectangular performance space of a television studio. The voice-over comes from the director's booth, which also contains the sophisticated instruments to control all of the production elements. And the tripartite structure signifies a rehearsal, a dress rehearsal, and the stability of the final performance, which will incorporate the definitive blocking, sight lines, and sound effects. In this respect *Ghost Trio* especially resembles *Footfalls*, which similarly uses the progression of three closely related stagings to make the image come out right in the final set. The actor's movements are intentionally theatrical in *Ghost Trio;* he sits still in a tense pose and even leaps up, puppet-like. His major role here is to convey the alternation between tension and loss of tension:

> II. 2. F *raises head sharply, turns still crouched to door, fleeting face, tense pose. 5".*
> 3. V: No one.
> 4. F *relapses into opening pose, bowed over cassette.*
> 5. V: Again.
> 6. *Same as 2.*
>
> —*Ghost Trio*, p. 58

Anticipating a visit, F rises to look out of a window and a door. Both initially open into blackness and nowhere, blind studio space. A woman's even, unimpassioned voice narrates his thwarted expectation: "No one." What we will finally "see" through this window and through this door has been carefully edited in through montage: the close-up of a boy's face and what is clearly meant to be man-made rain. The mirror which reflects nothing is another self-conscious device, an edited-in impression of a ghost's invisibility. Conventionally, of course, television cameras are invisible, yet the medium normally avoids making this obvious: no close-ups of mirrors, for instance. Beckett shows neither the figure's reflection in the glass nor the television camera in the mirror, calling our attention to the skillful editing work this medium can so easily accomplish. Sound effects made in a studio are also self-consciously theatrical. Real rain never sounded like this, and the only places where we can hear such window and door creakings are on the sound tracks of "B" movies, especially in the genre of horror films. Footsteps and door knocks are similarly prefabricated and similarly melodramatic. The crescendo and decrescendo of Beethoven's piano trio, with its precise backtracking of bars we have heard before and its perfect collaboration with specific camera shots, has been deliberately prepared for us in a state-of-the-art sound studio, not on a cheap cassette.

So much has been technologically arranged for us in *Ghost Trio* that we sometimes forget the genesis of this process in Beckett's script. Many of the actions, like V's sentences and phrases, typically occur in pairs. F repeats the motion of raising his head and bowing it at the beginning of both the Action and the Re-action, the wall is seen twice in close-up, the complete set of F's action (going to door, window, pallet, and so forth) occurs twice, F's face is seen clearly two times, and the boy knocks on the door and shakes his head at F twice. The actions most frequently repeated are of the simplest nature: F standing, F looking, F bowing his head. The music, moreover, never occurs with the action in *Ghost Trio*. It also never occurs in the same time span as Voice's lines, but is instead always stopped by it, except in the Re-action, where music finally comes into its own.

One of the most interesting aspects of *Ghost Trio* is the attention Beckett pays to temporal spacings, and the regularity of rhythm he creates. Most numbered actions are followed by a notation for a pause, always five seconds long except for a few ten-second pauses. Where this longer interval is indicated, there is an extreme intrusion of either high or low tension to underscore a particular action. The temporal regularity is not based on the length of a given shot, or even on F's actions themselves, but rather on the space between actions and movements. The rhythm in *Ghost Trio* is thus established on defined intervals of non-action, much like rests in music. Similarly, Beckett indicates periods of extended silence, such as the one which closes the play, again for emphasis. In the German version, which Beckett directed, this final interval is tracked by a camera which slowly moves away from the actor to reveal the full figure sitting alone, further extending the silence. Because F is always listening for something in a gesture which parallels our own, the act of listening is the most prominent feature in *Ghost Trio*. In this play the absence of sound takes on as much character as its presence, which has been used all through this ghost drama only with the utmost discretion. The symmetry of the visual surface, the building and release of tension, the doubling back and repetition, and above all the attention to rhythm, place *Ghost Trio* in firm command of television's most attractive potential, the control of sound in coordination with motion. In this play Beckett's statement remains intensely visual, but it is equally musical and mathematical. On the television screen illusion builds its density from allusion as Beckett gives to rigid technology a personality, a ghostlike but still humanized form based on the most poetic elements of a simple geometric pattern.

III

In . . . *but the clouds* . . . the rich cadence of Beckett's poetics of television technology can be seen in even sharper relief. Here the physiognomy of emotion arising from seeming abstraction is taken one step further. The gray, rectangular surface of a familiar chamber has been transformed into a circular set whose single prop is the reflection cast by studio lighting. "All true grace," Beckett told Peter Hall, "is economical."[33] The play, originally called *Poetry only love*, takes its title as well as the theme on which it works a strong variation from the final stanza of Yeats' "The Tower":

> Now shall I make my soul,
> Compelling it to study
> In a learned school
> Till the wreck of body,
> Slow decay of blood,
> Testy delirium
> Or dull decrepitude,
> Or what worse evil come—
> The death of friends, or death
> Of every brilliant eye
> That made a catch in the breadth—

> Seem but the clouds of the sky
> When the horizon fades,
> Or a bird's sleepy cry
> Among the deepening shades.[34]

As Martin Esslin has suggested, the play draws much of its vitality from Paul Valéry's concept of the *ligne donnée,* the given line on which another imagination imposes its will.[35] Beckett, however, owes more than a line to Yeats. The television play, like the poem, deals with a "troubled heart" in conflict with "eyes / That are impatient to be gone":

> Does the imagination dwell the most
> Upon a woman won or a woman lost?
> If on the lost, admit you turned aside
> From a great labyrinth out of pride,
> Cowardice, some silly over-subtle thought
> Or anything called conscience once;
> And that if memory recur, the sun's
> Under eclipse and the day blotted out.
> —"The Tower," p. 195

In . . . *but the clouds* . . . a man's voice murmurs, "Look at me" and "Speak to me," imploring the fleeting image of a beloved to restore memory back to life with "those unseeing eyes I so begged when alive to look at me."[36] And now the variation on "The Tower": whereas Yeats, "lured by a softening eye, / Or by a touch or a sigh, / Into the labyrinth of another's being," finds "an answer in those eyes" to "rise, / Dream and so create / Translunar Paradise" in his art, the lonely creature who tramps in and out of Beckett's circle of hellish light is left only with "a begging of the mind."

> 24. v: For had she never once appeared, all that time, would I have, could I have, gone on begging, all that time? Not just vanished within my little sanctum and busied myself with something else, or with nothing, busied myself with nothing? Until the time came, with break of day, to issue forth again, shed robe and skull, resume my hat and great coat, and issue forth again, to walk the roads.
> — . . . *but the clouds* . . . , p. 54

Beckett's isolated figure departs as he had earlier arrived, with nothing, "no sound" and no revelation. What he finds in these cold eyes is emptiness, the great mystery of "unseeing" that Murphy meets when he stares into Mr. Endon's eyes. For Beckett's hero there will be no soaring tower and no Byzantium, only a fading horizon of memory, embers in "the deepening shades."

Produced in its original English version by the same team that worked together on *Ghost Trio* (Donald McWhinnie as director, with Ronald Pickup as the Man [M] and Billie Whitelaw as the Woman [W]), . . . *but the clouds* . . . shares with it some of the same technical options. While *Ghost Trio* was filmed in color but printed in black and white, resulting in a tremendous variation in shades of gray,[37] . . . *but the clouds* . . . was designed for broadcast in the sharper contrast of two tones. Yeats' poetry replaces Beethoven's music; it, too, works as powerfully unheard as heard. . . . *but the clouds* . . . features two voices, the male one who speaks and the female one who poignantly mouths Yeats' lines in silence. In . . . *but the clouds* . . . the heard melodies are sweet, but those unheard are sweeter. They are also, Keats notwithstanding, far more dramatically effective. The unvoiced lines come from the lips of the close-up image "*of a woman's face reduced as far as possible to eyes and mouth.*" Almost subliminal at first, the scrim of this face soon appears as a lingering transparency, a diaphanous illusion inlaid on the image of the male figure who patiently summons its presence: "Such had long been my use and wont" (pun intended). Within the television illusion there is, then, another illusion, the intrusive mask of a female head. It is now the deliberate turn of the man's voice we hear, rather than any Shakespearean Horatio we can also see, to make the appeal of "Stay, illusion!" we remember from *Hamlet.*

M's voice in . . . *but the clouds* . . . does more than wait. Like his female counterpart in *Ghost Trio,* this masculine register directs the action we see. But V in this case is now identified as M's, the voice of a man "*sitting on invisible stool bowed over invisible table.*" In this "*dark ground*" he wears a "*light grey robe and skullcap,*" a costume draped by M1 when we first meet him "*in set*": "*Hat and greatcoat dark, robe and skullcap light.*" As he sits in the dark for "*5 seconds,*" M is composing: "When I thought of her it was always night" is quickly amended to "When she appeared it was always night." The ghost in this story is given a bit more autonomy in its second go-round. The first version, V tells us, is "not right." It simply doesn't *look* right. For V has an expert and extremely visual imagination; as he speaks his image, it suddenly comes to televised life on the screen:

> *Dissolve to S [set] empty. 5 seconds. M1 in hat and greatcoat*
> *emerges from west shadow, advances five steps and stands fac-*
> *ing east shadow. 2 seconds.*
> — . . . *but the clouds* . . . , p. 53

"No," says V, "that is not right." "She" needs to *appear* in her own right, and the word is all-important here. The visualization is repeated, exactly, except that the camera will hold the revised scene for "*5 seconds*," not "2." V is now free to write additional material into his words and pictures: "Right."

Beckett's composer in . . . *but the clouds* . . . will not shy away from using a personal pronoun. "I came in," he repeats, "Came in, having walked the roads since break of day." What he brings "home," however, is "night." He stands "listening," then, hearing nothing, finally goes to the closet to change from outdoor attire to a costume more fitting the atmosphere of night-thoughts ("Shed my hat and greatcoat, assumed robe and skull"). Word and image represent two separate grammatical dimensions of time as delivered here: words speak in the past tense, pictures and stage directions in the more luminous present. "Facing the other way," M1 returns "exhibiting the other outline." Profiles are signifiers: in the absence of stage props, they point out the vectors of space in the unnatural light of the set, "*about 5 m. diameter, surrounded by deep shadow.*" M1 follows through on the movements dictated by V, but he is fated to do so in a circular void. Movement in this technological sphere is also timed in specific intervals of two seconds or five seconds: space in this medium can only be apprehended as an experience in time. In . . . *but the clouds* . . . Beckett, moreover, does not fill up the frame with the mime M1 performs according to V's rules. The lighting for this series of images is maximum "*at centre,*" dark at the "*periphery.*" Whenever M1 goes to the closet, the sanctum, or out the door, he bleeds into darkness, negative space, "where none could see me." The irony here is that M1 effectively becomes M when he crouches in his so-called invisible sanctum: that is where we discover him imagining his story at the beginning of the play, and that is where we see him going when he disappears into the "north shadow." He is not alone after all. Unknown to him, the television camera has become an unseen voyeur, recording for the viewer a "*near shot from behind.*" This is how we will first see him in a gesture of listening—listening, like Hamm, to a voice "dripping" inside his head.

There are, of course, things we do not see. We do not see the
closet (east shadow) and we do not see the door ("West, roads."").
Beckett makes darkness suggest other spaces, peripheries where other
scenes are to be enacted. Shadow space frames in a circle of light the
action we see through that larger frame of the rectangular television
box. Beckett graphically isolates his image here in a bleak visual landscape that serves as a further emblem of the figure's solitude. On the
television screen shadow space is negative space, but Beckett uses it
in . . . *but the clouds* . . . to confuse our sense of just what constitutes the positive and the negative. Removing a video image from its
usual visual context, Beckett sets it free of any expository function in
order to make us contemplate it in its pure state. Conceiving blacks
and whites as forms of color, Beckett exhorts us to look at the clarity
of the figurative means. Affirming the primacy of representation over
abstraction, . . . *but the clouds* . . . allows us to see even in unseen
things how language controls vision.

What Beckett designs for us to see in this play is as precisely
plotted as the images captured on videotape in *Ghost Trio*. . . . *but
the clouds* . . . uses only three camera shots, a near shot from behind
for M, a close-up for the woman's face, and a long shot for the empty
set or the set with M1. Each of the three shots is the "*same shot
throughout.*" The use of this particular close-up, however, is something new for Beckett, especially as prepared for transmission in the
BBC production studio, where Billie Whitelaw's face appeared as a
transparent shot superimposed on another video image. Camera work
therefore presents us with something more complicated here than three
images which move us, as in *Eh Joe,* progressively inside M's imagination. The shots of M and W meet in collage, further eroding the
barriers between one illusion and the next.

The close-ups, moreover, are as extraterritorial with time as they
have been with space. These exist, in fact, as "three cases," each with
a distinctive temporality. Sometimes they appear in the blink of an eye
("*2 seconds*"), sometimes as a lingering pose ("*5 seconds*"), and
sometimes long enough for the mouth to form, after a moment, the
words ". . . clouds . . . but the clouds . . . of the sky . . . but the
clouds." In this third case V murmurs, synchronous with W's lips,
"but the clouds," during the mouth's second movement on the screen.
After decoding this tripartite repertory for us, V says: "Let us now run
through it again." The camera obliges, but not so scrupulously as we
might expect. Before the inaudible mouthing of the lines from "The
Tower," V unexpectedly intones, "Look at me," paraphrasing Krapp's

cry of "Let me in." And after this quiet Yeatsian interlude, V's prayer is suddenly changed to "Speak to me," a heart-rending appeal answered only by silence, then a quick dissolve to M. "Speak to me" is another Shakespearean echo in Beckett's work, this one from *Hamlet;* it is the line Horatio addresses twice to the ghost of the murdered king, a supplication similarly met with silence:

> Stay, illusion!
> If thou hast any sound, or use of voice,
> Speak to me;
> If there be any good thing to be done
> That may to thee do ease and grace to me,
> Speak to me . . .
> —act 1, scene 2

V's supplication shows us, moreover, that Beckett has read not only his Shakespeare closely, but his Eliot as well, the Eliot of "A Game of Chess" in *The Waste Land* who inspires Pozzo's line of "Think, pig" in *Waiting for Godot:*

> "My nerves are bad to-night. Yes, bad. Stay
>   with me.
> Speak to me. Why do you never speak. Speak.
> What are you thinking of? What thinking. What?
> I never know what you are thinking. Think."[38]

In . . . *but the clouds* . . . the response of empty silence to M's appeal is followed by mention of a previously undocumented "fourth case," the most typical and the most foreboding, the one in which W, like Godot, fails to keep her appointment:

> 52. v: Right, There was of course a fourth case, or case nought, as I pleased to call it, by far the commonest, in the proportion say of nine hundred and ninety-nine to one, or nine hundred and ninety-eight to two, when I begged in vain, deep down into the dead of night, until I wearied, and ceased, and busied myself with something else, more . . . rewarding, such as . . . such as . . . cube roots, for example, or with nothing, busied myself with nothing, that MINE, until the time came, with break of day, to issue forth again, void my little sanctum, shed robe and skull, resume my hat and greatcoat, and issue forth again, to walk the roads. (*Pause.*) The back roads.
> — . . . *but the clouds* . . . , pp. 55–56

Beckett's "MINE" is doubly ambiguous: in one sense it is a rich source of supply, but in another it is a pit from which all resources have been taken, as well as an encased weapon designed to destroy. "That MINE" V discovers is nothingness, but it is also that "Mene, mene," the ominous warning written on Belshazzar's wall that Hamm mentions in *Endgame*. The reference is to Dan. 5:26: "MENE; God hath numbered thy kingdom, and finished it."[39]

In . . . *but the clouds* . . . Beckett confronts his television audience with the concision of an image, an image which condenses even further the dimensions we remember from Yeats' poetic experience. Its sixty camera shots, the shape of an hour, or a minute, localize abstraction and present us with a true iconography, a complete language in pictures. It is difficult to tell, however, if image imitates words or words imitate image: which illustrates which? Words, which seem to be in charge of what happens on the circular performance space, are, ironically, as "canned" in this medium as are the pictures themselves. Fated always to be delivered the same way, recorded words exist in this play as spoken by V. But they are, in fact, part of M's evolving composition. In the process of writing, M = V. He inevitably tries to capture in language the picture he brings to mind, "that MINE," in his own imagination. The words we hear in this play therefore serve a mediating function between the image M invents or remembers and that quite different picture broadcast before us on the screen. Beckett locates language at its source, in the writer's vision. He uses not only Yeats and Shakespeare, but Dante as well: this empty set of studio light is a dark circle in hell. As M sits at his "invisible" table, he is sitting, like the characters in Yeats' *The Words upon the Window-Pane*, at a seance, calling out to a face and a voice to appear: "Look at me," "Speak to me." Yeats' play offers us a stunning parallel:

DR. TRENCH: I thought she was speaking.
MRS. MALLET: I saw her lips move.[40]

But Beckett's face and voice have been programmed to appear through the intercession of a quite different medium, the mechanical one of television. On the television screen, word and image are made to participate in a dynamic relationship that is symbiotic and essentially poetic. Mutually supportive, each has been recorded in advance to foster a new kind of illusion where we might have least expected it, "that MINE" of television technology.

IV

Beckett directed a German version of . . . *but the clouds* . . . in 1977, several months after the play was taped by the BBC in December 1976. Entitled *Nur noch Gewölk,* this telecast uses the final fourteen lines of "The Tower" and makes another departure from the BBC version in that Yeats' lines are not read against the face of a woman, but rather against the figure of the man bent over. The German version also has a male figure *"in set"* who walks with a much more ironic step. Despite the author's variations on his English script, much of the lyricism of the original was lost in *Nur noch Gewölk,* relying as it did on a clumsy, though standard translation of Yeats. A far more successful work for German television was the screening of *Nacht und Träume,* which was written for and produced by Süddeutscher Rundfunk in 1982 and transmitted on May 19, 1983. *Nacht und Träume* creates its unique atmosphere through the collaboration of specific musical and poetic motifs, a combination of the melodic structure of *Ghost Trio* with the lyrical pattern of . . . *but the clouds* . . . . In *Nacht und Träume* a male voice conveys Schubert's music, the last seven bars of a lied by the same name (op. 43, no. 2), while the lines of verse come from Schubert's source, Matthäus von Collin (1779–1824): ". . . come again, holy night! / Sweet dreams, come again!"[41] The play focuses, as its title makes clear, on night and dreams; it opens with a black-and-white shot of an old man sitting in still another "chamber" in the series Beckett has made so "familiar," a dark, empty room. Lit "only by evening light from a window set high in back wall," the work dispenses with written dialogue, but speaks to us instead through the interplay of its two primary visual images, each one the mirror reflection of the other ("right profile," "left profile").[42] The first one we encounter represents the dreamer (A), the second the dream; the dream felt is meant to contrast the "dreamt self" (B). B, as M1 sometimes does in . . . *but the clouds* . . . , appears on the screen to exhibit "the other outline," the dream image set against the waking world, recorded in this medium, inevitably and ironically, as merely another black-and-white illusion broadcast on the screen.

Short as it is, thirty scripted directions involving five "elements" (evening light, A, B, "dreamt hands" and the last seven bars of the lied), *Nacht und Träume* can nevertheless be divided into three scenes followed by the epilogue of two quick dissolves. The initial scene, which corresponds to the first shot we see, displays on the screen's left foreground the right profile of a man, faintly lit ("head bowed, grey hair"), seated alone at a table: "Clearly visible only head and hands and section of table on which they rest." Beckett discreetly refrains from filling up the frame, highlighting his "elements" by encircling them in a somber ring of televised darkness. Silence is broken; we hear a male voice softly humming, followed by the direction, "Fade out evening light." In this diminishing light music changes its mask from "softly hummed" to "softly sung, with words." The situation here has been predicted much earlier in the Beckett canon: "He's singing a lied," we recall from *How It Is*. The melodic line can now be more precisely identified as Schubert's, in this case the last three bars of the lied, beginning with "Holde Träume . . ." ("Sweet dreams"). A bows his head further to rest on hands and remains minimally lit ("just visible") as his dream and scene two begin. A curtain of even fainter light delivers up A to the "deep sleep" of *Footfalls* and of Hamm's story in *Endgame:* "Deep in sleep. . . . But deep in what sleep, deep in what sleep already?"[43]

The dream image, exhibiting the dreamer's left profile "faintly lit by a kinder light," is superimposed "well right of centre" on the upper corner of the screen, one shadow image intruding its uneasy presence on its simulacrum. The action of scene two is about to begin. As if it were a modernist version of some medieval religious painting, a "dreamt hand" appears above B's head from "dark beyond" and rests "gently" on it. B raises his head, then the mysterious hand, identified in the script only as "left" (L), just as mysteriously withdraws and disappears. From "the same dark" another hand, the right one (R) this time, appears with a cup and conveys it "gently" to B's lips: "B drinks, R disappears." R reappears with a cloth, wipes "gently" B's brow, then disappears with the cloth, bleeding out of the picture. B raises his head further to gaze, the script now confirms, at an "invisible face." The next six movements (12–17) outline the plot of the dream self's silent assignation:

12. B raises his right hand, still gazing up, and holds it raised palm upward.
13. R reappears and rests gently on B's right hand, B still gazing up.
14. B transfers gaze to joined hands.
15. B raises his left hand and rests it on joined hands.
16. Together hands sink to table and on them B's head.
17. L reappears and rests gently on B's head.

—*Nacht und Träume*, p. 306

The dream fades out; the scene, the climax, and the enigma of this rendezvous are at an end.

The third scene opens with a fade-up on A and the evening light. The dream is over; A signals this by raising his head to its opening position. We hear the lied softly hummed, then the evening light fades out once more. The actions are repeating themselves: again we begin to distinguish the words of the lied softly sung, and again we see a fade-down on A "as before." A dreams again; fade up on B "as before." But this scene will offer us something more than a second glance at the same brief encounter. This is repetition, but it is repetition with a difference, repetition with an alternative perspective. Through trick photography the dream world is unexpectedly enlarged, "losing A" to take over the full visual landscape. Not only do we see B invade A's territory, but we also see how a dream *becomes* the video reality. The camera has moved in slowly to offer us a closer view, a "Look again," as *Ghost Trio* states it, at the strange interlude of a dream. This time the television has tuned itself "accordingly." Once more we dream with this dreamer, once more we watch hands embrace, but in this repeat performance every action is projected "in close-up and slower motion." We see again, but we see with a difference. The image is the same, yet the image is transformed.

Scene three closes with the opposite camera movement in a slow withdraw to the opening viewpoint, "recovering A." The camera zooms back to catch the dual tableau of A and B as Beckett makes us see the dream image recede into its original television space. We confront for one last time the simultaneity of the dreamt self superimposed on the larger dream felt, an unexpected detour that returns us to the dual image with which this video game began. Yet whose territory invades whose when the camera brings us back to the shot of a simultaneous image we have looked at before? Does reality replace the dream, or is one illusion merely being substituted for another? Is it in the waking world or in the dream world where we see most fully—where we see, as in *Footfalls*, "it all?" "Kehre wieder, heilge Nacht! / Holde Träume, kehret wieder!"[44] Is it A's televised life or B's that is the ultimate dream? "They give birth astride of a grave, the light gleams an instant, then it's night once more." Beckett's "elements" in *Nacht und Träume* have been used before. The slow withdraw of the camera therefore prepares us for the finality that will take place in the denouement of this play's epilogue. First the dream figure fades out, then the "real" figure follows in fatal disintegration. Suddenly we are all alone, facing neither dream nor dreamer, only our own reality in the shape of an

empty rectangle where "something" has just taken its course on the
screen. The images dissolve; everything is finished. "Time is over,"
Endgame states more explicitly, "reckoning closed and story ended."
Beckett now has his viewer, like his lonely hero in . . . *but the clouds*
. . . , bring "night home."

Nacht und Träume televises a pictorial language dramatizing in-
ference rather than argument. A cup of water and a hand wiping a
brow are ripe with referentiality, but the possibly Christian symbolism
is never made explicit. The movements suggest an archetypal scheme,
but fail to yield it, offering us the enchantment of apparition in its
place. Freeing an eye looking for sentimentality of subject, the camera
work is simple, direct, even modest in scale. The measurement in television space, its disposition and the objects in it, also suggest a mathematical formula, but this strict geometry is similarly withheld. In *Nacht
und Träume* Beckett's imagery is not simply representational or an-
ecdotal, but more purely formal in its attempt to capture the essence
of dream play. Reacting to the evocative nature of the video images,
the viewer responds to their gestural energy: the more you study them,
the more ambiguous they become. *Nacht und Träume* therefore emphasizes a dream's and a play's phenomenal quality, their substantive
primacy over the terms a waking world uses to describe them. In pur-
suing the preeminence of such images, *Nacht und Träume* again reveals Beckett's indebtedness to Yeats:

> The unpurged images of day recede;
> The Emperor's drunken soldiery are abed;
> Night resonance recedes, night-walkers' song
> After great cathedral gong;
> A starlit or a moonlit dome disdains
> All that man is,
> All mere complexities,
> The fury and the mire of human veins.
>
> Before me floats an image, man or shade,
> Shade more than man, more image than shade . . .[45]

The images seem vague as telecast, but always concrete, as if their
visualization, not their meaning, were the dramatist's true subject. All
of the significance in *Nacht und Träume* seems to lie in its being a
drama, not in what it is a drama of. Writing with the basic material
of television, video images, Beckett makes us sense the verbal poten-

tial of all that he renders so palpably visual. The medium of television requires another kind of lyrical language here, a spatial and temporal one, for its most effective means of communication. The video image speaks more precisely because it says less, and in saying less it says everything in the way this medium can be made to say it. It is the camera, substituting film for rhetoric, that provides punctuation and emphasis here. The only "voice" Beckett needs in *Nacht und Träume* belongs to music, the concluding bars of a Schubert lied. The rest is silence, where night and dreams take place.

V

Beckett's *Quad* plays, two related works that premiered on German television on October 8, 1981, under the title *Quadrat 1 + 2*, are, by comparison, literally teeming with movement, color, and percussion. The plays, originally done in Stuttgart by Süddeutscher Rundfunk, were later shown by the BBC in England on December 16, 1982. The work in this instance is more like the scheme for some avant-garde modern dance than anything even vaguely recognizable as traditional dramatic form. But then we remember that one of the origins of Western theater lies in the dithyramb and the choral dance. Missing from Beckett's text, if we can indeed speak of it as such, is, however, the recitation of any spoken dialogue, strange, poetic, or otherwise. The *Quad* plays present us instead with a choreography of madness, four players, "mimes," Beckett said, "not dancers,"[46] on an empty set "each following his particular course" but always turning his back on the midpoint of a square ("Length of side: 6 paces").[47] "It was feverish," said Jim Lewis, the cameraman who had earlier worked with Beckett on *Eh Joe, Ghost Trio*, and . . . *but the clouds* . . . , "feverish monotony." The center, as in Yeats, simply cannot hold; Beckett merely identifies it here as a supposed "danger zone." As each player arrived at a point close to the center, he made a "jerky turn to his left as a diversion away from it." At first it seemed "they were merely avoiding one another, but gradually one realised they were avoiding the center. There was something terrifying about it . . . it was danger."[48] Like "J. M. Mime," the sketch conceived for Jack MacGowran about 1963 and now in the Beckett collection in the Trinity College manuscript room in Dublin, the "book" for this show is reduced to a diagram and a series of mathematical permutations:

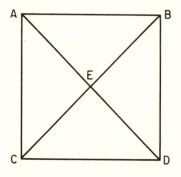

COURSE 1: AC, CB, BA, AD, DB, BC, CD, DA
COURSE 2: BA, AD, DB, BC, CD, DA, AC, CB
COURSE 3: CD, DA, AC, CB, BA, AD, DB, BC
COURSE 4: DB, BC, CD, DA, AC, CB, BA, AD

—*Quad,* p. 291

Each player is defined by a predetermined formula for movement and, in *Quad I,* at least, by a specific percussion "to sound when he enters, continue while he paces, cease when he exits." In his script Beckett calls for four sounds: "say drum, gong, triangle, wood block." The actual instruments used were two Javanese gongs, an African wood block and an African talking drum, and, as Beckett added whimsically, "a wonderful wastebasket—from Rathmines."[49] "Pianissimo throughout," the percussion is "intermittent in all combinations to allow footsteps alone to be heard at intervals." *Quad I* also features color, a first for Beckett in this medium. *Ghost Trio* had been shot in color and the television version of *Not I* had originally been printed in color, but before broadcast the decision to go with color had been changed. Both were finally printed in black and white.

Like the cowled Auditor in *Not I,* the four players for *Quad I* wear gowns "reaching to ground," "hiding faces," but in this instance 1 is white, 2 yellow, 3 blue, 4 red. The color of the costumes, moreover, further distinguishes the figures from one another and corresponds in the script to each one's assigned light: "Each player has his particular light, to be turned on when he enters, kept on while he paces, turned off when he exits." Each figure holds himself in the same posture Billie Whitelaw used in *Footfalls,* their bodies bent forward as if "resisting cold wind."[50] The square itself is a dim area lit "from above fading out into dark," the four supposed sources of "differently coloured light clustered together." To the permutations of number, Beckett's script therefore intended to add "all possible" combinations of color and sound, even though the use of four lights proved to be impossible in production, as Jim Lewis reports:

We couldn't use the colored lights. First the combination of white plus blue plus red plus yellow produced an effect of an indefinite shade of orange. I worked on it and got a closer delineation but then the frequency of light going on and off with the entrance and exit of each player proved too distracting and had to be abandoned.[51]

In turn each player, as "alike in build as possible," enters the arena of movement, then leaves it, bleeding his color off the television screen as he exits accompanied by his assigned sound: "Some ballet training desirable."[52] The piece was in fact composed for the Stuttgart Preparatory Ballet School and was produced there in June 1981. The camera records the action from one oblique angle centered above the set "raised frontal" and "fixed." The running time is initially set as "approximately 25 minutes," on the basis "of one pace per second and allowing for time lost at angles and centre." Later Beckett admits the timing has been "overestimated": *Quad I* requires a "fast tempo," "15′ approx." Nothing more is explained; everything happens "as though the irrationality of pi," to use Beckett's phrase from his dialogues with the art critic Georges Duthuit, "were an offense against the deity."[53]

    Quad II, "a variation" Beckett abandoned "as impracticable" in the Faber edition of *Collected Shorter Plays* published in 1984, is something of an afterthought, and an opportunistic one at that. When the German technicians checked the color print of the film on a compatible monitor to make sure that the play would work for transmission on black-and-white sets, they were intrigued by what they found. Beckett, his own director for this project, was summoned back to the studio. "Yes," Beckett said, "marvelous, it's 100,000 years later."[54] The actors, two men and two women, were called back for another run-through, this one to be printed in black and white: "Constant neutral light throughout." *Quad II* has a short running time, "slow tempo," "5′ approx," and a single mathematical formula, "series 1 only." This time there are no instruments, only a metronome and the rhythmic sound of sandals grating on the floor of the set, the frenzy of *The Lost Ones* before "all goes dead still." Although *Quad II* revives the same four players, they now appear costumed in "identical white gowns" to accent the neutrality of a dehydrated image: no color, no percussion, only the sound of feet falling not so faintly this time around in "a continuing beginning towards transparency."[55]

Quad II makes sense in terms of *Quad I,* and vice versa. Both are hilarious and frightening, especially as done in Beckett's German production, where the script's "percussionists in frame" barely "visible in shadow" were discreetly hidden at the point of each right angle outside the square, further isolating the source of so much seemingly gratuitous energy. The exhausting series of permutations and combinations suggests a similar use of this relentless numerical force in *Watt,* but in his brief sequel to *Quad I* Beckett introduces an enormous range of possibility for individual "elements" of loss and gain within a "piece for four players, light and percussion." In these wordless plays there is no real script, only the *pretext* of one. There is, however, a performance, one, moreover, which is meant to be regularized and fixed forever on videotape. The performance we see on television *is* the text, for in *Quad I* and *II* the verbal element has been ultimately suppressed. The only final statement the permutations within this medium offer is in the impermutability of screened presentation. In his plays for the live theater, works which are designed to be produced more than once, Beckett will introduce a new concept of what constitutes a lyrical dramatic text, one which borrows heavily from such experimental work in film and video to develop and sustain a poetics of technology which becomes a poetics of theater space as well. "Some of my means are trivial," Joyce said, "and some are quadrivial."[56]

CHAPTER SIX

Monologue, Impromptu, and Mask

I

A Piece of Monologue and *Ohio Impromptu* demonstrate how Beckett's work in the mechanical media has shaped scripts written for live performance. What has been potential becomes concrete: in these works the playwright sets aside the technology for recording dialogue and in its place subjects his actor's voice to the same metronomic considerations. Controlled by a precise rhythm and marshalled by the repetition of image and sound, the language of each play has been designed to mark the tempo of an action which is fundamentally verbal. In Beckett's early plays the effect of the action is in the dialogue, but here the situation is different: the effect of the dialogue *is* the dramatic action. Within the language of Beckett's late plays we therefore handle referential details with reverence, since we are granted so few. What is normally considered stage direction is contextually written as dialogue, which will develop and contain the rising action as well. Usually one searches for elements of structure, such as exposition, introduction, rising action, and recognition, in the dialogue rather than in the stage directions. But in these plays the relationship between the two, a "movement impossible to follow let alone describe,"[1] is the source of the drama and the tension. In *A Piece of Monologue* and *Ohio Impromptu* the conflict is not in a character's problem; the conflict is in language.

Structurally, it would be easy to trace the genesis of plays like *A Piece of Monologue* and *Ohio Impromptu* in Beckett's work for film and television: the stage geometry of black, white, and shades of the color gray, the circle of light to illuminate a small performance space, the screen enlarged to accommodate the three-dimensionality of a proscenium frame, the discretion in withholding from the set any extraneous physical detail (a virtue of the early plays as well), and the elevation of negative space to magnify and enhance the isolation of an actor's presence. Yet the relationship between Beckett's work for theater and his work for film and video runs much deeper than this, for it has to do more conceptually with the function of discourse and the role it is designed to play as a given drama unfolds. In the mechanical media it is the camera rather than the word which controls the action and configures meaning. The plays for television, when they choose to accent a language that is verbal rather than more purely imagistic, do so on a sound track programmed, like everything else in this medium, in advance. Words may contribute to the making of a condensed video image, but they cannot on the screen create it spontaneously on their own. The camera, by comparison, exercises an enormous range of authority here: its capacity for selectivity, emphasis, isolation, lyricism, subjectivity or its opposite, objectivity, is all but inexhaustible. As used by Beckett, moreover, one of the camera's chief priorities lies in the evolution of masks, the various faces and outlines a dramatic character may be required to exhibit depending on the angle and the distance from which a physiognomy is being taped. Close-ups, medium shots, slow fades, withdrawing shots, dolly-ins and dolly-outs: each camera action allows the figure to display a different mask which simultaneously reveals and conceals. Even when the pose is exactly the same, bent and rigid as it is in *Ghost Trio* or double-silhouetted as in *Nacht und Träume*, the face we study changes with the varying gradations of light, range, amplitude, and depth of focus. In film and video the actor is always the passive receptor of a mask: it is the privilege of Beckett's camera to convey characterization here.

In *A Piece of Monologue* and *Ohio Impromptu*, works for the live theater, masks will be worn quite differently, but quite as unconventionally. In these plays it is the actor rather than the camera that defines his own stage space, however minimal that may be. The first of these plays features a speech and a palpable Speaker, but not necessarily a "character" in the usual theater sense of the word. Beckett's language is the single protagonist in this monodrama; the figure who stands before us is the mask language wears to get itself recited onstage. Every tale needs a teller; every dramatic narrative, a narrator; every recitation, a speaker. In the theater there must be some mechanism for delivering the lines. "What is there to keep me here?" Clov asks. "The dialogue," Hamm intones responsively. The player in *A Piece of Monologue*, significantly, does not move: he stands stock still, "lip lipping lip," "mouth agape," to serve as the motionless but mediating force between Beckett's language and us.[2] Seen only in a "*faint diffuse light*," his dim physical reality is balanced, reflected, compromised, and finally parodied on the opposite end of the platform by a "*skull-sized white globe*," "*faintly lit*," "*same level, same height.*" One of the most important functions of the mask as it is worn in the Greek theater is the amplification it offers to a poet's words through the projection of a human voice, and this is precisely the classical role assigned to it here. Speaker, immobile but nevertheless still breathing, is a mask the actor assumes to give Beckett's lyrical language a stage voice. Character has been upstaged by discourse.

Reducing the actor to a mask, a mask for his language, Beckett has provided *A Piece of Monologue* with a script that cries out for the examination of a drama inherent in what the author himself called a text, a "text for the stage."[3] Beckett himself wondered whether he had written a piece of prose or a piece of monologue. Only in performance does the script's potential for theatricalization become clear. It is language, then, that provides not only the direct action that sets the play in motion, but also the indirect action of a word-play-within-the-play, making the piece a far more sophisticated vehicle for the stage than a term like mere "recitation" seems likely to imply.

> Birth was the death of him. Again. Words are few. Dying too. Birth was the death of him. Ghastly grinning ever since. Up at the lid to come. In cradle and crib. At suck first fiasco. With the first totters. From mammy to nanny and back. All the way. Bandied back and forth. So ghastly grinning on. From funeral to funeral. To now. This night. Two and a half billion seconds. Again. Two and a half billion seconds. Hard to believe so few. From funeral to funeral. Funerals of . . . he all but said of loved ones.
>
> —*A Piece of Monologue*, p. 70

"I had an image of a man alone onstage," said David Warrilow, the actor who presented this play in its premiere at La MaMa in New York in December 1979. "You couldn't see his face. He was talking about death."[4] Beckett did not actually write *A Piece of Monologue* for Warrilow, but he did later say that he did not at all mind if the actor "says so." The work, he pointed out, was "really part of something else," something else that had to do with death and dying.[5] What interests us in the theater, however, is not so much the topic of Speaker's discourse, a subject Beckett has taken up many times before, but rather the peculiar blocking for its delivery. How the masked player is directed to talk about death this time around constitutes the highly original dramatic structure of *A Piece of Monologue*. The recital is the action, but it is not the only action. The real drama is in the "text."

Like John Ashbery's "Paradoxes and Oxymorons," Beckett's play is "concerned with language on a very plain level,"[6] the plain level in this instance constituting the finite dimensions of a proscenium frame. The unusual nature of this dramatization is reflected even in the title, where *piece* toys with the French *pièce*, hence "a play of monologue." In Beckett's French translation the piece is called *Solo*, a pun on English "so low," a cue for the actor's delivery. Other bilingual puns, or would-be puns, are less edifying, going from bad to worse (*de mal en pis*). The French *pièce* is the English "piece"; the English "piece" is the French *pis*, as in *pis aller*, the last resource of monologue and a "pisser" (English again) to perform. In this work Beckett addresses his attention to the communicative possibilities of dramatic speech, how far language can go in sustaining tension on a darkened set. The challenge for the actor lies in how much of the playwright's compression can be conveyed in oral interpretation. What are the limits and possibilities of such a linguistic enterprise as the performer reaches for a play's true life on the stage? Before we consider *A Piece of Monologue* as a "text" for performance, let us first examine it as a "text" by Samuel Beckett.[7]

In the theater we normally expect the actor to move, but in this case the actor stands still, the better for Beckett's language to move. The faintly lit actor is always hard to hear, and Beckett's stage strategy demands that we listen carefully. When actors stand still in such subdued light, we are forced to attend more rigorously to what they say. What Speaker says in *A Piece of Monologue* involves, moreover, a great deal of *talk* about movement: learning to walk; groping to the window; ripping photographs from a wall, then sweeping them in shreds under the bed, among the dust and spiders; rain pelting against the window panes or bubbling in the black mud; a lamp smoking; light diminishing as night slowly falls; lips quivering and breath hissing; a cry "stifled by nasal"; parting lips and thrusting tongue between them; backing away from edge of light and turning to face wall; the whole business of dying and going; the burial of the dead; and, above all, "the various motions described" in lighting a globe. Saying "Birth," the "rip" word which sets the whole thing going, is "no more no less" than "lip lipping lip," the kind of action any speaker must inevitably make with his mouth when uttering voiced or voiceless stops such as "birth," "beginning," or "begone." On this platform Speaker's "word go" is "birth," but as the drama unfolds he "stands there waiting for the first word," more and more troubled by the script's verbal demands for "beginning" yet again. Beckett has pivoted the narrative within this play on the lamp, the movements necessary for lighting it, and its culpability in being snuffed out. It is a constant battle between the lamp and the impending darkness from the sunset. The flame keeps going out, the wick burns lower, and each time the light needs to be turned higher to provide appropriate illumination. Forever being consumed, it burns as soon as it is relit in a tantalizing but nevertheless pointless ceremony of sacrifice and redemption. "A bright light is not necessary," we remember from *Malone Dies*; "a taper is all one needs to live in strangeness, if it faithfully burns."

Within the actions reported by Speaker, a series of repeated patterns and images structures each expository detail as well as our impression of a dramatic whole. The lamp-lighting ritual is recounted three times and there are also three funerals. The second lighting and the second funeral are condensations of earlier descriptions; incidents lose their materiality until mere allusion suffices to express previously substantial renditions. The first time the lamp is lit, the verbal action requires twenty-four lines; the second time, fourteen; and the third time Speaker elliptically murmurs merely "lights lamp as described." Such extreme economy of speech happens again when all three funerals are reduced to nothing more than an image: "bubbling black mud." The figure in this story lights three matches and the narrator hints of three loved ones. The two rituals, the lamp lighting and the funeral, have physical counterparts onstage: the vertical lamp and the horizontal bed which is mostly out of view, just as the coffin mentioned in Speaker's monologue is "out of frame." Furthermore, the lamp and the grave are both composed of three parts: the globe, the chimney, and the lit wick; the ditch, the coffin, and the dead body. The complex structure of this speech will also confront us with a verbal paradox in the shape of a trio of interrelated lexical elements:

> Never but the one matter. The dead and gone. The dying and the going. From the word go. The word begone. Such as the light going now. Beginning to go.
>
> —*A Piece of Monologue*, p. 79

The word "begone," while derived from the word "go," is phoneti-
cally close to the word "begin." "Beginning to go" combines phonetic
and lexical possibilities of all three. "Birth," the synonym for the key
"word go" here, was indeed "the death of him," as Speaker has been
quick to remind us three times before. "Again," the signal for repetition as well as a cue scrupulously endorsed by Speaker, features
prominently in this monologue. "Words are few," but between the first
one, "Birth," and the last one, "gone," Beckett has encapsulated the
pattern for a universal biography, a "fragmentary tragedy," as Wallace
Stevens has stated it more expansively, "within the universal whole."[8]
"These fragments," Eliot writes in *The Waste Land*, "I have shored
against my ruins."

Such compression of language for maximum dramatic effect is by
now one of the familiar rituals on Beckett's stage. The lamp-lighting
ceremony is a not-so-oblique metaphor for the sudden illumination offered by this playwright's continuing invention of stage dialogue, forever threatened by extinction but always on the alert for a last-minute
reprieve: "No. Next to none. No such thing as none." Words keep
getting complicated and literary despite Speaker's reluctance to deploy
them. "At suck first fiasco" may sound innocent enough at first, but
it becomes far less so once we consider the prominence the word "suck"
has earlier had in the opening pages of *A Portrait of the Artist as a
Young Man:*

> Suck was a queer word. The fellow called Simon Moonan that name be-
> cause Simon Moonan used to tie the prefect's false sleeves behind his back
> and the prefect used to let on to be angry. But the sound was ugly. Once he
> had washed his hands in the lavatory of the Wicklow Hotel and his father
> pulled the stopper up by the chain after the water went down through the hole
> in the basin. And when it had all gone down slowly the hole in the basin had
> made a sound like that: suck. Only louder.[9]

The refrain of "Wick turned low" and "Turns wick low" in *A Piece
of Monologue* returns us not only to the same source in Joyce, but
more significantly to a writer's own "beginning": County Wicklow,
Ireland, Beckett's birthplace. "County Wicklow," says Mr. Casey to
Stephen Dedalus, "where we are now." The pieces of allusion are
"beginning to go": "suck" brings to mind not only Lady Macbeth's
speech ("I have given suck and know / How tender 'tis to love the
babe that milks me . . ."), a Shakespearean source that will soon in-
spire the configuration of a "milkwhite globe," but also Beckett's own
Molloy and the hilarious seaside episode of his sucking stones. Once

we consider a word like "suck" along with the sexual innuendos of "mouth agape" and "lip lipping lip," the "fiasco" of this word's connotations is complete. In *Malone Dies* the writer-hero's very existence depends on the same word ("I part my lips, now I have the pillow in my mouth. I have. I have. I suck. The search for myself is ended"), and later in the same novel Beckett makes us entertain the amorous ministrations of no less a figure than Sucky Moll. "Mouth agape" is also Mouth *agapē*, the Greek word for love. "Words are few," but their domain in *A Piece of Monologue* is hardly meant to be singular. Several of them have been used by Beckett before, and this particular run-through is not at all apologetic in displaying them "again," this time creating ever new verbal entanglements.

When Speaker, like the figure in his story, "stands there facing blank wall," he is in fact staring out at his audience through the imaginary fourth wall of the box set, "Into black vast. Nothing there. Nothing stirring. That he can see. Hear." Clov has stood here before, and in the same position, purporting to see "a multitude . . . in transports . . . of joy." Hamm, noting that the discovery of such meta-dramatic rapture has been made by a telescopic lens in league with wishful thinking, undercuts such windy exaggeration: "That's what I call a magnifier." The language of *Endgame* will be referred to more than once: Hamm yearns to face the blankness of a blank wall and Clov fiercely admits that what he sees out of *his* window is the same "light dying." "Nothing stirs" in *Endgame* and there is "nothing stirring" in *A Piece of Monologue*—nothing, that is, other than language.

Constructing a new stage speech from the remnants of Beckett's other works, it is indeed the language of *A Piece of Monologue* that goes "ghastly grinning on." The family pictures torn from the wall memorialize Buster Keaton's action in *Film*; "Back at window staring out" makes us look back to *Still* and forward to *Rockaby*, a script that will ask "Whom else" in place of this work's "Where else?"; and the "Mouth agape" is, of course, merely the starting point of an elaborate disquisition on the "what? . . . who? . . . no! . . . she!" performability of *Not I:*

> Dark whole again. Blest dark. No. No such thing as whole. Stands staring beyond half hearing what he's saying. He? The words falling from his mouth. Making do with his mouth. . . . Stares beyond into dark. . . . Mouth agape. A cry. Stifled by nasal. . . . Parts lips and thrusts tongue between them. Tip of tongue. Feel soft touch of tongue on lips. Of lips on tongue.
> —*A Piece of Monologue*, pp. 76–77

"Starless moonless heaven" resembles the "Moonless starless night" of *Company*, as does the Miltonic rhetoric of "Dies on to dawn and never dies," the same line the prose text will convert into the past tense: "Died on to dawn and never died." Up "at nightfall and into gown and socks" verbally echoes the physical action M "*in set*" undergoes in . . . *but the clouds . . .* , just as the rain mentioned here does in words what Beckett has a camera do to film an important frame in *Ghost Trio*, another work whose atmosphere is permeated by "Ghost light. Ghost night. Ghost rooms. Ghost graves. Ghost . . . he all but said ghost loved ones." A "faint hand" intrudes as mysteriously within Speaker's monologue as it will later do physically in *Nacht und Träume*. And like *That Time*, *A Piece of Monologue* is another work that manipulates stage time as opposed to time within the work itself. Performance makes us conscious of the various elements for marking time: the different "that time"s referred to in Speaker's narrative, the specific language we use to refer to time ("again," "light," "dark," "birth," "death," and the fateful possibilities of tenses past and present), and the time it takes to see a play or read a script. Time, as in *Hamlet*, is, however, "out of joint" here. Numbers also measure time: "Thirty thousand nights" and "Two and a half billion seconds" compute a life of approximately 80 years (actually 79 years of seconds and 82 years of nights),[10] though this mathematical fantasia is a sugarplum Beckett saves for his scrupulous reader rather than for the careful listener sitting not so comfortably in his seat in the theater. A "ditch" and a "pallet" draw us even further back into Beckett's world: Molloy ends up in a ditch and Gogo claims to have spent a night in one in *Waiting for Godot*. In *Eleuthéria*, *Malone Dies*, *Film*, *Eh Joe*, *Ghost Trio*, and *Company*, palletlike beds or cribs (Anglo-Irish "cots") are never far off, though in this monologue a "brass bedrail" briefly catches some of the limelight, but not much more than Mag and Dan in *Molloy* or Nell and Nagg in *Endgame:*

> Could once name them all. There was father. That grey void. There mother. That other. There together. Smiling. Wedding day. There all three. That grey blot. There alone. He alone. Not now. Forgotten. All gone so long. Gone. Ripped off and torn to shreds. Scattered all over the floor. Swept out of the way under the bed and left. Thousand shreds under the bed with the dust and spiders. All the . . . he all but said loved ones.
>
> —*A Piece of Monologue*, p. 72

"Alone gone," the last words the actor will be enjoined to utter on this platform, are a familiar topos to conclude a familiar verbal ritual. The lamp faintly lit in Speaker's monologue has been a memorial lamp after all. We see its variations in *Malone Dies*, *That Time*, and *Company*.

Beckett, as much a "biologist in words" as the Joyce he celebrated by the same phrase,"[11] can therefore be counted on to offer us a "choice of images."[12] But what is central to *A Piece of Monologue* is the hierarchal structure the playwright now assigns to them. In the language of this play not every image is created equal. The singular one that we see in the theater, a Speaker tied down to a dimly lit set, enriches several of the images we hear about in his speech, and vice versa. Every mention of a globe and a wick turned low (the counterpart to a taper on an Elizabethan stage), every instance of light "beginning to go," and every reference to the speech act itself is foregrounded by its theatricalization on the platform before us. Sight validates sound here. Certain images in *A Piece of Monologue* therefore participate in an existence which is binary, visual as well as verbal. We seem to be called upon to contrast the duality of a privileged set of images with those rendered exclusively in words. Is it the theater image or the verbal image that has the most staying power? What happens to us, phenomenologically, when we sit in the theater and suddenly recognize that a verbal image has been elevated to the status of a stage image, an image, as it were, come to life before our very eyes?

> I have of late—but wherefore I know not—lost all my mirth, forgone all custom of exercise; and indeed it goes so [heavily] with my disposition that this goodly frame, the earth, seems to me a sterile promontory, this most excellent canopy, the air, look you, this brave o'erhanging [firmament], this majestical roof fretted with golden fire, why, it appears no other thing to me than a foul and pestilent congregation of vapours.
> —*Hamlet*, act 2, scene 2

Is the primacy of perception, as in Hamlet's speech calling our attention to the physical structure of the Globe Theatre, in what we see, or is it, rather, in what we intuit from what we hear? Though we might be tempted, at first glance, to make our pact with the stage effects so palpably wrought by such persuasive theatricalization, the actual situation may not be nearly so simple as this criterion alone would seem

to suggest. One of the most striking metaphors we will remember from
A Piece of Monologue is likely to be an exclusively verbal one—one,
moreover, which draws sustenance from no less a source than Shakespeare. The source is Portia's intensely lyrical speech about mercy
from *The Merchant of Venice:* "Rain . . . dropping gentle on the place
beneath."[13] Words will need no accompanying illumination here. This
is already stage language for an accomplished speaker from another
"globe," Shakespeare's theater.

It is, in fact, this alternation of images, some visual, some verbal,
some whose existence is somewhere between the two, that brings so
much dramatic vitality to *A Piece of Monologue*. It is also the taut line
of tension that ultimately bridges the gap between this work as a text
by Samuel Beckett and as a text for performance. When a player onstage talks about movement on a set whose props imply that such action is potential, even imminent, he inevitably builds suspense, offers
exposition, and controls our line of vision:

> Gropes back in the end to where the lamp is standing. Was
> standing. When last went out. Loose matches in right-hand
> pocket. Strikes one on his buttock the way his father taught
> him. Takes off milkwhite globe and sets it down. Match goes
> out. Strikes a second as before. Takes off chimney. Smoke-
> clouded. Holds it in left hand. Match goes out. Strikes a third
> as before and sets it to wick. Puts back chimney. Match goes
> out. Puts back globe. Turns wick low. Backs away to edge of
> light and turns to face east. Blank wall.
>
> —*A Piece of Monologue*, p. 71

Speaker is describing the props that we see, yet it is only his verbal
dynamism that animates their static presence in the theater. Dramatic
action depends for its life on stage language. Words, as Beckett has
previously demonstrated in his radio plays, can create pictures as graphic
as any actual visualization theater may accomplish in performance.
Here, too, Beckett shows his reliance on the dramatic conventions of
the classical theater: it is always the messenger's speech that creates
the best pictures in the spectacle of a poet's words. "The motion alone
is not enough," we remember from *Footfalls*, "I must hear the feet,"
the specifically poetic feet, "however faint they fall."

No image, however, can give us more information than the medium that conveys it can carry. Poetic dialogue onstage is language in
space and time and therefore participates in a metrics beyond the text,
the rhythm of performance. It is the presence of an actor in *A Piece*

of Monologue which will finally dignify Beckett's language with the stage spatiality it demands. Beckett sees the different media in which he works in relation to each other. If his stage dialogue is to function as a new scenic space, as in film and video, he must establish between the visual and the verbal a system of links that is extremely precarious and, as a result, dramatic. When, for example, Speaker concentrates on the sun "long sunk behind the larches," the "new needles turning green," and especially on the blackening of the ceiling, he foreshadows the ending of his own monologue, when each night in production the stage will be bathed in similar darkness and similar doom:

> Lamp smoking though wick turned low. Strange. Faint smoke issuing through vent in globe. Low ceiling stained by night after night of this. Dark shapeless blot on surface elsewhere white. Once white.
>
> —*A Piece of Monologue*, p. 73

As Speaker and speech focus on the "low ceiling," we are tempted, albeit tentatively, to look up at the rafters. Language controls vision. Everything that is muffled and muted by the faint light on this set therefore explodes with mesmerizing force whenever verbal description highlights a feature of this particular mise-en-scène. Dreamlike but never wistful, the set and the figure whose platform it becomes contribute what is essential to this drama: the strange and disquieting tension between the playwright's words and his icy and disturbing tableau. Within this monologue and on this set there is "no such thing as none" and "no such thing as whole." A thematic gray pervades, "unaccountable," always a "faint light in room. Whence unknown" and "faint sounds. Whence unknown." We feel without knowing. The play stations us in that remoteness "Beyond that black beyond" where, seen through the scrimlike atmosphere of a smoke-clouded globe, "Ghost light," "Ghost nights," and "Ghost rooms" are summoned to their ghost life for one more turn on Beckett's stage.

Within the confines of Speaker's monologue, certain effects can be accommodated only in words, in that language which is explicitly written, as opposed to that "language" which is explicitly staged. In production *A Piece of Monologue* allows us to study, even before words are spoken, a stage set which never changes: "*Ten seconds before speech begins.*" The only modification provided by the stage directions has the same set lit with dying intensity as preparation for the play's closure:

Thirty seconds before end of speech lamplight begins to fail.

Lamp out. Silence. Speaker, globe, foot of pallet, barely visible in diffuse light.

Ten seconds.

Curtain.

—*A Piece of Monologue*, p. 69

The images Speaker evokes in his monologue, however, are by no means subject to the physical restraint imposed by the limitations of this play's one set. In developing scenes through the exclusivity of words, his speech borrows from Hamlet's a canopy, a grave, and a "congregation of vapours" in order to play with time and space through a surprising number of perspectives and a seemingly dauntless horizon. Can this be Hamlet watching from "on high" Ophelia's funeral procession?

> Again and again. Again and again gone. Till whose grave? Which . . . he all but said which loved one's? He? Black ditch in pelting rain. Way out through the grey rift in dark. Seen from on high. Streaming canopies. Bubbling black mud. Coffin on its way. Loved one . . . he all but said loved one on his way. Her way. Thirty seconds. Fade. Gone.
>
> —*A Piece of Monologue*, p. 78

In this instance it is words rather than a camera that draw us into the text for an unprecedented shot of reality. From which angle of vision is this burial being viewed? From the "on high" of a window mentioned earlier in the narrative? If so, why is this lofty burial perspective rendered only in one of its two previous incarnations in the speech?

> Again and again. Again and again gone. Till dark slowly parts again. Grey light. Rain pelting. Umbrellas round a grave. Seen from above. Streaming black canopies. Black ditch beneath. Rain bubbling in the black mud. Empty for the moment. That place beneath. Which . . . he all but said which loved one?
>
> Dark parts. Grey light. Rain pelting. Streaming umbrellas. Ditch. Bubbling black mud. Coffin out of frame. Whose? Fade. Gone.
>
> —*A Piece of Monologue*, pp. 75–76

In this third and most concise version of a funeral scene, is Speaker's frame of mind centered on the frame of a window, the frame of a length of film, or the coffin made out of a frame of wood? We have a description in words—in fact, we have three descriptions—but what we do not have is an explanation.

The action that takes place onstage in the presence of these words follows a similarly intricate pattern. What we actually see take place in *A Piece of Monologue* is how Speaker is slowly transformed into the principal image of his own discourse. "Trying to treat of other matters," it is Speaker who becomes the next in the series of images that fade and are gone. Speaker is narrator, but Speaker is also victim. Throughout his speech "fade," a technical lighting effect for stage, film, and video, has often been used as a command to signify the end of a scene; the monologue itself might be viewed as a montage of scenes all beginning with the word "birth" and ending with the word "gone." But death and going, come and go, are all that matter now: all else seems to "fade" into insignificance.

> Never were other matters. Never two matters. Never but the one matter. The dead and gone. The dying and the going. From the word go. The word begone. Such as the light going now. Beginning to go. In the room. Where else? Unnoticed by him staring beyond. The globe alone. Not the other. The unaccountable. From nowhere. On all sides nowhere. The globe alone. Alone gone.
>
> —*A Piece of Monologue*, p. 79

"Such as the light going" is a crucial lighting cue: it is time to turn down the lights for the "*thirty seconds*" during which the "*lamplight begins to fail.*" Thus as the light onstage recedes, so too does the monologue, this Speaker's life. He murmurs his last word, "gone," a statement frozen in the eternity of moments constituting the following ten-second tableau. Then all is gone: light, monologue, and man.

Yet the final and perhaps most noble death here belongs to language. We normally think of birth and death as opposites, but apparently things are different in this dramatic world. Beckett's language has an uncanny way of resurrecting itself, as we have heard it do so many times within this "strange" monologue. Retardants within its structure have been merely that: retardants, not executioners. They have led this text straight toward progressive reduction rather than annihilation. Less presupposes the more that comes before, the play we have just seen performed. There is, then, "no such thing as none," only less: "No. Less. Less to die. Ever less. Like light at nightfall." A simile intrudes. Forever being snuffed out and lit again, dramatic language, like the lamp that features so prominently in this play, is "ne-

void," a combination of *never* and *void*. *Rest in peace*, the encoded
"rip" word, never comes.[14] Even "Alone gone" must suffer the same
fate and endure the same linguistic wheel of fortune. The "Alone" is
now "gone" because of the communion that makes theater happen.
Time has been counted in nights, the evenings of performance.

A Piece of Monologue makes us concerned with images, not actions, how the making of an image not merely takes the place of, but
becomes the dramatic action. In the theater the strongest image will
always be the one we see framed in the proscenium. And in Beckett's
staging of this image, Speaker, significantly, "*stands well off centre
downstage audience left*," the conventionally strong place for the introduction of a protagonist. Threatening our hero, the antagonistic props
which will seal his downfall stand, again conventionally, "*to his left*":
the skull-sized white globe and, at our extreme right, the white foot
of a pallet bed. Here is the proper stage environment Beckett's language has been searching for. Only on such a set will the composite
of words and scene have the power to confirm a speaker as his own
"other." Words become pictures, pictures become words. All of this
has been summed up before, and as far back as *Waiting for Godot:*
"They give birth astride of a grave, the light gleams an instant, then
it's night once more." Pozzo's image has been expanded for the making of a new play, *A Piece of Monologue*, another of the "thirty thousand nights" of theater offering a different speaker the opportunity to
dramatize on a stage platform the light of birth and the inevitable darkness of a grave.

What of this speaker? Who will memorialize his presence when
the curtain comes down? Beckett is counting on his audience to do so,
for all the while this speaker has been "heard in the dark"[15] by us. His
monologue has been designed to be performed, a rhetorical event meant
to be listened to rather than read. While much in the muscular strength
of his speech as a text specifically *written* by Samuel Beckett may
elude the audience in performance, how an image in this text supports
the image that we see is not likely to pass us by. The verbal image
which comes closest to the image we see in the theater is the one that
lingers on when the curtain comes down: a script by Samuel Beckett
suddenly comes to life as a text for performance. Just as the distinct
rhythm of Speaker's poetic narration celebrates the images drawn from
the past in aposiopesis, a tension line beyond words ("All the . . . he
all but said the loved ones"), so too will our silent witnessing of theater
confirm an illusion, however fleeting and faint, which has been made
indelible in a few moments of stage time. Between two interdependent
images, the one we see and the one we only hear about, the actor's

presence adds a new twist to dramatic irony in which a speaker of
stage dialogue describes his own fate, albeit unknowingly. The vehicle
for image making becomes the ultimate image, something more, finally, than a mask for words: the speaker becomes his own image,
live, palpable, vulnerable, and real. Instead of revealing a psychological state, a tired and rather conventional use of the monologue, the
device has been reinvented to certify Beckett's dramatic intensity.
Lucky's "for reasons unknown but time will tell" has become "unaccountable" in the shape of a quite different monologue. The speaker
for this dramatic recital brings us ever closer to the source of his words,
the poet masked carefully behind them. What we hear in *A Piece of
Monologue*, a play which gives the narrator of a poem a human form,
is pure Beckett, the lyrical voice in which he speaks to us so hauntingly
in his late works for the stage.

II

Ohio Impromptu offers us a different kind of monologue, one whose
shape is as unprecedented as its structure is unusual. Here Beckett
makes two figures wear identical masks, yet only one player recites
the playwright's lines. The gift of language, however, is bound to a
"worn volume," the words inscribed in a textbook prop the actor is
fated to speak in his assigned role as Reader.[16] The printed text for
this *lecteur d'anglais* is "an old quarto-type thing" which he performs,
as Beckett wrote to David Warrilow, "calmly, soothingly, like a bed-
time story."[17] "*As alike in appearance as possible*," the second actor
plays Listener and does the other thing we do with Beckett's words:
we read them, and we listen to them. Not quite a soliloquy in the sense
of *A Piece of Monologue*, *Ohio Impromptu* presents us with something
more elementary as confrontational drama than a solitary game a human voice plays with stage time. In this unconventional two-hander
actors portray dual aspects of language which are shown in the work's
mute denouement to be one. "—Hypocrite lecteur, —mon semblable,
—mon frère!"[18] Baudelaire's famous poetic dictum to his reader (whose
name in French, like Listener's, begins symbiotically with an "L") is
therefore the inspiration for such a laconic dramatic display. Baudelaire's "hypocrite lecteur" is doubly rich in its connotations. Beckett's
"lecteur" is in every sense a "hypocrite," the *actor* and *answerer* of
classical Greek theater summed up in the word *hypokritēs*. Beckett's
Reader, moreover, is discovered onstage in the company of his own
"other"; "lecteur" has brought his own listener with him. We watch

him and we study his mirror image as first there is "little," then once
again "nothing," that is finally "left to tell."

Beckett wrote *Ohio Impromptu* for the international symposium
devoted to his work which was held on the campus of the Ohio State
University in 1981. To say that he designed this piece for the occasion
is, however, not entirely accurate. Always uneasy about writing something on commission, so to speak, Beckett merely promised the or-
ganizers of the conference that he would "try to come up with something."[19] The play had its world premiere before an audience of Beckett
specialists in the Stadium 2 Theater of the Drake Union at OSU in a
single matinee performance on May 9, 1981. Directed by Alan Schneider, David Warrilow played Reader and Rand Mitchell took the part
of Listener. The same team brought *Ohio Impromptu* to the Centre
Pompidou in Paris, to Chicago, and later to New York, where it en-
joyed a successful run at the Harold Clurman Theatre on a triple bill
with *Catastrophe* and *What Where*, opening on June 15, 1983. The
cast then presented the show at the Coolidge Auditorium of the Library
of Congress in Washington, D.C., the following March. Later the show
traveled to the Edinburgh Festival, where the three plays opened on
August 13, 1984, for a limited run of eleven performances at the Church
Hill Theatre. The plays were also seen in London, opening the same
month at the Donmar Warehouse.

Beckett told a surprised Alan Schneider that the original audience
gathered in Columbus would laugh when the curtain went up on *Ohio
Impromptu*.[20] He was right. Taken by the austerity of the situation,
two look-alike "philosophes" bent over an ancient tome at a table where
a soigné Latin quarter hat lies abandoned, the audience in Ohio could
appreciate the irony of the stage event. Was this a disguised Beckett
reading on the Left Bank to a blind James Joyce? "Stay where we
were so long alone together," the book for this show reads, "my shade
will comfort you." "That's where I used to go to walk with Joyce,"
Beckett told Martha Fehsenfeld about the island in Reader's narrative.[21] Ohio, as Beckett would certainly know, is a river mentioned by
Joyce in *Finnegans Wake*, and in the first chapter of *Ulysses* Buck
Mulligan reminds Stephen Dedalus not to forget his own "Latin quarter
hat."[22] OHIO (in caps) occurs twice in *Finnegans Wake*. A right-mar-
gin note reads, all in capitals, in this configuration:

COME SI
COMPITA
CUNCTITI-

TITILATIO?
CONKERY
CUNK,
THIGH-
THIGHT-
TICKELLY
THIGH, LIG-
GERILAG,
TITTERITOT,
LEG IN A TEE
LUG IN A
LAW, TWO
AT A TIE
THREE ON A
THRICKY
TILL OHIO
OHIO
IOIOMISS.[23]

"The title is a kind of joke," observed Alan Schneider. "Beckett simply wrote it on the spur of the moment for Ohio State; the title has no connection with the content."[24] The scenario for this play, however, is prefigured as far back as *Malone Dies*, in the telling description of the Lamberts, *père et fils:* "There they sat, the table between them, in the gloom, one speaking, the other listening, and far removed, the one from what he said, the other from what he heard, and far from each other."

In the discussion which followed the performance in Ohio, part of the "riverrun" of *Finnegans Wake*, Beckett's audience was quick to respond to the playfulness of the term "impromptu," bringing to (academic) mind such earlier compositions for the French stage as Molière's *Impromptu de Versailles*, Giraudoux's *Impromptu de Paris*, and Ionesco's *Impromptu de l'Alma*, or even a contemporary English play for radio, John Arden's *The Bagman, or the Impromptu of Muswell Hill*. As a theatrical form, an impromptu should appear light, improvised, almost extemporaneous, even if these effects are achieved through premeditation. Beckett's impromptu, however, is really none of these things. It is "on the spot," etymologically, only in the sense that it lies *in promptu*, in readiness, before the spotlight. In *Ohio Impromptu* the framework is comic while the drama that takes place within it is, as comedy often is, totally serious.[25] Beckett manipulates the form to reshape it for his own satisfaction, making us observe a stage phenom-

enon with a scrupulousness that may have escaped us before. Although
the curtain rises to reveal a surprising tableau that may initially pro-
voke laughter, Beckett soon changes our reaction by refocusing the
drama on a tension that has been built into the set. The story this
speaker recites from his "worn volume" will unwittingly implicate him
in its verbal action, defining the limits of his own stage existence by
foreshadowing the silent *gestus* of a final parting that has all the while
been waiting for him in the wings.

Beckett achieves his precision in *Ohio Impromptu* through the impact of language on his audience, the words which ask us to impose
a symmetry between the poetic fragments we hear and the theater image we see. What is shown onstage is a simple action, though an un-
common one. There is no conversation, little physical movement, and
no change in lighting. The effect is created through suggestion. The
major dramatic question is not raised by the figures onstage in the
language one of them speaks, but is developed instead by the observer:
it is we who must postulate a harmony between what we see and the
"sad tale a last time told." The fiction within this drama, which parallels the action onstage, is not by itself difficult to understand either.
The story begins in the past and ends in a future which foretells the
play's conclusion: the congruity is achieved by an audience which tries
to make sense out of the ambiguous relation between treatment and
chronicle. The drama relies on a witness to make categorical a stage
opportunity that remains everywhere conditional. "We are," as Beckett
wrote in his monograph on Proust, "rather in the position of Tantalus."
But it is essentially Beckett's binary structure that has made all the
technical arrangements for us "to be tantalised."[26]

In *Ohio Impromptu*, to paraphrase Artaud's revolutionary proc-
lamation, the theater image therefore finds its double:

> L *seated at table facing front towards end of long side audience*
> *right. Bowed head propped on right hand. Face hidden. Left*
> *hand on table. Long black coat. Long white hair.*
>
> R *seated at table in profile centre of short side audience right.*
> *Bowed head propped on right hand. Left hand on table. Book*
> *on table before him open at last pages. Long black coat. Long*
> *white hair.*
>
> —*Ohio Impromptu*, p. 27

The duplication of masks here is not meant to signify any duplication
of roles, though it is meant to initiate, and graphically, the series of
doubles that will function as the structural principle for this work. Nor-

mally we think in stage terms of drawing attention to the physical dif-
ferentiation that, through natural stature and vocal quality as well as
costume, wigs, and makeup, exists or can be made to exist between
two players. Helena must be taller than Hermia in *A Midsummer Night's
Dream*, Thea Elvsted's hair must be more luxuriant than Hedda Gab-
ler's, and Didi should be (conventionally, at least) leaner and lanker
than Gogo. Even when a play calls for actors to masquerade as twins,
we must think of them as variation upon variation rather than in terms
of exact resemblance if we hope to suppress the broad comedy of Plau-
tus' *Menaechmi*, the lightheartedness of *The Comedy of Errors*, or the
grotesquerie of the gum-chewing Toby/Roby and the blind Koby/Loby
in Friedrich Dürrenmatt's *The Visit*. Ella Rentheim is Gunhild's twin
sister in *John Gabriel Borkman*, but in developing two distinct per-
sonalities Ibsen highlights everything about their Wagnerian profiles
that builds tension through opposition. Balance through contrast, even
when the physical types are as different as the Peggy Ashcroft and
Wendy Hiller who played these roles opposite Ralph Richardson in the
1975 National Theatre production, not only has the virtue of avoiding
confusion for the audience, but more basically sustains the anxiety we
internalize as we watch a performance take place. Ibsen is concerned,
of course, with character rather than caricature, with the elaboration
of plot and the expansion of theme as vehicles for revelation. In Beckett, however, the emphasis falls more formally on how much does not
have to happen onstage for a play to have dramatic potential. Ever
since *Godot* he has been asking his players to do more and more with
less and less. In *Ohio Impromptu* Beckett bares the dramatic bone down
to a glance, a gaze, a hat, a knock, and a book: what we "read" in
each of these elements displays, nonetheless, the stunning theatrical
power a rich symmetrical pattern can contain; how far an image, and
a simultaneous image within that image, might be able to go in holding
the stage. In this short play Listener's "knock," as we read in Theodore Roethke's *Praise to the End!*—another worn volume of poetry—
is unexpectedly "open wide."[27] Its presence in this play brings to mind
still another reference to Joyce. Beckett told Richard Ellmann in 1954
about one occasion when Joyce dictated a small part of *Finnegans
Wake* to him. There was a memorable knock on the door, which Beckett apparently did not hear.

Joyce said, "Come in," and Beckett wrote it down. Afterwards he read back
what he had written and Joyce said, "What's that 'Come in'?" "Yes, you said
that," said Beckett. Joyce thought for a moment, then said, "Let it stand."[28]

The "knock" we hear in *Ohio Impromptu* is in fact the aural counterpart to the double image we see. Reader and Listener have established between themselves some tacit understanding regarding the knock's dual domain. When Listener knocks, Reader responds by reacting in two ways. He pauses, then doubles back on the phrase he has just uttered, triggering its repetition. The knock resounds through time and space to interrupt the flow of narration by underscoring what comes before and creating suspense for all that may follow. Halting the narration, it signifies a beat in the action, but it also signals a continuity through partial duplication. Certain features of this story are delivered as a tale twice told. Less mechanical and more efficient than Krapp's clumsy interference with electronic recording tape, the sound of an actor's fist on a table not only segments the story and causes Reader to repeat what Listener needs to hear again, but also taps out the rhythm of a highly memorable phrase:

> R (*reading*): Little is left to tell. In a last—
>
> L *knocks with left hand on table.*
>
> Little is left to tell.
>
> *Pause. Knock.*
>
> In a last attempt to obtain relief he moved from where they had been so long together to a single room on the far bank.
> —*Ohio Impromptu*, p. 28

The same, however, is in this context really quite different. The melodic line we have heard before can never be heard as it was the first time around. The doubling back has not simply doubled back. When a phrase in this "lyric of fiction"[29] is retrieved, it inevitably cuts deeper. The knock prepares us for its second coming, but the action itself emotionalizes meaning by dramatizing progression in place of linear duplication. The words are the same, but as we hear them echo in theater space, the same now offers us something more, something in the guise of a lyric refrain.

> *Pause. Knock.*
>
> In his dreams he had been warned against this change. Seen the dear face and heard the unspoken words, Stay where we were so long alone together, my shade will comfort you.
>
> *Pause.*
>
> Could he not—

Knock.

Seen the dear face and heard the unspoken words, Stay where we were so long alone together, my shade will comfort you.

Pause. Knock.

—*Ohio Impromptu*, p. 30

"Then turn and his slow steps retrace," another turn of phrase Reader will be urged to make reverberate onstage, therefore defines his acting job as speaker for this monologue as much as it does that of the protagonist allotted a similar role in the fiction the same words create. The part calls for an actor to go through his paces of turning a page twice and also reciting a line twice: "Then turn and his slow steps retrace." Dialogue, too, can be counted on to resound onstage with a surprising number of echoes and double entendres. "Stay where we were so long alone together" memorializes the triumphant rhetoric of Vladimir's "Together again at last!" In *Waiting for Godot* the figures will "celebrate" one another with the human warmth of an embrace. By the time of *Ohio Impromptu* the actors meet only a "shade" in a figure of speech. What they embrace in this last of all encounters is language, the "poetry," as W. H. Auden wrote in celebration of W. B. Yeats, that "makes nothing happen."[30]

What happens on the level of language also takes place on the level of stagecraft. The tableau, of course, confronts us with the spectacle of two actors "*as alike in appearance as possible.*" But these two players as seen by the audience appear subtly different. Though both bow their heads, propping them up on the right hand, Listener sits facing front, Reader in profile. The image is a counterfeit rather than a counterpart; what we see is a near-double instead of a doppelgänger. An impromptu, we remember, is an open form, unfixed and susceptible to various representations. The incongruous sitting positions define the antagonists, and, as the play begins, their opposing roles—one as listener, one as reader—separate them further. Extremities are becoming important here: a left hand knocks and the same limb checks R from turning back the pages. "Your arm! Any arm! A helping hand! For five seconds! Christ, what a planet!" moans Mrs. Rooney in *All That Fall* and, in a change of tone, May apostrophizes another "poor arm" in *Footfalls*. In *Ohio Impromptu* much will be made of other extremities: Reader and Listener sit at one end of the table, the book rests open toward its last pages, and the man in the story looks out of his single window on the "downstream extremity of the Isle of Swans." Even though the hero perceives the joyous union of the river, he cannot get beyond the end of the island, hence he turns and, like the passage repeated in the text, he must "his slow steps retrace." A masculine complement to the figure in *Footfalls*, he paces left to right, right to left, the other extremities R and L inevitably signify in any dramatic text.

All of the extremities in *Ohio Impromptu* are twofold. The dramatis personae wear long black coats and have long white hair, hence extremities of color and length. Fictional man walks on the island in daytime and fears the night, hence extremities of time. The section detailing his relapse into night-fear is especially full of multiples of two: "Now with redoubled force the fearful symptoms described at length page forty paragraph four." The "redoubled force" of the symptoms suggests that the terror of night is now two times as extreme as it had been when initially doubled on page forty. And the entire sentence will be repeated twice, parcelled out spatially in the text and temporally in performance by the duet of Listener's knocks. "White nights," too, suggests a double meaning. The counterpart through literal translation of the French *nuit blanche*, a sleepless night, it is also a pun on Whiteknights, the location of the Beckett Archive at the University of Reading. Such a meaning would be truly apposite for a play originally performed in America before an audience of Beckett specialists, many of whom had spent hours poring over the rich holdings at Whiteknights. So that "White nights now again his portion" resounds onstage with "redoubled force": it is Beckett's chosen fate to deliver his portion, his holograph manuscripts and typescripts, to a library in England. Reading, the name of a city in Berkshire, is, obviously, another pronunciation for what features so prominently in this play, the act of *reading* from a highly poetic prose text.

Ohio Impromptu abounds in doubles and near-doubles. "Simile qui con simile è sepolto," to use Dante's line from the *Inferno:* "Like with like is buried here."[31] The play itself is framed in two fades of equal length, a ten-second fade-up and a ten-second fade-out; there are two "*plain armless white deal chairs*" and a plain white deal table, "*say 8' × 4'.*" Although there are props onstage that defy such rampant dualism—the "worn volume" and the black "wide-brimmed hat"—there are, nonetheless, only two of them. Each balances the other in its postpositive singularity. Within Reader's text sleeping contrasts with waking, a "dear face" becomes the unnamed "dear name," there are words spoken and words best left "unspoken," and the "Little is left to tell" permutes itself to the ultimate curtain line, "Nothing is left to tell."

In this work the number two in its many literary configurations and scenic displays exercises, like the "irrationality of pi" that Beckett mentions in his dialogues with Georges Duthuit, "a kind of Pythagorean terror."[32] Assigning symbols to numbers, it was the ancient Greek philosopher who identified the binary nature of the number two with that which deceives, that which is false, that which wears a mask. Such duplicity through duality is extended in *Ohio Impromptu* even to literary derivations and allusions. Baudelaire's "—Hypocrite lecteur,—mon semblable,—mon frère!" is not one analogue, but two. Eliot employs the same line preceded by the stigmata of "You!" in *The Waste Land*, where it brings emphatic closure to "The Burial of the Dead."[33] Beckett has depended on serial allusion before, most notably in Estragon's poetic reliance on Yeats. "The wind in the reeds" refers to *The Wind Among the Reeds*, the collection of Yeats' early poems, but it does so only by way of the Gospel According to St. Matthew. In a similar way the "Speak to me" of . . . *but the clouds* . . . is Shakespeare, but it is also the Eliot of "A Game of Chess," the second section of *The Waste Land*. In *Ohio Impromptu* the "isle of Swans" is Proust, but it is also Mallarmé and suggests further complications with the planetary signs we associate with *Mercier and Camier*, *Murphy*, and *Enough*. And yet it is the gemini rather than the swan that shed so much symbolic light on this play. Even some of the Shakespeare used in *Ohio Impromptu* comes to us via Joyce. When Reader and Listener stare out at one another in the final moments of the drama, their wordless action suggests a reversal of Murphy looking into the eye "unseeing" of Mr. Endon; it also suggests a reversal of the "rage of Caliban at not seeing his face in the mirror"—Buck Mulligan's remark when he brings a glass away from Stephen's "peering eyes" in the same chapter of *Ulysses* which inspires Beckett's use of a Latin Quarter hat.[34]

Beckett's incorporation of *Macbeth* will also travel a double literary journey into the past before coming to rest in the dialogue of *Ohio Impromptu*. Lady Macbeth's "What's done cannot be undone," to be used by Beckett later in *Ill Seen Ill Said*, will be retraced by this text's "What he had done alone could not be undone. Nothing he had ever done alone could be undone. By him alone." Beckett has used a variation of this speech before, in *Malone Dies*: "the moment comes when one desists, because it is the wisest thing to do, discouraged, but not to the extent of undoing all that has been done." Other Shakespearean echoes will be double-barreled in another way, combining in one concise phrase a comprehensive "reading" that receives subsistence from two disparate sources:

> Relief he had hoped would flow from unfamiliarity. Unfamiliar
> room. Unfamiliar scene. Out to where nothing ever shared. Back
> to where nothing ever shared. From this he had once half hoped
> some measure of relief might flow.
>
> —*Ohio Impromptu*, p. 29

"For this relief much thanks. 'Tis bitter cold, / And I am sick at heart"
expresses Francisco's gratitude to Bernardo in the first act of *Hamlet*,
a scene which soon prepares us for another "shade," the ghost of a
murdered king and father. The Duke's speech in the last scene of *Measure for Measure* completes the trope in a telling phrase that brings
the action of *Ohio Impromptu* to its prompt conclusion: "Like doth
quit like, and *Measure* still *for Measure*." The derivation of Beckett's
stage language, his "measure of relief," is becoming necessarily more
oblique. Here, too, more and more is designed to happen with less
and less. Beckett's dramatic language continues to draw its sustenance
from many of the rich sources that nourish his earlier works for the
theater. But just as the specific points of allusion are becoming progressively more difficult to identify, so, too, is the problematic situation which develops between minimal stage action and narrative economy. As the actual drama moves ever more closely into the text, into
the language which brings not only harmony but sharp definition to
the "actions that a man might play," a more somber tension overwhelms, ironically, the entire fabric of the mise-en-scène.

The most important duality in *Ohio Impromptu* is, of course, that
which exists between fiction and drama, between the story being told
and Beckett's "Unfamiliar scene." It is finally on this conflict that the
major dramatic tension of this piece will depend. Each relies on the
evocation of a separate dramatic vocabulary, the one based on a language read from a book, the other rendered in a language of physical
gesture. *Ohio Impromptu* therefore offers us the best demonstration we
have so far in Beckett's late work of the separate but interrelated do-
mains of two kinds of image making in his theater, the one we hear
and the one we see. Between these two languages, the one written in
dialogue and the one choreographed in movement, Beckett places his
accent on symmetry and integration. Each advances the other by offering mutual support to foster the interdependency of a vivid stage
metaphor.

It is not the intention here, merely for the sake of argument, to
set up any artificial barriers to describe the many levels of dichotomy

to be found in Beckett's stage language, for his script contains several uncanny exceptions to what otherwise seem to be its rules. Reader, for example, has considerably more to do onstage than his initial assignment may at first lead us to suspect. He, too, must play a kind of listener, for when he reads from this "worn volume" he hears the sound of his own voice and also responds to the importunity of his partner's measured beats. He may even at one point show some initiative by testing his skill as a close reader of texts:

> In this extremity his old terror of night laid hold on him again. After so long a lapse that as if never been. (*Pause. Looks closer.*) Yes, after so long a lapse that as if never been.
> —*Ohio Impromptu*, p. 31

Listener, similarly, is another kind of reader, one who scans sound cues, what this text calls "worn volume." What he knows how to "read" best are pauses, intonations, and inflections of the human voice. As Reader recites, "Could he now turn back? Acknowledge his error and return to where they were once so long alone together," Listener picks up the signal he has been silently waiting for. He readies himself for hand action, stopping Reader from turning back the pages to a passage "described at length page forty paragraph four," a line which, like those we remember from *Murphy*, *Watt*, and *Footfalls*, calls our attention to the mechanics of written literature. This is no passive listener, but an active participant in the drama. His knocking on the table, moreover, establishes him firmly in command as the prompter for each verbal action that takes place in this impromptu.

The language of gesture, of all that is visual and nonverbal, can similarly wear a mask, sometimes the same literary one we have had occasion to notice before. The knocks we hear in this play summon up soundscapes from earlier drama, the "one of these days youth will come knocking at my door" of *The Master Builder*, and especially the knocking on the south gate in *Macbeth*, a rich source of allusion for so much in Beckett's late plays. It is not only verbal language that Beckett borrows from Shakespeare, but other kinds of stage language as well. As in *Macbeth*, the knock interrupts the action onstage, this time not to acknowledge a break in the scene, which in this case never changes, but to confirm once again its reification in words. The peroration in *Ohio Impromptu* will take place, however, in silence, in the mime show which plays out a fictional episode R has shown such diligence in reciting:

> So the sad tale a last time told they sat on as though turned to
> stone. Through the single window dawn shed no light. From
> the street no sound of reawakening. Or was it that buried in
> who knows what thoughts they paid no heed? To light of day.
> To sound of reawakening. What thoughts who knows. Thoughts,
> no, not thoughts. Profounds of mind. Buried in who knows what
> profounds of mind. Of mindlessness. Whither no light can reach.
> No sound. So sat on as though turned to stone. The sad tale a
> last time told.
>
> —*Ohio Impromptu*, p. 34

A "sad tale," we remember from *The Winter's Tale*, is "best for winter," corresponding to the atmosphere of Beckett's chilling tableau. In
the tale that has been read aloud, moreover, Beckett provides us with
the dramatic foreshadowing that prepares us for the rhetorical function
of a silent gesture. What we are left with, then, is an illuminated manuscript, a text supported by accompanying illustration at close of play.
It is also a tableau vivant, the language of a book rendered visually in
a symmetrical image, two faces chiseled, like a Brancusi sculpture, in
one block of cold stone. Sometimes Beckett, who draws in this play
on his experience as a writer for film and video, makes us rediscover
that there are moments even in the live theater when the spoken word
is not needed.

What has been spoken on this stage, however, sets the scene for
the conclusive metaphor of movement. The spoken text, establishing
a precedent and a pattern of thinking about words and movement on
this platform, will at long last achieve the dramatic event, the climax,
which makes its reality complete. "Action," to use the phrase David
Bevington takes from *Coriolanus*, "is eloquence."[35] Beckett's mime
opportunity reverses the sequence in which we remember it from
Shakespeare: in *Hamlet* "The Murder of Gonzago" starts with a run-
through in silent movement followed by a parallel demonstrativeness
in the company of words. *Ohio Impromptu* saves silence for the end,
where all contraries meet in one. Language art and theater art come
together in a mime of reconciliation that brings together all of the nuances characteristic of the binary nature of this enterprise. And in this
recognition scene the protagonists, in a sense, take off their masks.

> *Simultaneously they lower their right hands to table, raise their
> heads and look at each other. Unblinking. Expressionless.*
>
> *Ten seconds.*
>
> *Fade out.*
>
> —*Ohio Impromptu*, p. 35

In this case the progress toward dramatic resolution really resolves nothing, intensifying uncertainty rather than explaining it "all strange away." The mute recognition scene involving two silent actions—raising the head and lowering the right hand—a reversal of the movement in *Still*, remains, therefore, the ultimate mystery. Like Winnie looking into Willie's face at the conclusion of *Happy Days*, we never learn just what it is Reader and Listener see in their blank stare. The "worn volume" R consults has spoken previously not of thoughts, but of some cryptic realm of consciousness called "profounds of mind." Have they looked into one another's eyes, conventionally, as windows to the human soul? Perhaps "profounds of mind," with its faint echoes of Yeats ("the mind's eye," "the eye of the mind," and especially "the deeps of the mind") is meant to evoke the poet's spirit for one more time on Beckett's stage. Or has Beckett's "profounds of mind" presented us with a new gloss on Joyce's "agenbite of inwit" in yet another reference to the first chapter of *Ulysses*, where Joyce's term refers to conscience?[36] Middle English "inwit" stands on its own for a whole series of dualisms, in one sense reason, understanding, intellect, and wisdom, but in another sense heart, soul, cheer, and courage. Beckett's "profounds of mind," however, is followed by "mindlessness," "Whither no light can reach. No sound," suggesting yet another Joycean parallel through inversion, a process which by its very nature accentuates extremities.

Whatever the tentativeness of Beckett's recognition scene, limits which *Ohio Impromptu* shows to be full of dramatic energy, one can be far more certain about the resolution that takes place on the verbal dimension of his stage language. Here the tension between fiction and drama is reconciled by the introduction of a third genre, the language of poetry. For Pythagoras the number three represents unity, in contrast to the chaos of two,[37] and it is in this third level of lyrical unity that *Ohio Impromptu* finds its primary strength, "How in joyous eddies its two arms conflowed and flowed united on." Like the eddies in this stream, fiction and drama meet through poetry in the river of stage time, Beckett's Anna Livia Plurabelle.

Ohio Impromptu confronts us with an uneasy reality in the shape of a haunting dramatic metaphor: in its book we learn nothing of what comes before and we know nothing of what comes after. The play offers us only the presentness of an enigma, but one whose outlines and imagery become progressively clear in a rhythm designed for performance. In the theater it is Beckett's voice, however, that commands our attention and confirms the dual roles we are everywhere encouraged to play, the same parts of reader and listener. "Me to play,"

Hamm begins. Before the curtain comes down, silencing the playwright but annihilating the audience as well, Beckett's players will be asked to don other masks, to create "other only" images.[38] The "sad tale" may be nearing its end, but the book itself, as in *Ohio Impromptu*, is never quite closed.

CHAPTER SEVEN

"Other Only" Images

I

The politics of making an arresting theater image is both the theme and special focus of *Catastrophe*. Beckett composed this play in French, a departure from his general practice since *En attendant Godot* and *Fin de partie* of using English as his original language for the live stage. Dedicated to Vaclav Havel, this short play opened on July 21, 1982, for a single performance at the Avignon Festival in Provence. The low-budget production was mounted by Stephan Meldegg, starring Pierre Arditi as the Protagonist, Gerard Desarthe as the Director, and Stephanie Loik as the Assistant. *Catastrophe* was Beckett's contribution to a day in honor of the dissident Czech playwright, imprisoned since 1979 for his writing, which appears in his own country only in samizdat editions. Other dramatists, including Ionesco, similarly premiered their own one-acts to protest Havel's incarceration by the Czech authorities. Havel's "subversive activities" included his membership in the Committee for the Defense of the Unjustly Prosecuted (VONS) as well as his signature on the Charter 77 manifesto, of which he was one of the three original spokesmen. On one of the rare visits he was permitted, Havel told his wife how deeply moved he was by this show of support from his Western European colleagues, but he was not to read the new plays until he left Pankrac Prison, Prague, almost four years after his sentence began.[1] Out of jail, Havel wrote a response to *Catastrophe,* a play called *Mistake,* and English translations of both works were printed together in the *Index on Censorship* for February

1984. The journal included a letter Havel wrote to Beckett in April 1983, six weeks after his release, in which he described

the shock I experienced during my time in prison when, on occasion of one of her one-hour visits allowed four times a year, my wife told me at Avignon there took place a night of solidarity with me, and that you took the opportunity to write, and to make public for the first time, your play *Catastrophe*. For a long time afterwards there accompanied me in prison a great joy and emotion and helped to live on amidst all the dirt and baseness [sic].

Catastrophe and *Mistake* were produced as a double bill at the Stockholm Stadsteater on November 29, 1983, as part of an evening of solidarity with Havel and his fellow members of the Chapter 77 human rights movement in Czechoslovakia.[2]

Before its appearance in the *Index on Censorship,* however, Beckett's English translation of *Catastrophe* had already been published in *The New Yorker* on January 10, 1983. Six months later Alan Schneider directed the play in New York. The cast included David Warrilow as the Protagonist, Donald Davis as the Director, Margaret Reed as his Assistant, and Rand Mitchell as the offstage voice of Luke, though at various times Alvin Epstein and Kevin O'Connor played the Director and Leigh Taylor-Young, Jenny Martel, and Julia Indichova his Assistant. Barney Rosset reprinted the English script of *Catastrophe* in the *Evergreen Review* in spring 1984, several weeks before the publication date for the one-volume Grove edition of *Ohio Impromptu, Catastrophe, and What Where.* His final copy for the play, however, contains in both instances an error: "This crave for explicitation!" is misprinted as "This crave for explication!" In the English typescript Beckett's word is *explicitation,* and the same in the French, a bilingual neologism which appears correctly in *The New Yorker* as well as in the Faber and Grove editions of *Collected Shorter Plays.*[3]

Just how political is the theater image Beckett creates in *Catastrophe*? Even without the dedication to Havel, the play confronts us with a disturbing syntax of tyranny and intrigue. Gone are the tender yet often menacing rhythms of the plays that come before. In this script the poetry will be found somewhere else, in the stunning vocabulary of a climactic gesture. This director, a great dictator who makes a show of his own self-importance, puffing on a cigar and strutting about in a *"fur coat"* with *"fur toque to match,"* enters the set in a bureaucratic tizzy.[4] "Step on it," he hurries along his female assistant with thinly disguised macho irritation, "I have a caucus." Later when he shouts, "Where do you think we are? In Patagonia?" he alludes to another scene of recent repression, Argentina, which Henry mentions in *Embers*. In the radio play an unexpected serpent similarly insinuates itself into the seemingly uncorrupted garden of the "Pampas": "We never found your body, you know, that held up probate an unconscionable time, they said there was nothing to prove you hadn't run away from us all and alive and well under a false name in the Argentine for example, that grieved mother greatly."

The Protagonist in *Catastrophe,* who stoops forlorn on a cold "plinth," hands limp, head down, a new image for Lucky in *Waiting for Godot,* is subjected to the brutality of some unspecified back room humiliation. In sharp contrast to the attire of his Torquemada, P's costume—he is draped by an ominous *"black dressing gown to ankles"*— is the ashen uniform of a concentration camp victim. In this torture chamber the female assistant, no angel of mercy, dons the inevitable white cloak of the immaculate but by no means innocent collaborator. The relationship between the director and his assistant is, moreover, the power play of some petty backstage drama. The two continually speak in a common and cryptic style that shrouds their relationship in ambiguity as each vies with the other to control the stage space and the figure who suffers before them on the block. Their interaction is a parable of the making of a theater image. Sometimes it is also a parody of it, a "gag" in which the Director self-consciously poses at being a tyrant while the Assistant overdoes it in playing her part as an "extra":

A: Like the cranium?

D: Needs whitening.

A: I make a note. (*She takes out pad, takes pencil, notes.*) Whiten cranium.
She puts back pad and pencil.

D: The hands. (A *at a loss. Irritably.*) The fists. Get going. (A *advances, unclenches fists, steps back.*) And whiten.

A: I make a note. (*She takes out pad, takes pencil, notes.*) Whiten hands.
She puts back pad and pencil. They contemplate P.

D: (*Finally*). Something wrong. (*Distraught.*) What is it?

A: (*Timidly.*) What if we were to . . . were to . . . join them?

D: No harm trying. (A *advances, joins the hands, steps back.*) Higher. (A *advances, raises waist-high the joined hands, steps back.*) A touch more. (A *advances, raises breast-high the joined hands.*) Stop! (A *steps back.*) Better. It's coming. Light.
A *returns, relights cigar, stands still.* D *smokes.*

A: He's shivering.

D: Bless his heart. *Pause*.

A: (*Timidly*.) What about a little . . . a little . . . gag?

D: For God's sake! This craze for explicitation! Every i dotted to death! Little gag! For God's sake!

A: Sure he won't utter?

D: Not a squeak. (*He consults his chronometer*.) Just time. I'll go and see how it looks from the house.

—*Catastrophe*, pp. 30–32

A repeatedly urges her supervisor to seek out the opportunities that arise in rehearsal, to take advantage of the practical to evoke the metaphysical. Sitting momentarily in his cushioned armchair or suggesting ever more horrifying nuances for P's beleaguered posture, A struggles in vain to usurp D's authority, an inept Mosca to this totalitarian Volpone. When the Director leaves the set to check the effect from the stalls, "*not to appear again*," his offstage voice assumes the frightening impersonality of absolute assertion. In the second part of the play D therefore becomes even more ruthless, forcing his minion to do the dirty work. Manipulated by his voice, she becomes as malleable as the disturbing image of P which she, with her false sense of security, had previously sought to control. All the while, of course, the Director's hands remain clean, and they are fated to remain so for the rest of the play. Like Willie before the curtain goes down on *Happy Days*, he is dressed, so to speak, to kill, for he has a mysterious "caucus" to attend. The "show" he has just evaluated is not the major event of his happy day. "Once more," this attendant lady says to the accommodating Luke, "and he's off."

It should come as no real surprise that Beckett's work seems to take such a direct turn toward commitment in *Catastrophe*. Initially performed at an activist event, a day of protest, the play's surface is clearly more "engaged" in Sartre's sense of the term[5] than almost anything else Beckett has written. The tone here is a far cry from Malone's high-spirited "Up the republic!"[6] Yet the rich subtext of Beckett's work for the stage has had from the start the full potential for political allegory. What a contemporary audience might take for an ontological void in the set of *Waiting for Godot*, for example, can be appreciated as a more immediate stage metaphor once we consider the defoliated landscape of post-Holocaust Europe. "Nature has forgotten us," Hamm will complain in *Endgame*. "There's no more nature," Clov responds with desperate finality. "No more nature!" Hamm retorts. "You exaggerate." Perhaps this is not hyperbole after all. Estragon's name in the early pages of the notebook for *Godot* is Lévy,[7] the wandering Jew whose journey ends in Auschwitz, Dachau, and Mauthausen, where Beckett's close friend from Trinity College days, Alfred Péron, was detained following deportation from Paris. He died soon after liberation.[8] Brecht was one of the first to recognize the historical applicability of Beckett's mise-en-scène. Before he died in 1956, Brecht wanted to adapt *Waiting for Godot* by socially anchoring the characters and their lines. In the Marxist counterplay Gogo would become a worker, Didi an intellectual, Pozzo a large landowner.[9] In 1971 Peter Palitsch, once Brecht's student, finally produced a Brechtian *Godot,* complete with *gestus* and estrangement.[10] The round poem Didi recites at the opening of act 2 is not only recycled by Beckett into *The Unnamable,* but is also used by Brecht in *Drums in the Night* and adapted as an acting exercise:

> A dog went into the kitchen
> And stole an egg from the cook.
> The cook took his cleaver
> And cut the dog in two.
> The other dogs came
> And dug him a grave
> And put on it a headstone
> With the following epitaph:
>
> A dog went into the kitchen . . .

Substituting an egg for Beckett's "crust of bread" and a cleaver for Didi's "ladle," Brecht's version of the traditional eight-liner is to be recited each time as it might be said by a different character in a new situation. The exercise of repeating the *Rundgedichte,* wrote Brecht, might be useful in learning the fixation of a method of portrayal.[11]

One does not have to go as far as Brecht did to draw out the typology of oppression in Beckett's dramatic repertory. Lucky's fate on the Board, for instance, hardly qualifies him for such a cruel misnomer. "I suppose he is called Lucky," Beckett once said in response to a query about this character's name, "to have no more expectations."[12] From the Chinese torturer in *Eleuthéria* to the blinding spotlight in *Play,* tormentors and interrogators seem to lurk at almost every corner of Beckett's proscenium, both on and off the stage. Violence is in the air. Croak in *Words and Music* achieves an uneasy harmony by beating his two elements into submission, Dan Rooney emerges as a prime murder suspect in *All That Fall,* an unseen hand sadistically teases a mime in *Act Without Words I,* a suicide leaves a trace of suspicion behind her in *Eh Joe,* and four characters inflict a living hell on one another in the *huis clos* of *Endgame.* One of them, Nell, even gets bundled back into an ashbin, the cover closed tightly on top of her.

> HAMM: Have you bottled her?
> CLOV: Yes.
> HAMM: Are they both bottled?
> CLOV: Yes.
> HAMM: Screw down the lids.
>
> —*Endgame,* p. 24

"I can't be punished anymore," Clov says in his opening speech in *Endgame.*

In the fiction torture takes a turn for the worse. Molloy uses his fists to beat his mother over the head with the lame excuse of assisting her "notion of mensuration"; in *How It Is* a notorious can opener meets its mark; in *The Lost Ones* a "little people of searchers" is crowded together into the inferno of a flattened cylinder; and in *Company* a fablist "fabling in the dark" lies flat on his back in an isolation chamber. Here silence is experienced not as solitude, but as solitary confinement, a punishment for what *Not I* calls not suffering "enough" or not suffering—"imagine"—"at all." If Beckett's characters are encircled by Lucky's "net," the hell which finally closes in on them is far more personal than political. This dark world all around them is quite different from the underground network Youdi, Gaber, and Moran belong to in *Molloy,* or the one Beckett himself joined as a member of the French resistance during World War II.[13] Detention in Beckett is also more typically psychological than political, yet in *Catastrophe* we are struck by the rarefied mixing of the two, a characteristic of more advanced violators of human rights. The psychiatric ward has become in this instance the extension of some vast penal system, hence the "white overall" of a "female assistant" in the gulag of Beckett's play. *"Age and physique unimportant,"* the stage directions tell us three times—the trinity of dehumanization could not be more agonizingly complete.

Yet as always in Beckett, such one-dimensional readings are bound to be reductive, and they will prove to be so in *Catastrophe* as well. The energy of this little drama cannot be contained by anything as neat as a swift denunciation of repressive regimes, however attractive such a statement from Beckett might be. This play has more to do with the collaboration that goes into the making of a concise theater image than it does with the drafting of political manifestos. "Art has always been this," Beckett said long ago in his essay on Denis Devlin, "pure interrogation, rhetorical question less the rhetoric." "It is naturally in the image," he elaborated, "that this profound and abstruse self-consciousness first emerges with the least loss of integrity."[14] *Catastrophe* is far more a discourse on method, specifically theater method, than an argument about ethical imperatives from an agent provocateur. Theater tactics, not power politics, are implicated here. "But my dear Sir, my dear Sir, look at the world," Nagg sums up in a famous punch line from *Endgame*, "and look . . . at my TROUSERS!"

In *Catastrophe* the stage is transformed into an intimate rehearsal space. Beckett surprises us by the explicit realism of the tableau even more than by the political overtones the dramatic action soon gives rise to. On first viewing, the play seems, of all the works since *Not I*, the most accessible from a naturalistic point of view. Yet such an assumption is quickly discredited; this is no "tonight we improvise." In a series of carefully calibrated movements, Beckett makes us study, instead, how horrifying the stage image can become, how pitiful the stimulus can be, before the audience is ready to cry, "hold, enough." "Terrific!" this impresario cheers. "He'll have them on their feet. I can hear it from here." And yet the naturalism of this rare glimpse of a play-in-the-making is highly questionable. No sooner has this director spoken his lines of triumph than we hear, coming from nowhere, the "*Distant storm of applause*." We move from Pirandello to Ionesco, from the tentativeness of a run-through to the recorded sounds of unseen spectators which bring down the curtain in *The Chairs*. The biggest surprise, however, is still to come. At the sound of a witness to his own persecution, "*P raises his head, fixes the audience. The applause falters, dies*." With P's one gesture Beckett displays his fundamental classicism and reveals the intention behind the title for his play. In a true catastrophe the protagonist must *act*, even though such action brings on his extreme misfortune, his utter destruction or death. The Director was therefore wrong when he trumpeted, "There's our catastrophe. In the bag." What he had been aiming for was "a catastrophe of the old comedy," Edmund's description of his brother Edgar in *King Lear*. What he gets instead is quite different. He failed to anticipate the most momentous event of this dramatic unfolding, the protagonist's action highlighted by the following stage directions:

> *Long pause.*
>
> *Fade-out of light on face.*
>
> —*Catastrophe*, p. 36

The image of depersonalization has been made personal in an ironic reversal of previous events. We move from observation to participation, the movement toward tragedy.[15]

"People say about Beckett," Alan Schneider observed when he directed *Catastrophe* in New York, "'Isn't he gloomy!' But you must find the line between despair and acceptance. We're cooking up reverberations, creating images on the stage." Schneider encouraged his actors, Donald Davis as the Director and Margaret Reed as the Assistant, to keep Beckett's images in mind as they went about the task of creating their roles:

Donald, you are slimy, so much so that when you get up to leave Maggie wipes the seat of the armchair, and even turns it over before she sits down. As to you, Maggie, you must convey the sense of possibility and impossibility in the bloody job you are given to do. Particularly when you ask whether the claw-like hands might not be joined together. D of course likes the prayer-like gesture, requiring only that the hands be brought breast-high, to the level of the man's heart.[16]

P's "two claws" are a surprisingly autobiographical reference, for Beckett's "fists" suffer from the same "fibrous degeneration" as his hero's, the "crippled hands" made memorable in *Worstward Ho*. So gnarled were the author's hands in 1984 that it was painful for him even to autograph copies of his works, contributing to his sense of frustration at a long spell of writer's block. "I write a word," he told one critic, "and then I cross it out." Rosette Lamont, who saw Beckett in Paris the year before, called the malady by its French name, "Dupuytren," after its discoverer.[17] Catastrophes may be experienced as personal, but onstage the search for their authentic metaphors translates them into universal terms—the "render," as Beckett says in *Malone Dies,* necessarily "rent." "Bless his heart," the Director in *Catastrophe* intones reverentially. He has A place P's hands to heart and indulges himself with a personal statement of a man-made pietà. "Leave him like that," Hamm had said earlier—and of his dog—"standing there imploring me." "No forcing," this same image-maker will observe a little later, "no forcing, it's fatal."

Making theater happen in *Catastrophe* is therefore a fairly complicated business, for on this stage, which seems to be divided in half, it involves blocking not one scene, but two. The actor portraying P is caught up in a one-character play which, although it *looks* like Beckett's late theater style, is designed to sit in the frame of a far more realistic set. This second drama will make use of a third playing space, the offstage one where Luke, a conscientious but contemptuous "techie," operates his spots, his dimmers, and his gels:

> D: It's coming. Is Luke around?
>
> A: (*Calling.*) Luke! (*Pause. Louder.*) Luke!
>
> L: (*Off, distant.*) I hear you. (*Pause. Nearer.*) What's the trouble now?
>
> A: Luke's around.
>
> D: Blackout stage.
>
> L: What?
>
> > A *transmits in technical terms. Fade-out of general light. Light on* P *alone.* A *in shadow.*
>
> D: Just the head.
>
> L: What?
>
> > A *transmits in technical terms. Fade-out of light on* P's *body. Light on head alone. Long pause.*
>
> D: Lovely. *Pause.*
>
> —*Catastrophe*, pp. 34–35

Lighting is so important to the construction of this image that it has a separate character assigned to it, one, moreover, whose famous namesake carries a packet of New Testament associations. One of the four characters Beckett invents in this play, and the only one assigned a proper name, Luke is also one of the four authors of the Gospels—significantly, the "one of the four" who *did* say that "one of the two" thieves had been saved (see *Godot* and Luke 23:43). A physician and the companion to the apostle Paul, Luke, moreover, was popularly supposed to have been an artist, hence his role as patron saint of painters. It is in this sense that "Luke's around" in Beckett's work. Northern European art frequently portrays the evangelist sketching the Virgin Mary, herself the principal figure in any conventional notion of a pietà. In *Catastrophe* it will be Luke's lighting that controls the emerging tableau, and it will be his lighting again which will hold the image before it fades. "The lights are . . . very important here," Alan Schneider said in rehearsal for his production of *What Where*, "we are lighting poetry."[18]

The lights which illuminate the set for *Catastrophe* therefore discover two complex theatrical moments, each one the vigorous complement for the other.[19] Limited, like the frozen figure of Hermione before she moves into life in the last scene of *The Winter's Tale*, to the dimensions of a plinth, a raised and privileged platform, the actor performing P plays an expressionistic mime whose most impressive effects are statuesque. His hovering action is an attitude performed: physicalization breeds character through the multifaceted lexicon of a silent gesture. Here anguish is more than just another routine in a world in which "all is" ultimately "corpsed."[20] This protagonist is acting, but he is definitely not *playing*. "Something," to quote from Beckett's poem, is "there": "not life necessarily."[21] P's "*black wide-brimmed hat*" establishes his link with the manufactured heroes of *Ohio Impromptu,* and his whitened "cranium" resembles the facial mask Hamm wears in *Endgame*. Trapped in a wordless drama of visual menace, his color is "ash," what a Blakean painter gone mad sees in *Endgame:*

> I once knew a madman who thought the end of the world had come. He was a painter—and engraver. I had a great fondness for him. I used to go and see him, in the asylum. I'd take him by the hand and drag him to the window. Look! There! All that rising corn! And there! Look! The sails of the herring fleet! All that loveliness!
> (*Pause.*)
> He'd snatch away his hand and go back into his corner. Appalled. All he had seen was ashes.
> (*Pause.*)
> He alone had been spared.
> (*Pause.*)
> Forgotten.
> (*Pause.*)
> It appears the case is . . . was not so . . . so unusual.
>
> —*Endgame,* p. 44

In *Catastrophe* the "unseeing eyes" of . . . *but the clouds* . . . turn into the "unceasing eyes" of *The Lost Ones,* where "flesh and bone" similarly "subsist." To flesh out P's part, however, Beckett relies on the language of movement, the repertory of gestures, and the use of stage space we associate with his earlier plays. P first appears as a draped figure, as Nell and Nagg are introduced to us in *Endgame* and as Auditor stands throughout *Not I*. His final look into theater space not only parallels the close-up shots we have seen before in Beckett's work for film and video, but also repeats Krapp's blind stare, Winnie's final posture of confrontation, and the disembodied head's inscrutable glare in *That Time*. In rehearsal "that look," the climax of *Film* as well as *Catastrophe,* proved to be, not surprisingly, the most difficult stage direction to implement.[22] Suggesting defiance and hopelessness as well as evoking the Aristotelian responses of pity and fear, P's ac-

tion may be merely another "gesture of helpless compassion," the kind
of movement Beckett's other wordless giant, Auditor, performs four
times in *Not I*. It was necessary for him, too, to stand stock still on a
raised platform, though his "plinth," like Mouth's in the same play or
head's in *That Time*, has been cleverly camouflaged by the sophisticated machinery that makes such theater imagery possible on a modern
stage.

A and D are played by actors working in a different performance
style, the method occasioned by the contingencies of fourth-wall realism. It is the dialogue, to paraphrase the spoken language of *Endgame*, which keeps them there. Here verbal artistry is nourished by
words we have heard Beckett's characters utter before. "Say it," by
way of the "I say it as I hear it" of *How It Is*, is lifted from *Mercier
and Camier*, as is the verso of "I don't like the look of them at all,"
the barman's trenchant comment to Mr. Gast. "Like the look of him?"
A eventually asks D in her opening line which follows a long pause
of figurative contemplation. As they study P in silence, we watch them
watch him in an act without words that is really a play-within-a-play.
As the sense of menace increases, so do the images evoked by their
language. The scene builds its tension through reverberations from
Endgame and *Waiting for Godot*, Hamm's directions to Clov and Pozzo's commands to the unfortunate Lucky:

> D: (*Off, plaintive.*) I can't see the toes. (*Irritably.*) I'm sitting in
> the front row of the stalls and can't see the toes.
> A: (*Rising.*) I make a note. (*She takes out pad, takes pencil, notes.*)
> Raise pedestal.
> D: There's a trace of face.
> A: I make a note.
> *She takes out pad, takes pencil, makes to note.*
> D: Down the head. (A *at a loss. Irritably.*) Get going. Down his
> head. (A *puts back pad and pencil, goes to* P, *bows his head
> further, steps back.*) A shade more. (A *advances, bows the head
> further.*) Stop! (A *steps back.*) Fine. It's coming. (*Pause.*) Could
> do with more nudity.
> A: I make a note.
> *She takes out pad, makes to take pencil.*
> D: Get going! Get going! (A *puts back pad, goes to* P, *stands ir-
> resolute.*) Bare the neck. (A *undoes top buttons, parts the flaps,
> steps back.*) The legs. The shins. (A *advances, rolls up to below
> knee one trouser-leg, steps back.*) The other. (*Same for other
> leg, steps back.*) Higher. The knees. (A *advances, rolls up to*

above knees both trouser-legs, steps back.) And whiten.

A: I make a note. (*She takes out pad, takes pencil, notes.*) Whiten
all flesh.

—*Catastrophe,* pp. 32–34

Such "desiccation of the envelope," to quote from *The Lost Ones,*
"robs nudity of much of its charm as pink turns grey," the color of
ash and the color of this play.

Dressing the stage to prepare for performance, an endgame once
more, A and D are in fact part of the larger theater image which emerges.
Their "great reckonings" in this little room have been, like P's on his
"plinth," everywhere programmed in advance.[23] The stage existence
they share with P in this two-part invention is, moreover, a dynamic
one, for their relationship with their finished product is far more fluid
than any dichotomy between the naturalistic and expressionistic modes
might seem to indicate. When D steps off his platform into darkness,
repeating Vladimir's movement in *Waiting for Godot,* stage reality
changes as he extends the boundaries of this proscenium into the stalls.
His voice now speaks from some great beyond, some vast echoing
void. Though Luke's voice has previously foreshadowed some other
"space," D's now looms "there" with a new kind of urgency and dread.
During rehearsals Alan Schneider said that the audience must feel dis-
oriented by this change of venue:[24] we are meant to be intimidated, to
feel the eeriness and experience the terror. The effect of two simultaneous sets, each inlaid on the other, is enriched by the addition of
another dimension of performance when sound expands the territori-
ality of the double image. Before long we hear applause in the shape
of a tempest. There is danger in this empty space.

Catastrophe is a rehearsal, but one that comes to us in the guise
of a completed play, a complex metaphor portraying politics as theater
and theater as politics. Every director plays the tyrant and every member of the company is a collaborator, just as every political movement
makes its own iconography. The play is a frame-tale, but in this case
it is difficult to tell which border frames which show, where illusion
ends and reality begins. The dress rehearsal *becomes* the performance
with the surreal intrusion of a play-audience's reaction, a contrast to
our own. The naturalistic tableau has not been so realistic after all,
merely another realm of stage illusion, and not the most persuasive
one at that. In this arbitrary genre A and D have merely served as
multiple observation posts, points from which to evaluate not how it
is, but how it looks, how it appears to be on this "bitch" of a stage

platform.[25] According to David Warrilow, Beckett was highly amused
with the editors of *The New Yorker* when they wrote to him requesting
a change in the word "caucus," which they felt would not be understood by their readers in the context of his featured script.[26] Beckett
authorized no changes. Despite its possible allusion to the Caucasus,
to Russia and the KGB, a "caucus" is inevitably a race with time, and
that is precisely what a rehearsal in the theater is. Reblocking the show
and revising it all for "company," A and D put their protagonist through
his paces in order to make their scene come out right in the end. "I
make a note," the actress playing Assistant mumbles repeatedly as she
marks up her copy of an ever expanding promptbook. Yet as she does
so we are struck by two competing meanings, two double images lurk-
ing in the word *sentence,* one grammatical, the other political. Working hard on a tight schedule to make art happen, these theater buffs
draw upon the echoes still ringing in our ears from the material which
has come before, the "That is not quite accurate" of *The Lost Ones*
and the "No, that is not right" of . . . *but the clouds* . . . : "Let us
now make sure we have got it right." This last run-through, however,
is destined to be in vain. The Protagonist will no longer cooperate. In
one autonomous gesture this trooper raises his head, subverting the
pathetic little drama prepared for him and performing another of his
own liking. An image in this medium will not be so easily contained.
Every player gives it an interpretation of his own, its real life on the
stage. That's how it is in the theater: "and if ever mute laugh I wake
forthwith catastrophe. . . ."[27] P refuses to be manipulated; he will risk
a chance to master his own theatrical fate, a real *actor* and a true
protagonist in what Malone calls a "catastrophe" too, and "in the ancient sense no doubt."[28] "One loses one's classics," Winnie sighs after
recommending Aristotle to Willie. But then she remembers: "Oh not
all. (*Pause.*) A part. (*Pause.*) A part remains. (*Pause.*) That is what
I find so wonderful, a part remains, of one's classics, to help one
through the day."

One of the principal effects of the Protagonist's action in *Catastrophe* is the face that unexpectedly emerges, an image, as Beckett has
Gogo "say it," of "all humanity." Ironically, it will be lighting that
performs the necessary gesture here, for it is a bright spot that isolates
and clarifies the image, holding it in stage time and suspending it in
stage space. It is lighting, too, which patterns the next essential mime,
the image which slowly and quite deliberately fades, what we will
remember from this play when the curtain comes down. Drama is by
its very nature concerned with movement, but the lighting, as it fades,

provides a fixed image. In the simplicity of such gestural energy the
play informs through ambiguity, tracing the progress of universal tragedy in stark but still human terms: the movement from light to darkness
that finally overwhelms us all.

II

What Where will explore the theatricality of a fading image on another
level of reality, Beckett's own, as the playwright draws us further and
further into the recesses of a single tableau. Constantly permuting as
Bom, Bim, Bem, and Bam enter and exit, the image their movements
foster is always changing but always relentlessly continuous. The
threshold of variance is so low that what the audience perceives remains the same, not different. "The same," as Beckett writes in *Ill
Seen Ill Said,* "but less." "To say the least." Though such a statement
might be made of Beckett's late plays taken as a whole, the series
seems infinitely various when compared to this gray display:

> *Players as alike as possible.*
>
> *Same long grey gown.*
>
> *Same long grey hair.*[29]

Written as *Quoi où* in French, *What Where* should have had its first
performance at the Graz Autumn Festival in Austria, but when Alan
Schneider needed a third play to round out the presentations of *Ohio
Impromptu* and *Catastrophe* in New York, Beckett agreed to give it
to him if Graz consented. When the Austrian producers graciously re-
linquished their rights, Beckett translated the play into English. Schneider
received the script, never having read it before, a day before rehearsals
were scheduled to begin.[30]

What Where has been calculated on a rhythm designed to come
out in performance, a uniformity which must avoid becoming monotonous. Here it is sheer stage presence which acts as a modulation for
the monotone. "I wish I could use a metronome," Alan Schneider said
to his actors while directing the play. "I'd like to establish a pattern
that you are called upon to repeat."[31] In this work Beckett's interest,
as he told Charles Marowitz concerning the "stylized movement" he
tried "to get at" in the 1962 Paris revival of *Godot,* is "not so much
in mime but in the stratum of movement which underlies the written
word":

Producers don't seem to have any sense of form in movement. The kind of form one finds in music, for instance, where themes keep recurring. When, in a text, actions are repeated, they ought to be made unusual the first time, so that when they happen again—in exactly the same way—an audience will recognize them from before.[32]

In *What Where* a variety of elements, some lexical, some seasonal, and some more strictly choreographic, contribute to the formulation of a sustained pattern of repetition and recognition. On this set all directions end in mathematical symmetry and all paths arc woven into geometric blocking within another quad, this time a rectangular playing space, "*3m × 2m, dimly lit, surrounded by shadow, stage right as seen from house.*" Downstage left, "*dimly lit, surrounded by shadow,*" an overhead megaphone, V, hangs suspended from the rafters. The play begins with "*General dark*" followed by "*Light on V.*" Just as a spotlight, albeit offstage, was previously in *Play*, the megaphone is the protagonist here, an electronic mechanism amplifying sound as well as stage silence, the white noise. V, like Speaker in *A Piece of Monologue*, "*stands*" secure and secured in the traditionally strong place on a conventional stage. Without the diagram that accompanies the script the piece is almost impossible to visualize:[33]

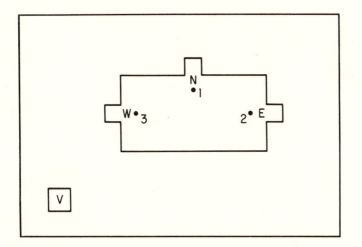

Such an abstract rendering of stage space becomes humanized when four players present themselves on the rectangle turn and turn about. "We are the last five," V announces enigmatically in the voice-over that sets words going once "*general dark*" is erased by "*light on V*"

alone. Speaking as Prologue, V begins to formulate a variation on a round poem, as Didi does in act 2 of *Waiting for Godot:*

> We are the last five.
> In the present as were we still.
> It is spring.
> Time passes.
> First without words.
> I switch on.

As light opens on the playing space (P), two images, as we have seen in *Catastrophe,* merge into one: opposed to V on one side of the stage the quad now displays "Bam *at 3 head haught,* Bom *at 1 head bowed,"* the former displaying a posture we remember from *Ping, Ill Seen Ill Said,* and *Worstward Ho.* But V is dissatisfied with this arrangement:

> Not good.
> I switch off.
>
> *Light off P.*
>
> I start again.
> We are the last five.
> It is spring.
> Time passes.
> First without words.
> I switch on.
>
> *Light on P.*
> Bam *alone at 3 head haught.*
> *Pause.*
>
> Good.
> I am alone. It is spring.
> Time passes.
> First without words.
> In the end Bom appears.
> Reappears.
>
> —*What Where,* pp. 42–43

In the course of this work V is Beckett's formidable agent for salvation or damnation. On this platform it will control all the blocking for the *what* and the *where.* V synchronizes everything that we see, and V dictates every placement for the self-correcting image of which it forms so crucial a part. V, however, is nothing but words, dialogue broadcast through mechanical speakers. Language precedes vision and is in fact vision. In this mise-en-scène Beckett makes us *look* at words, at least at that illusory aspect of them which seems to fill up the empty space occupied only by a precision instrument, the *"small megaphone"* which is the medium not only for their message but, more significantly, for their visionary domain. "Not good," this disembodied force will have its stubborn say, "I start again." "Saying," as in Beckett's trilogy, "is inventing."

Where is V, a human voice projected somewhere offstage but heard onstage, coming from? How are we meant to understand its simple declarative opener, "We are the last five"? This last song in which we are "given the works" will reveal only four players, Bam, Bem, Bim, and Bom, not the fifth member of the vowel series taking a "bum" rap offstage:

> BAM: Well?
> BOM: (*Head bowed throughout.*) Nothing.
> BAM: He didn't say anything?
> BOM: No.
> BAM: You gave him the works?
> BOM: Yes.
> BAM: And he didn't say anything?
> BOM: No.
> BAM: He wept?
> BOM: Yes.
> BAM: Screamed?
> BOM: Yes.
> BAM: Begged for mercy?
> BOM: Yes.
> BAM: But didn't say anything?
> BOM: No.
> V: Not good.
> I start again.
>
> —*What Where*, pp. 45–46

Perhaps the fifth member of this shadow cabinet is the last in the long history of Beckett's bums, the victim whose unseen suffering predicts the inevitable catastrophes awaiting other doomed players. This fifth element, on the other hand, may be simply the "Voice of Bam," as Beckett identifies V on his short list of dramatis personae. V, to complicate matters, is also roman numeral five. In the theater that which is quintessential may very well be the audience sitting, according to Beckett's diagram, at the south, the only direction missing from his sketch. Or perhaps we need search no further for the "last" of the "five" than the megaphone, certainly the character in the piece with the strongest personality and the one whose name, like so many other Beckett heroes, begins with an *M*. In 1984 Beckett said "the megaphone is deaf" but added that it seems "to represent something from beyond the grave," in which case its role as mysterious protagonist rests secure. When the play was done in 1984 at the Edinburgh Festival, moreover, this towering megaphone swayed menacingly back and forth, maybe accidentally, but fortuitously all the same.

When V speaks as prologue to introduce the "last five," he also speaks as stage director and prompter. Once again Beckett stations his dramatic action in a rehearsal room, this one a recording studio in which a single megaphone hangs overhead but unexplainably off-center. Why the speakers for this recording session appear in identical costumes, in full regalia so to speak, remains unclear. Quickly preparing his company for the mood of the scene they must enact, V quite appropriately initiates the sequence with spring. Yet every season here is a winter of discontent featuring circularity rather than change. "Always winter," Mouth says in *Not I*, "some strange reason." All seasons are the same, just as all directions—North, West, East—yield the same set of consequences. "What is this late November doing," Eliot writes in "East Coker," "with the disturbance of the spring. . . ."[34] In the five essential movements which comprise *What Where*, Bam ends where he began, as Eliot does in the *Four Quartets* ("In my beginning is my end"). Beckett's cyclical pattern is structured as follows:

1. Bam alone
2. Bom/Bim.
3. Bim/Bem.
4. Bem/Bam.
5. Bam alone.

As in *The Lost Ones* (by way of Sir Thomas Browne), the piece is "quincuncially" arranged "for the sake of harmony." Here, too, "rumour has it or better still the notion is abroad that there exists a way out." Parodying the multiple exits and entrances of some country-house farce, the movements in this *La Ronde* are deathly, suggesting that no player is "free." Those who inflict torture are fated to be tortured when they, too, cannot "say it." "It, say it," we remember from *The Unnamable*, "not knowing what." In the sanctity of a private world, revealing anything is torture. Those who enter the quad with "head haught" are destined to return humbled, "head bowed." All permutations, like all rectangles, look alike. "The sun shone," *Murphy* begins, "having no alternative, on the nothing new."

V, however, knows the conventions of his genre well, and in structuring his exposition, the "what" and the "where" of his play, he draws upon a rich dramatic history to give substance to the enterprise at hand. As in *Hamlet,* the murder of this Gonzago begins with a dumb show, "First without words." V, like Hamlet, is there to cheer his actors on ("Good") and there to offer advice and submit revisions ("Not good. I start again.") When the rehearsal "reappears" with words, V is similarly supportive as he struggles to find the language to match the image that we see. He expresses delight ("Ah!," as in *Ghost Trio*) at a particularly felicitous delivery and emphatically urges his actors to move on to the next scene once they have mastered the tempo of the one at hand ("v: So on."). As a director V can therefore be counted on to be compassionate, for he has a real sensitivity to the difficulty these players face in learning the give and take of such demanding stichomythic lines. Each role requires enormous concentration and discipline. As the actors struggle with the rhythm of the text, the "what" of the narrative on the "where" of this rectangle, words suddenly appear in unprecedented and unnatural sequences. "Where," for example, comes in this script just where one would normally expect to find "what":

> BAM: Take him away and give him the works until he confesses.
> BEM: What must he confess?
> BAM: That he said where to him.
> BEM: Is that all?
> BAM: And where.
> V: Good.
>
> —*What Where,* pp. 55–56

This script is also full of resonances from other Beckett works, the pun on Watt, the use of Bem/Bom from *How It Is,* and the history of discovering "it all" that features so prominently in *Footfalls.* In performing their dialogue in *What Where* the players must be careful not to give such allusions an exaggerated importance. They must stick to the task of creating a new illusion of their own.

V is moving this play, and his actors and audience with it, inevitably toward winter, where every "journey" ends. It is here that Bam stands alone, *his* head finally bowed. It is here, too, that the company of "we" makes a surprising permutation to the poignancy of a lonely

"I." We recognize for the first time that what V has been busy staging for us is an autobiographical skit, one that proceeds, like all dramatic art, through metaphor. V is clearly Bam's voice; the Bam we have followed onstage is V's projection of his own inner self. The movements have been, as in *Endgame,* "for nothing." "Now as always," Hamm warms up to *his* final soliloquy, "time was never and time is over." "I am alone," V closes. "In the present as were I still." Bam's voice trails off as he fatally rewrites key lines we have listened to before:

> It is winter.
> Without journey.
> Time passes.
> That is all.

> —*Catastrophe,* p. 59

This is Krapp's den once more, a megaphone having replaced the single bulb swaying gently overhead. This play, however, is a fundamentalist's "come and go," one without the intrusion of any of the props constituting a traditional notion of a tableau. When the image fades on this set, "we're in Limbo," as Alan Schneider said. "This is Prometheus and his bird," he told his actors. "There's no way out. This is an eternal search that will not yield an answer. All of you are defying the inevitable."[35]

In *What Where* the dramatis personae are not so much characters as they are "figments," Beckett's own word to describe what they are doing "there" on his stage:[36] "Figment dawn dispeller of figments and the other called dusk," other figments from *Lessness.* Robot-like, the "figments" in *What Where* recite the words and repeat once more the "actions," as Hamlet says, "that a man might play." While it is indeed possible to trace the political dimensions implied by this work's steady focus on so much offstage torture, its energy in performance makes peripheral any specific allusion to the excesses of Marxism, as it does any flirtation with the hilarious farce of the Marx Brothers, yet another gang of four. Especially when performed with *Catastrophe, What Where*'s political overtones seem to loom center stage. Yet in this play any parable of terrorism, Marxist or otherwise, is delivered in strictly symbolic terms. And as in the making of any image, it is not the five W's that matter, the what and the where, the who, the when, and the why, but the how. "He's not dealing with literal meaning," Alan Schneider said of Beckett. "He's dealing with image, metaphor—a kind of equivalent of music and painting in theatrical terms."[37]

What Where leaves us with only an image, one from which to draw sustenance as we confront the enigma of a dream, or of a play. In this work exposition is forever delayed. The only thing we can depend on is the haunting rhythm of stage presence, a mystery without solution in a world, as the intrepid Winnie quotes, "without end." Although the figures within the piece seem to know what they're about, we look on, as we do in the *Quad* plays, in fascination and dismay. The mystery within the "play" is therefore paralleled by our mystery about the play, the highly imagistic essence that informs the intrigue of its very what and its very where. A simple declarative statement will simply not do, for the final statement rests only in the definition offered by the presentation. This resulting image grows in stature, too, once we place it in the long series of theater works that seem to stretch the genre beyond minimalism in the plays since *Not I*. Once we have been "given the works," Beckett's works, none of his dramatic metaphors, concrete yet always singularly visionary, can ever be paraphrased, nor can their unique brand of lyricism be explained away:

> *Light off* P.
>
> *Pause.*
>
> *Light off* V.
>
> —*Catastrophe*, p. 59

Here are the echoes "for to end yet again": "Silence once broken will never again be whole."[38] The strange melody of Beckett's what and where is therefore meant to implicate in the play's final couplet the puzzled *who*, the audience which tries in vain to resolve the meaning of the theater event it has just witnessed. Action—the playwright's dramatic action—is arrested in silence. Darkness seems redoubled once this image, too, like all his others, fades away. "All that goes," as *Enough* states it, "before forget":

> Make sense who may.
> I switch off.
>
> —*Catastrophe*, p. 59

III

In early 1984 Beckett was approached by the Süddeutscher Rundfunk (SDR) about the possibility of doing another play for television. Reinhart Müller-Freienfels, the director of SDR and a strong supporter of other Beckett projects for German television, was planning to retire, and the author was asked if he had anything on hand to round off the producer's career. "It might be possible," Beckett replied. "I shall have to think about it." In March he suggested doing an adaptation of *What Where,* but only if he could have Jim Lewis as his cameraman. Because of Beckett's ill health, the project did not go forward until the following year. Translated into German from the French *Quoi où* by Elmar and Jonas Tophoven, *Was Wo* was finally directed for television by the author himself in what emerged as a heavily revised form of the stage play.[39]

On the television screen *Was Wo* confronts the spectator with a highly unpredictable image. The full figures have disappeared. All that remains from the original conception is an idea about cyclical patterns and a rhythm of repetition for enactment and mechanical resolution. No longer projected through a megaphone suspended from the rafters, the Voice of Bam is now "envisioned" as a large, diaphanous face on one side of the screen whose bloated presence contrasts with a trio of smaller but much more brightly illuminated faces stationed to his lower left. Martha Fehsenfeld offers the following description of how Beckett's play looked on the screen:

What Where (Was Wo) on television begins with the image of a man's head facing three-quarters left in the left-hand upper corner of the picture. The head is life-sized, shrouded in dimness, indistinct. The eyes are closed. There is no discernible expression. He seems to be asleep or in deep thought, removed from the present. There is no visible hairline, only the outline of the face, much softened by shadow. The features are seen as if through a diffusive lens.[40]

This radical departure from the playwright's original script arose, however, only as an afterthought. In Beckett's first plan for SDR (1984) the draped figures were meant to appear on the screen. Beckett had even thought of a possible model for the costumes: the statue of John Donne in St. Patrick's Cathedral in London. He sent Jim Lewis a photocopy of what he had in mind. "He thought he might like something like this for the players, but he wasn't sure," Lewis reported. "He wants them all to look just alike, though, he's definite about that. And he wants every movement to be rigid—a kind of mechanical ballet. And he wants the feet bare."[41]

By the time Beckett was able to take up the project again (1985) he had thought of a crucial change. "The figures should not appear," he said, "only faces faded in and out of the screen," perhaps accompanied by the sound of a drum. He considered using some sort of headdress and was intrigued by the possibility that this, too, might have a facial shape. He was momentarily interested in a Turkish tarboosh, a red hat similar to the fez worn by some Muslim men. But the tarboosh, Beckett said, was "too realistic," as was the device of a scarf. Both were eliminated from further consideration. Beckett was also concerned with different color values for the screening of *Was Wo*. He mentioned Rimbaud's "Voyelles" ("A noir, E blanc, I rouge, U vert, O bleu: voyelles . . ."[42]), a poem which links sound to color, and he actually wrote "Cf. Rimbaud's sonnet" in the margin of his notebook for this production, now at the Beckett Archive at the University of Reading. But "no green," Beckett insisted, thinking perhaps of Dante's color for hope. Rimbaud's poem thus surfaces as an important allusion in *What Where*. Beckett's Bam, Bem, Bim, and Bom make a similar play of sound-sense relations: "a," "e," "i," "o" but, significantly, no "u," no "you." "Voyelles" was, moreover, a poem Joyce liked to recite aloud—and often, according to Beckett. In *All Strange Away* Beckett had previously paid tribute to Joyce's partiality for Rimbaud. In this particular context the prose piece makes another pointed reference to "Voyelles": "Fancy dead, to which now add for old mind's sake sorrow vented in simple sighing sound black vowel a. . . ."[43]

In the end, however, all "gadgets" were removed. Everything was pared down "to the bare minimum," as Beckett told Martha Fehsenfeld. "In the end everything went—no color, no headdress, even the drums went. Everything out but the faces." The resulting image for the television screen, the kind of "meremost minimum" Beckett celebrates in *Worstward Ho*, owes its existence to Jim Lewis' technical precision and inventiveness:

I cut a small hole, an aperture, in a piece of cardboard, and placed each cardboard in front of each camera. We used four cameras at the same time, and we lined the aperture up to fit the particular face. We had to cut the opening to fit the face, the physiognomy of each face, because they weren't that much alike. He wanted them as much alike as possible. We couldn't get that exactly, but the apertures helped increase the similarity. Then we did makeup, rounding out the head, getting rid of the hair, the ears, darkening the outline to recede into black, hooded the faces. It looked like a science-fiction sort of thing.[44]

The major challenge in taping *Was Wo* was to establish visually that Voice was Bam's face, only changed. "How changed?" quickly became the problem in search of a technical solution. "Perhaps it could be blurred or wrinkled," Beckett suggested. The rectangular playing area was faintly lit throughout, but with a fade-up to Voice. The "action is a remembered one," the playwright noted, and he began to quote, according to Walter Asmus, from Thomas Moore: "Sad memory brings the light of other days around me." When the production team wondered if the show might be done with only one actor, Beckett demurred: "One actor will only confuse, unless one can be made up as four. We need resemblance, not identity." In the actual screening one actor, Friedhelm Becker, did in reality play two parts, Bam and the Voice of Bam, but in this case the desired "resemblance" resulted more from Jim Lewis' technical solution than from any apparent doubling of roles.

The adaptation of *What Where* for television results in some startling effects and gives the play new and sharper resonances. On the stage Beckett had never really been satisfied with the role the cold and impersonal megaphone had been called upon to play. On screen Beckett more clearly establishes that this is a story about Bam remembering. "All this happened long ago," the playwright pointed out. On television *Was Wo* turns inward, personalizing and depoliticizing the stage play even further. Torture becomes more explicitly self-inflicted, a function of memory, remorse, and the relentless need to tell a story. Removing all of the comings and goings stage blocking had required, offstage and onstage action are now brought closer to the spectator and made more immediate and intimidating. We concentrate not on a repeated body movement but on a held facial expression. Heads imply a mind and the hell that lies within. This is a far more somber winter journey.

Eyes open/eyes closed, a necessary substitution for what stage space had previously displayed as head haught/head bowed, also renders Beckett's image more evocative of an inner dialogue between self and soul. The inclination of a head would, in any case, be impossible in this concept, for any movement here would result in the face "bleeding" off camera. Eyes open/eyes closed, for example, would have been similarly ineffective onstage. When actors face not the audience but one another, such subtle eye movements are difficult, if not impossible, to see. To a certain extent the studio in which *Was Wo* was taped resembled the "torture chamber" for the staging of *Not I*. The actors in this case were mechanically stationed, this time on barber chairs with attached headrests especially built for the occasion to hold them securely in place. Unlike the stage play, the characters in this video portrayal keep their position. They do not take the place of other characters. Becker, playing the Voice of Bam, had the biggest challenge of all. The voice of the image had to be done separately, so

Becker had to mouth the complete text on a playback. He also spent twelve agonizing minutes on camera without blinking his eyes. Only at the end of the videotape did a tear begin to form.

The quality of the voice, too, was mechanically arranged. Beckett emphasized the "exhaustion" of this sound, an "energy up slow" for spring and summer, then down, reduced almost to what he called a "faint gasp." The end "must be simple," Beckett said. "Slow, no pauses." The lonely monotony coming out of the void should be "like a robot, clear and hard." The "face" for this voice must be "unreal" and "distorted." Striving always for simplicity and reduction, the television play thus evolved during production. Beckett gave his crew enormous latitude. Unlike his method of working on his previous projects for SDR, where he began with a firm technical sense of what he wanted, he encouraged much greater collaboration here. "It's your invention," he told Jim Lewis concerning the "solution" for Voice. But he quickly added, "Make it smaller."[45]

What Where for television makes us conscious of the ever-increasing expanses of darkness in Beckett's imaginative world. Progressive reduction makes things simpler, but it also makes them more bleak. As the play moves from stage to television screen, the void encroaches on a visual horizon once filled with a playing space offering, by comparison, a much wider range of human potential. Such discipline, however, serves to clarify an important tension in the original stage play: the narrative progression that makes of Bam's lines both a story and an autobiographical event. Bam is "Sam," the B is "Beckett"; and Bam's voice, like so many others we have heard on Beckett's stage, is speaking, as always, through metaphor. Seasonal imagery, which Beckett said was meant to reflect Schubert's *Winterreise* song cycle, points forward, as it inevitably does, to the ages of man, now "seen" to be as fleeting and elusive as an image on this screen—only twelve minutes' duration. In the end all fadings were abandoned except the most important one, the final one: you couldn't tell when it finally wasn't there. "All gimmicks gone," Walter Asmus said when *Was Wo* was finally ready for broadcast. "All?" Beckett wondered. "You can't tell."

IV

In April 1986 Pierre Chabert directed a production of four Beckett plays at the Petit Rond-Point in Paris: *Berceuse*,[46] *Quoi où, Impromptu d'Ohio,* and *Catastrophe*. The real event of this evening was clearly *Quoi où*. Featuring the bilingual David Warrilow as Bam, Chabert's interpretation was based on a new script provided by the playwright.

Returned to its original life on the stage, the new *Quoi où* was strongly influenced by Beckett's work in Stuttgart the year before. As soon as the performance began, it became clear that this was going to be an entirely different play. In this variation the megaphone is gone, replaced by a deliberately artificial circle of orange light at stage right to "hold" and "represent" Voice. At extreme stage left there are no human figures, only three heads suspended in space in a posture more reminiscent of *That Time* than *Play*. Beckett had mercilessly edited his script in order to present a very different arrangement of stage time and space.

But the biggest surprise was still to come. The play was funny. Everything was speeded up and the offstage action seemed far from threatening: there simply was not much time for the audience to think about it. This new tempo for performance displayed an altogether lighter touch—perhaps, at times, even a little too coy. The horror seemed to have gone out of *What Where* completely. Here was a new Beckett "play" and, irony of ironies, here was the author reassuring his audience that even at this eleventh hour it still might be worth "going on," at least in the theater.

The 1986 *Quoi où* shows more graphically than any previous Beckett play the profound impact his work in television continues to have on his use of theater space, the many ways in which such experience determines his sense of tableau. In this third trial of *What Where*, Beckett expands a mechanical image to accommodate the contingencies of live action on a box set, translating stage to television, then back to stage once more, where "it all" began. In Paris David Warrilow's gravelly voice was background music for a stark but still humorous interlude, providing a strong contrast to the psychological texture of the televised *Was Wo* and the political implications audiences were perhaps a little too quick to respond to in *What Where*'s first incarnation in New York.[47] In the three versions of this play figures and faces—what *Rockaby* so aptly calls "other only windows"—are not only switched "on" and "off" but around. Yet no one version is definitive or complete. Beckett's quest is always to explore the potential of a theater image, to simplify it, to reduce it, above all to clarify it. When Jim Lewis asked him if he would do more television after *Was Wo*, Beckett said "something about doing something with the pure image. He's said that before. And then he wrote to me just this week and said, 'Das letzte das mal.' How would you say it? 'Next to the last.'"[48] "C'est bon," to quote the refrain from *Quoi où*—those "images that yet / Fresh images beget."[49]

CHAPTER EIGHT

Play as Performance Poem

In *Rockaby* Beckett's mature style achieves a somber elegance and a quiet dignity that is both original and sharply defined. Although this piece was produced before *Ohio Impromptu, Catastrophe,* and *What Where,* its dimensions develop a bold stage image which is at once more elusive, more disturbing, and more essentially profound. The play, which had its world premiere performance in Buffalo, New York, on April 8, 1981, continues Beckett's preoccupation with a small-scale play written specifically for a prerecorded voice in conflict with live stage action. A strange mixture of the carefully controlled and the spontaneous, the drama, whose sole protagonist is a woman dressed in black and whose only scenery is a rocking chair, restricts its subject matter and directs our attention instead to the formal integrities of the play as a text for performance. Light, sound, movement, and action must therefore be understood within the context established by this deliberately circumscribed space, an acting area in which a single image is expressed, explored, and advanced. Clear, articulate, definite, and precise, the visual impact becomes progressively haunting in its lonely simplicity. Simultaneously remote yet urgent in its personal appeal, a human shape is transfixed by the strong and pitiless light of a cold lunar glare, Yeats' "per amica silentia lunae." Much is made out of almost nothing.

What *Rockaby* gives up in breadth it makes up in fineness. The closely valued harmonics in the interplay of all that is visual and verbal, the use of light, the rocking of a chair that is controlled mechanically, the function of movement to emotionalize meaning, and the incorporation of electronics in the form of a magnetic recording tape are developed tactfully and richly. Beckett has employed part of this strategy before, most notably in two stage plays immediately preceding *Rockaby*, *That Time* and *Footfalls*. Yet the technique crafted here has its roots much earlier in his repertory. As far back as *All That Fall* (1956), Beckett had experimented with the dramatic potential of the recorded voice, the way in which electronically generated sound removes the intellectual barrier of the word. "Never thought about a radio play technique," he wrote to Nancy Cunard at the time, "but in the dead of t'other night got a nicely gruesome idea full of cartwheels and dragging feet and puffing and panting which may or may not lead to something."[1] The experience with technology set him going on the magnetic field of time and memory in *Krapp's Last Tape* as well. Although in his stage play Beckett had settled on a practical device for demonstrating the past's effect on the present as well as the present's commentary on the past, he did not in *Krapp's Last Tape* concern himself with the physical materialization of the inner voice central to so much of his writing. It is not until another play for radio, *Embers*, and especially his work for television, plays like *Eh Joe* and more particularly *Ghost Trio* and . . . *but the clouds* . . . , that inner voices become manifest in performance. Yet the voices we hear in these media, typically (though not always) signified by a dynamic switch in gender, are clearly not the protagonist's own. In radio and television Beckett's characters are usually prey to voices heard as identifiably "other." . . . *but the clouds* . . . demands special consideration here. In this television play the voice we listen to belongs to the man we see, yet his particular obsession is clearly with the voice of the woman whose image we see momentarily—and then only subliminally. The man we see on screen "mouths" her unspoken words, the final lines from Yeats' "The Tower," in a compelling voice-over that validates the progressive interiorization of Beckett's dialogue. It is only in a late work for the theater such as *Rockaby*, however, that voice and protagonist can securely be identified as one.

In order to understand what is unique to *Rockaby* there are some additional distinctions which must be made. In *Footfalls*, a play, like *Rockaby*, which features a female protagonist, May engages in a formalized duet with her mother's voice (another *m* + "other" = "mother"), even though the dramatic development of this work consists in demonstrating how these two voices come to resemble each other. In *That Time*, on the other hand, an "*Old white face*" hears but does not seem likely to control voices A, B, and C, which are, as the stage directions

indicate, "*his own coming from both sides and above.*" Unlike May,
a faint though by no means invisible "tangle of pale grey tatters," a
head suspended in space is by no means a complete human figure,
surrealistic overtones and relationships to *Not I* notwithstanding. And
unlike May, the fragmentary and disembodied Listener of *That Time*
does not talk, though he is, of course, a heavy breather. Beckett's late
style in the theater is, therefore, a limited yet surprisingly changing
one. Within the narrow and austere range he sets for himself, there is
in fact some variety. He does not repeat himself in *Rockaby.* The woman
seated in this rocking chair, evoking memories of *Murphy* and *Film,*
not only listens along with us to her own inner voice, but summons it
to start up again and joins with it to recite in a series of highly patterned
voice-overs. The play thus offers us a new dramatic solution to what
remained only momentarily accessible in Beckett's earlier works.
Rockaby, then, displays both the assurance and the increasing harmony
of what is for Beckett not only a persuasive artistic preoccupation, but
a new theatrical concept.

In *Rockaby* what looks, at first glance, like a radical simplification
of style turns out on further acquaintance to be a new and deeper complexity. The play is never quite as easy or apprehensible as it seems
to be on first encounter in the theater. It harbors depths that cannot be
quickly encompassed. In the world premiere production directed at the
Center Theatre in Buffalo by Alan Schneider as part of "A Samuel
Beckett Celebration" sponsored by the University-Wide Program in the
Arts and the Department of Theatre and Dance, SUNY/Buffalo, its
running time was only fourteen minutes, fifty seconds;[2] yet this play
for W (" = *Woman in chair*") and V (" = *Her recorded voice*") can
in fact be divided into four acts, each of which begins with the stage
direction, "*Long pause.*" The four long pauses are critical. They remind us that for Beckett the dramatic image is the primary thing. The
degree of radical concentration and intensity achieved in the pictorial
constituents of this theater style is meant to be studied, scrutinized,
and finally assimilated during each break in the action. In this short
script enormous attention is given to visual detail, for in this play the
image commands attention, something we will be forced to come back
to again and again.

Let us consider this image more carefully. Earlier I said that in
Rockaby the rocking chair was the only scenery. But that is not really
the case, for in Beckett's late theater style it is not really possible to
talk about scenery in the usual sense. *Rockaby* makes us conscious of
the fact that darkness, grays and blacks, shades, and other gradations

of sheerly theatrical light can be "scenery" too. What initially appears to be monochromatic is, on closer inspection, not really monochromatic at all, for light and color in *Rockaby* appear soft and faded but never dull. A "subdued" light uncovers the chair. The rest of this stage is "dark." A "subdued spot" rests on the face "constant throughout, unaffected by successive fades." Beckett in fact makes us see the same figure in different artificial lights, offering us an ever-shifting series of perspectives from which to encounter the image anew. For the opening fade-up the "Notes" to the script read "first spot on face alone. Long pause. Then light on chair." At the close of the play the movement is reversed. For his final fade-out Beckett specifies "first chair. Long pause with spot on face alone." Throughout the play other gradations of light are similarly meant to shift and vary, sometimes even to sparkle and gleam as the rocking chair is made to sway "to and fro." So insistent was this rocking in the original production that the actress, Billie Whitelaw, never rested her feet on the stage floor for one moment during the entire production.

When there is speech in this play, the face is "slightly swaying in and out of light," for movement in *Rockaby* is soon accompanied by the sound of a human voice, the woman's own: "whom else"? And this spectacle of light, sound, and movement also features color, or more precisely, shades. The "pale wood" of the chair is "highly polished to gleam when rocking." The woman's unkempt hair is "grey." Her face and hands are "white." Fabric and texture are selected and designed along the same lines for maximum visual stimulation. As worn by this draped and seated figure, the clothes appear in this shifting light as ever-changed and ever-changing. As the playwright's "Notes" state, the "lacy high-necked evening gown" is "black." At those moments during the rock when we see it in full light, we realize for the first time that it sports "long sleeves." But this is no two-dimensional "Whistler's Mother." Beckett's seated figure is kinetic: "Jet sequins . . . glitter when rocking." And then the baroque detail: "Incongruous frivolous head-dress set askew with extravagant trimmings to catch light when rocking." In the original Buffalo production, later seen in New York at La MaMa ETC, the hat worn by Billie Whitelaw even had a touch of lush Irish green.[3] To introduce "Jet sequins" and the kind of flamboyant "head-dress" associated with the Winnie of *Happy Days* into the stark visual landscape established by this play is profoundly and unexpectedly luxurious. In the presence of such somber light it seems like an act of free sensuality, almost heroic.

Sound in this work can be similarly triumphal. For in *Rockaby*

Beckett has written a performance poem in the shape of a play, a lyrical drama in which the language we hear not only offers us the background exposition for the image we see, but describes it neatly and
precisely as well:

> so in the end
> close of a long day
> went down
> in the end went down
> down the steep stair
> let down the blind and down
> right down
> into the old rocker
> mother rocker
> where mother sat
> all the years
> all in black
> best black
> sat and rocked
> rocked
> till her end came
> in the end came . . .
> —*Rockaby,* pp. 17–18

A striking visual metaphor materializes before our very eyes as we
watch a poem come to (stage) life. A visual image created by words
is therefore something far more substantial in *Rockaby* than the term
metaphor usually implies. For in this play we watch a verbal metaphor
become once again in the Beckett repertory concrete and palpable. In
a word, it has become real. Sound therefore structures sight in *Rockaby,* just as sight structures sound. Coming to us in the shape of words,
sound provides the proper context for the dynamic image we see; the
image we see provides the appropriate context for the haunting rhythms
we hear. The coincidence of all that is audible and visible is perhaps
even more carefully arranged than this, for there is in this play more
than one source of sound competing for our attention. Although the
largest part of what we hear is recorded, the little that is recited live
has been clearly calculated to sustain maximum dramatic tension. In
each of the four "acts" of *Rockaby* it is the "live" voice that gets the
"recorded" one going. Demanding and then intoning "More" a little
more softly each time, a distinct lessening of "more" that sounded in
Billie Whitelaw's rendition appealingly like "Ma," the woman's "live"

voice has the mantic power to set not only poetry in motion, but rocking chair as well. And it is this same "live" voice that creates *Rockaby*'s most striking dramatic action. The voice-overs of "time she stopped," heard a little more softly each of the seven times the phrase is intoned, as well as the echoes of "living soul" and the one which ends the piece, "rock her off," call attention to these lines by giving them psychological texturing and an emotional tenderness which greatly humanizes their meaning. For a few isolated moments of stage time we are back to the pyrotechnics of *Krapp's Last Tape*. In that play Beckett had already shown himself capable of having his hero extract a broad range of emotional response by similarly interfering with a tape. Though Krapp's interruptions are far more mechanical, the special effects he achieves in this way are the same—especially when lips move and no sounds come, as when he turns a page and presents "Farewell to . . . love."

In *Rockaby* the sounds come, and when they do so they form heard melodies which create an additional drama of their own. The almost linear progression in the narrative spoken by the recorded voice contrasts with the back-and-forth motion of the chair on which the actress—playing a woman "gone off her rocker" but "harmless"—is seated. The figure, moreover, never really changes; only our perception of it does as we build up the image through the steady accumulation of expository facts offered by the narrative. A story develops from scene to scene. And as it does so, the figure "moves" gradually inward. Here Beckett's verbal artistry is at its height, the lyrical opportunity he has been waiting for: *Rockaby* is Beckett's first play in which the language is not merely poetic, but a poem complete in itself. A limited lexicon is printed not as prose dialogue with the intensely lyrical rhythms we remember from *That Time* or *Footfalls*, but as a more traditional modern poem whose words move "to and fro," "high and low," to imitate the gentle sway of a rocking chair in graceful motion. Hard phonemes match the back-and-forth rhythm of the chair's rock: "stop her eyes / rock her off / rock her off." Each line of printed text thus coincides with one complete revolution made by the rocking chair's arc-shaped course. "All sides" of this verbal orbit move back and forth: lines are rotated, made to formulate new allegiances with other words, then recombined in a new synthesis before reassuming the original shape in which we first encounter them. Out of the cradle endlessly rocking, it is the language of the play that is always in full swing.

The pattern is easy to identify and even easier to hear. Acts 1 and

3 begin with the same four lines and will end in the same voiced-over couplet:

> till in the end
> the day came
> in the end came
> close of a long day . . .
>
> time she stopped
> *time she stopped* . . .
>   —*Rockaby,* pp. 9, 14, 11, 16

Acts 2 and 4 have been similarly designed to open with another patterned repetition, one which, moreover, cunningly reshuffles the words we have heard before in a slightly different permutation:

> so in the end
> close of a long day . . .
>   —*Rockaby,* pp. 12, 17

But here Beckett breaks the symmetry in order to signal the proper poetic closure of this play. While the second act concludes with the somber intonation of "another living soul / one other living soul," the final words of the piece offer us a surprise ending as unanticipated as the jet sequins and the flamboyant headdress we have already noticed as foregrounded accessories to this woman's black costume:

> saying to herself
> no
> done with that
> the rocker
> those arms at last
> saying to the rocker
> rock her off
> stop her eyes
> fuck life
> stop her eyes
> rock her off
> rock her off
>   —*Rockaby,* p. 20

This denouement needs no punctuation. The words, even the Anglo-Saxon expletive lifted so disingenuously from *Mercier and Camier,* have stopped. Murphy's rocking chair comes to rest. There is stage silence. There is also stage stillness. In the slow fade-out on the chair, the lights of a spot, like sudden stigmata, momentarily isolate the head, now "slowly inclined" to resemble—if not become—the narrative's "head fallen." At the end of most tragedies there is silence. The poem's performance is at an end.

In *Rockaby* Beckett therefore uses recorded sound to achieve a very spectacular stage effect. In this short play the special sound of a recorded voice becomes the true voice of feeling, the voice of lyric poetry. Yet its eerie tone, modulated but always metallic, is never entirely human. It is only the conflict between what we hear and what we see, the interplay between the "live" voice and its recorded counterpart, that makes the poetry not only lyrical, but dramatic. Here, indeed, is an "essential" moment, as Lukács might say, in which "the dramatic and the lyrical cease to be mutually opposing principles."[4] In *Rockaby* a woman seated onstage slowly becomes the image created by her own inner voice in a Yeatsian extravaganza in which man, in this case woman, is literally nothing until she is united with her own image. "Riddled with light," like Yeats' persona in "The Cold Heart," this figure, too, "cried and trembled and rocked to and fro." But as the stage lights darken, as the head slowly falls (in Billie Whitelaw's performance with an uncanny girlish look in apparent death), no soul claps hands and sings. This performance poem relies instead on the mechanics of sound, light, and movement for the skillful coordination of its most impressive stage action. Electronics, for example, will also be called upon to produce still another element crucial to the atmosphere of this work, the echo, that gradual diminution of sound which ends each act and parallels the play's fading light and slowing motion. The echo effect is in this context an especially dynamic one, for here *la voix humaine* literally turns inhuman as, through amplification, it reverberates in our ears through live theater space. With each contraction of sound, light, and movement, however, the audience's "famished eyes" gradually focus on an image almost holy, an image free of all nonessentials. For each loss in *Rockaby* progressively validates the purity of Beckett's dramatic style. With every softening sound, every fading light, every decrease in stage movement, the image unexpectedly expands as we study in production its simplicity and authenticity. The performance, moreover, *is* the poem. Language art and theater art have finally become one.

Beckett did not come upon this solution easily. The lyricism of this piece, as he was keenly aware, depends almost exclusively on the poetics of performance, the balance and symmetry of language cho-

reographed to stage movement. When, on August 5, 1980, Daniel Labeille, the producer, received in the mail the manuscript for *Rockaby,*
a work he initially planned to do with Alan Schneider and Irene Worth,
Beckett had appended to it the following brief caveat: "If they think
it worthwhile. If you think it worthwhile."[5] What Labeille had in mind
was the filming of the entire process of staging a Beckett play, from
first rehearsal to opening night, and he was of course delighted and
slightly overwhelmed to have a new work for the project. A sixty-
minute film was eventually made by D. A. Pennebaker and Chris Hegedus, shown for a limited run in April 1984 at the Thalia in New
York before its PBS broadcast the same year on May 28. When Schneider
reported to Beckett that Irene Worth found the work "quite humorous," the playwright was disturbed by her reaction and "disappointed
by her lack of perception about the mood of the play." *Rockaby,* Beckett commented, was "not a funny piece." When the actress became
involved with the movie of Ira Levin's *Deathtrap,* she asked that her
involvement with the project be postponed. The schedule could not be
worked out, and by late January 1981 Billie Whitelaw had been con-
tracted for the part, following Ruby Cohn's recommendation to Danny
Labeille that this casting was suitable.[6] Beckett, who did not, as is
popularly believed, write this play for Billie Whitelaw (as he had *Footfalls*), nevertheless liked the new arrangement: "Very pleased with switch
to Billie," he telegraphed to America. Rehearsals began in Billie Whitelaw's sitting room in London, where she was then starring on the West
End in Peter Nichols' *Passion Play.* The filmmakers were around, of
course, for the SUNY project, and the tapes for staging the play in
Buffalo were first recorded in a London studio. Billie Whitelaw, who
closed in the Nichols show on a Saturday night, arrived in America
the following Monday. This allowed only one more day of recording,
and only one day for editing. Schneider, like Whitelaw, a veteran of
many successful Beckett projects, told a conference assembled in Buffalo, "I try to get on the stage what Mr. Beckett intended—with some
degree of sensitivity." *Rockaby,* he continued, is a "short but full-
length play, a short piece with lots of detail."[7]

Because of the tight schedule and the relatively low budget, sub-
sidized in this case by a publicly supported university and additionally
funded by New York State through its University-Wide Arts Program,
Beckett was lucky with such a scrupulous and sympathetic band of
collaborators. To Danny Labeille he was especially generous, speaking
to him in Paris about an author's own designs for several crucial details
of production. "The woman in no way initiates the rock," Beckett told
him. "The memory initiates the rock." "It would be a good idea if

perhaps she wore a ring to suggest a past engagement," he commented, thinking perhaps of *Come and Go*. "Yes, let's use a ring," which the film would later allow us to see in close-up. As the same pattern is repeated every time, the eyes should be "more closed than open as peace progresses." Beckett also recommended that the production "lose the feet under the dress." The "rocker is mother's—no richness, no ornateness." It should, he said, be "plain." The playwright also commented on the headdress: "this must glitter . . . perhaps feathers."[8] Later Billie Whitelaw would remark on her own character's hair: "It's been done but 300 years ago." When she first saw the wig prepared for her she commented, "We've been here before, friends."[9] The "intensity of face spot is constant," Beckett said; there is a diminuendo of everything until stillness is achieved. "Her strength has left her," he admitted. Onstage all movement should simultaneously reach stillness and silence. "Use an echoing device in the theater," he urged. When Labeille asked Beckett where the sound was coming from, Beckett said: "Unlike *That Time,* sound source should not be localized and should come from general performance space." "How to do it?" the young American producer asked. "I don't know that," not surprisingly, was Beckett's response. But above all he stressed that "it is a lullaby."[10]

"Beckett blows the notes," Billie Whitelaw said in rehearsal. "I want them to come out of me." "Every time I'm in a Beckett play I feel as though I'm about to be shot out in a rocket." "I'm going to edit you," Alan Schneider told her. Doing Beckett, the actress suggested, is like "playing the right music."[11] "Once I've heard Beckett say it—just once—I've more or less got in my head the music of what it is he wants. That doesn't necessarily restrict me, but I think 'Right. I know what music they're playing.'" Whitelaw marked her copy of the script for *Rockaby* with brief, sometimes cryptic remarks, such comments as "reaching out—to other lonely creatures," "soft, monotonous, no colour, soothing, rhythmic," and toward the end of the play, "strongest drive toward death" and the single word, "Hurray!"[12] "I recognize," she continued, "bits from other plays."[13] On the film for this production Schneider spoke to Whitelaw about a Mother Earth figure, accepting death, and the inevitability of dying. Beckett's "mother rocker" is "moving like a harp," the actress mused. She thought about the possibility of "rocking toward death," completing the final arc of one's existence. Her own mother had died just before the premiere of the play and when the actress was going through her mother's possessions, she came upon a jar of cold cream. She suddenly realized that the last hand to touch it was her parent's. She placed the jar on her dressing-room table and, before going onstage to perform *Rockaby,* she dipped her finger in the cold cream. She did that for every performance, "for luck and for memory." *Rockaby,* however, is "not about dying," insisted Alan Schneider. "It's about accepting death." "You're not dead at the end," he told Billie Whitelaw, "you're accepting death." "The arc should lessen gradually—very gradually." Billie Whitelaw placed the emphasis elsewhere when she spoke to a reporter during a telephone interview from Buffalo. Commenting on the character she was portraying, she said, "She's rocking herself to death. There's more to it than that, but that's about it."[14]

The Schneider-Whitelaw production of *Rockaby* did not end its brief 1981 run in Buffalo, La MaMa ETC, or at the SUNY College at Purchase, where it opened for a one-night stand. The same production was also seen in London, where it was done for seven performances in the Cottesloe Theatre at the National during December–January, 1982–83. On February 16, 1984, the show returned to New York, where Billie Whitelaw made her first extended stage appearance in America. The evening featured three pieces, *Rockaby, Footfalls,* and a reading of the prose piece *Enough,* at the newly named Samuel Beckett Theatre in the old Artists and Directors Lab at 410 West Forty-second Street.[15] Next door, at number 412, *Ohio Impromptu, Catastrophe,* and *What Where* were still in repertory at the Harold Clurman Theatre. What so much late Beckett on Theater Row confirmed for the New York audience was the essentially poetic nature that gave definition to the metaphysical dimensions of his drama. Extending the boundaries of normal theatrical possibility, the plays in performance were not so much experimental as they were experiential. Somber yet eloquent, the chamber-like quality of these pieces became clear as they were mounted in the little theaters of Manhattan. On these stages the plays could take advantage of "the greater smallness," Beckett's own observation about the particular suitability of the Royal Court Theatre in London for the presentation of his work. "In the smaller theater," Beckett once remarked about the modest scale of another stage, this one for a revival of *Endgame* in Paris, "the hooks went in."[16]

In French *Rockaby* is called *Berceuse,* a title which invokes the triple meanings of cradle, lullaby, and rocking chair. The name also brings to mind van Gogh's *La Berceuse,* the famous portrait of Madame Augustin Roulin. Painted as a response to Gauguin's canvas depicting the same woman in a simpler color scheme and less exaggerated forms, van Gogh's bold and forceful painting captures the angular features of the face of Madame Roulin as she sits dressed, like Beckett's figure, in her "best black," but in this instance surrounded by a wildly decorative floral background, notable for its distorted shapes and energetic placement of reds and greens. In van Gogh's rendition, however, all of the pictorial emphasis is directed toward the face, a quiet landscape of provincial mystery and inner strength. Portraiture captures one dreamy pose of glance and gaze in a lyrical gesture of contemplation. The eyes are focused elsewhere. In Beckett's *Rockaby* van Gogh's squat and placid figure comes alive on a stage set, evoking the same image while presenting a tradition as well as a context for thinking about words, pictures, and movement. As the figure comes to rest, a moment is frozen in time as the head slowly falls and light slowly fades. On this stage one sometimes discovers that the spoken word is not needed.

"When I was working on *Watt*," Beckett said in 1983, "I felt the need to create for a smaller space, one in which I had some control of where people stood or moved, above all of a certain light. I wrote *Waiting for Godot*."[17] Yet it is not until his late works for the stage, the mature plays of the seventies and eighties, that Beckett's conception of dramatic action on a small plane achieves its full poetic spontaneity. Though the works since *Not I* may not have been conceived together, and though the style and subject matter of each one carries its own mood and its own inner determination, their various metaphors, so concerned with rest, night, and approaching death, reveal the almost epic adventure that lies behind a much larger work. The subtle references and echoes bring to what may at first appear to be "airy nothing" in Beckett's late style a "local habitation and a name," his own link to a continually variable and ever-expanding dramatic tradition. As his actors speak his language, each is both instrument and instrumentalist, player and prop. Each brings the private experience of a reader of lyric poetry to stage life for a few unforgettable moments of stage time. The words they speak and the motions they make are Beckett's poem.

"Every line of Beckett," Alan Schneider told Danny Labeille, "contains the whole of Beckett."[18] What is exciting in his late plays for the theater is the rigor with which he continues to push his dramatic art, to see how far he might be able to go in restructuring the medium in order to examine how poetry can still speak eloquently in this form. In this respect Beckett is one of a long line of twentieth-century writers concerned with making the drama poetic for the modern stage, a legacy in language which embraces Eliot, Isherwood, Auden, Fry, Lowell, and especially W. B. Yeats. Yet in Beckett's hands the attempt is directed as much toward the poeticization of the mise-en-scène as it is, more properly speaking, toward dramatic language. As he works his way from *Not I* forward, his exploration of the genre quickly develops conventions of its own. He "would now make," he told Alan Schneider, *Waiting for Godot, Endgame,* and *Happy Days* "shorter."[19] Moving on from "the old style," his own as well as others', the form Beckett chooses for his valedictory becomes a genre of its own, a genre that makes us recognize, finally, a new possibility for drama and poetry in that visionary realm that will always come to rest somewhere beyond minimalism.

Notes

Chapter One

1. Samuel Beckett, *Footfalls*, in *Ends and Odds: Eight New Dramatic Pieces* (New York, 1976), p. 47.

2. Beckett as quoted by Ruby Cohn in S. E. Gontarski, "Beckett's Voice Crying in the Wilderness, from 'Kilcool' to *Not I*," *Papers of the Bibliographical Society of America* 74 (1980), p. 28.

3. Alan Schneider, symposium on *Rockaby*, State University of New York at Buffalo, April 8, 1981. The other participants in this panel were Eric Bentley, Ruby Cohn, Saul Elkin, Martin Esslin, and Raymond Federman.

4. See John Fletcher, "Roger Blin at Work," *Modern Drama* 8 (February 1966), 403–8.

5. Samuel Beckett, *That Time* and *Not I*, in *Ends and Odds*, pp. 28, 21, 22.

6. Interview with Jessica Tandy after an audience discussion following her performance of *Not I*, in the Zellerbach Theatre, Annenberg Center, Philadelphia, on October 26, 1973.

7. Martin Esslin, symposium on *Rockaby*.

8. See Alan Schneider, *Entrances: An American Director's Journey* (New York, 1986), p. 252.

9. Samuel Beckett, *Waiting for Godot* (New York, 1954), pp. 9, 13, 40, and 12.

10. For an early study of this point, see Ruby Cohn, *Samuel Beckett: The Comic Gamut* (New Brunswick, N.J., 1962).

11. On the question of the "narrator/narrated" in Beckett's fiction, see Hugh Kenner, *Flaubert, Joyce, and Beckett: The Stoic Comedians* (Boston, 1962).

12. Samuel Beckett, *Endgame* (New York, 1958), pp. 61, 58, and 51–53.

13. Samuel Beckett, *Company* (London, 1980), p. 89.

14. Samuel Beckett, *Krapp's Last Tape*, in *Krapp's Last Tape and Other Dramatic Pieces* (New York, 1960), pp. 22–23.

15. *That Time*, p. 37.

16. Schneider, *Entrances*, p. 269.

17. Cited by James Knowlson, "Beckett as Director: The Manuscript Production Notebooks and Critical Interpretation," in *Beckett Translating/Translating Beckett*, ed. Alan W. Friedman, Charles Rossman, and Dina Sherzer (University Park, Pa., in press). See also his edition of *Happy Days: The Production Notebook of Samuel Beckett* (New York, 1985).

18. Samuel Beckett, *Happy Days* (New York, 1961), pp. 53–54.

19. For an illuminating discussion of Beckett's work in radio drama, see Martin Esslin, "Samuel Beckett and the Art of Broadcasting," in *Mediations: Essays on Brecht, Beckett, and the Media* (Baton Rouge, La., 1980), pp. 125–54.

20. Samuel Beckett, *All That Fall*, in *Krapp's Last Tape and Other Dramatic Pieces*, p. 33.

21. Donald McWhinnie, *The Art of Radio* (London, 1959), p. 133. See also Clas Zilliacus, *Beckett and Broadcasting* (Abo, Finland, 1976), pp. 68–69. My discussion of the making of *All That Falls* deals with the original BBC recording. Starring Billie Whitelaw as Maddy and David Warrilow as Dan, the play was produced again in 1986 in a production directed by Everett C. Frost. Distributed by American Public Radio, the first broadcast of the new version took place on April 13, 1986, to coincide with the playwright's eightieth birthday as well as to initiate the Beckett Festival of Radio Plays under the supervision of Martha Fehsenfeld.

22. Samuel Beckett, as quoted by Alec Reid in *All I Can Manage, More Than I Could: An Approach to the Plays of Samuel Beckett* (Dublin, 1968), p. 68.

23. See Nicholas Zurbrugg, "Beyond Beckett: Reckless Writing and the Concept of the Avant-Garde within Post-Modern Literature," *Yearbook of Comparative and General Literature* 30 (1981), pp. 37–56.

24. Esslin, symposium on *Rockaby*.

25. On the role of lighting in Beckett's plays, see James Knowlson, *Light and Darkness in the Theatre of Samuel Beckett* (London, 1972).

26. Samuel Beckett, *All Strange Away*, in *Collected Shorter Prose, 1945–1980* (London, 1984); "Three Dialogues by Samuel Beckett and Georges Duthuit," in *Samuel Beckett: A Collection of Critical Essays*, ed. Martin Esslin (Englewood Cliffs, N.J., 1965), p. 16.

27. Beckett's production notebook for *Happy Days*. See Knowlson, "Beckett as Director."

28. Peggy Ashcroft played Winnie at the National Theatre, London, in 1976. See Benedict Nightingale, "A British Grand Dame Comes Into Her Own," *New York Times,* January 20, 1985, sec. 2, pp. 1, 14.

29. Beckett's production notebook for *Waiting for Godot*. See Knowlson, "Beckett as Director."

30. See Beryl Fletcher et al., *A Student's Guide to the Plays of Samuel Beckett* (London, 1978), p. 138.

31. Schneider, *Entrances*, pp. 294–95.

Chapter Two

1. Interview with Jessica Tandy.

2. Ruby Cohn, *Back to Beckett* (Princeton, N.J., 1973), p. 206; Samuel Beckett, *Film* (New York, 1969), p. 11.

3. See Raymond Federman, "Samuel Beckett's Film on the Agony of Perceived-

ness," *James Joyce Quarterly* 8 (Summer 1971), pp. 363–70.

4. *Film,* p. 11.

5. Samuel Beckett, *Watt* (New York, 1969), p. 208.

6. Unless otherwise indicated, citations of passages in the trilogy are from the Grove Press edition of *Three Novels by Samuel Beckett: Molloy, Malone Dies, and The Unnamable* (New York, 1965). Beckett himself referred to *The Unnamable* as a major source for *Not I.* See James Knowlson and John Pilling, *Frescoes of the Skull: The Later Prose and Drama of Samuel Beckett* (London, 1979), pp. 197, 235.

7. For an interesting Jungian parallel to the psychological situation portrayed in Beckett's play, see M. Esther Harding, *The "I" and the "Not-I": A Study in the Development of Consciousness* (Princeton, N.J., 1965).

8. Interview with Jessica Tandy.

9. Ibid.

10. Martin Esslin, "Une poésie d'images mouvantes," in *Revue d'esthétique: Samuel Beckett,* ed. Pierre Chabert (Paris and Toulouse, 1986), pp. 391–403.

11. For the origins of Beckett's image in *Not I,* see Deirdre Bair, *Samuel Beckett: A Biography* (New York, 1978), p. 621; Knowlson and Pilling, *Frescoes,* p. 196; and Gontarski, "Beckett's Voice Crying in the Wilderness," p. 28.

12. Gontarski, "Beckett's Voice Crying in the Wilderness," pp. 35–36.

13. *Footfalls,* p. 47.

14. Ihab Hassan, *The Literature of Silence: Henry Miller and Samuel Beckett* (New York, 1967), p. 184.

15. See the "Introduction" by Michael Benedikt and George E. Wellwarth, eds. and trans., in *Modern French Theatre: The Avant Garde, Dada, and Surrealism* (New York, 1966), p. xxxi.

16. Cohn, *Back to Beckett,* p. viii.

17. See Randolph Goodman, ed., *From Script to Stage: Eight Modern Plays* (San Francisco, 1971), p. 143.

18. As reported by Ruby Cohn in an address entitled "Alan Schneider and Roger Blin" before the Samuel Beckett Society in Washington, D.C., December 29, 1984. See the same critic's essay, "Growing (Up?) with *Godot,*" in *Beckett at 80/Beckett in Context,* ed. Enoch Brater (New York, 1986), p. 15.

19. Samuel Beckett, *Play,* in *Cascando and Other Short Dramatic Pieces* (New York, 1968), p. 45.

20. Richard Admussen, "The Manuscripts of Beckett's *Play,*" *Modern Drama* 16 (June 1973), pp. 23–27. In the published version of *Play* Beckett has even indicated a precise choral arrangement for the recitation of dialogue. See *Play,* pp. 62–63.

21. Hugh Kenner, *A Reader's Guide to Samuel Beckett* (New York, 1973), p. 157.

22. "Statements by Samuel Beckett, Barney Rosset of Grove Press, and Robert Brustein of the American Repertory Theatre" appended to the program for JoAnne Akalaitis' controversial production of *Endgame* in Cambridge, Massachusetts (December 1984). See also Eileen Blumenthal, "The Beckett Stops Here" and Alisa Solomon, "For Interpretation" in the *Village Voice,* January 1, 1985, pp. 71, 74; Sylviane Gold, "The Beckett Brouhaha," *The Wall Street Journal,* December 28, 1984; Mel Gussow, "'Endgame' in Disputed Production," *New York Times,* December 20, 1984; Samuel G. Freedman, "Criticism of Beckett Cast Protested," *New York Times,* January 9, 1985; and Jeff McLaughlin, "Controversy Over *Endgame*" and "Play Goes On, With a Beckett Disclaimer," *Boston Globe,* December 10 and December 13, 1984.

23. Alan Schneider, "Working with Beckett," in *Samuel Beckett: The Art of Rhetoric*, ed. Edouard Morot-Sir, Howard Harper and Dougald McMillan (Chapel Hill, N.C., 1976), p. 280.

24. Billie Whitelaw, as interviewed for *The Sunday Times* [London], January 14, 1973. Quoted by Fletcher, *Student's Guide*, p. 197.

25. Interview with Jessica Tandy.

26. My information about the problems of staging *Not I* comes from interviews with Patrick Horrigan, stage manager of the original New York production, and with Richard Kirschner, former managing director of the Annenberg Center in Philadelphia.

27. In Mel Gussow, "Billie Whitelaw's Guide to Performing Beckett," *New York Times*, February 14, 1984, p. 21. See also Billie Whitelaw in the film of *Rockaby* by D. A. Pennebaker and Chris Hegedus (Pennebaker Associates, Inc., New York).

28. Interview with Jessica Tandy.

29. Samuel Beckett, *Stories and Texts for Nothing* (New York, 1967), p. 139.

30. Interview with Jessica Tandy.

31. *Malone Dies*, p. 254.

32. On Beckett's Paris productions of *Pas moi* in 1975 and 1978, see Ruby Cohn, *Just Play: Beckett's Theater* (Princeton, N.J., 1980), pp. 266–67, as well as Knowlson and Pilling, *Frescoes*, p. 198.

33. My information about the technical problems of taping *Not I* for television is from an interview (May 1976) with Tristram Powell, who worked on the BBC production.

34. *The Complete Poems and Plays of T. S. Eliot* (London, 1969), p. 32.

35. Samuel Beckett to Enoch Brater, May 1978. Martha Fehsenfeld received the same response from the playwright, as told to this author in December 1984. Cohn reports in *Just Play*, p. 213, that Beckett was so "captivated" by the television version "that he pronounced the telecast more effective than the stage play." Billie Whitelaw continues to say that Beckett prefers the television *Not I* to the theatrical production. It was, of course, the only opportunity the actress had to see herself in the role of Mouth. See David Edelstein, "Rockaby Billie," in the *Village Voice*, March 20, 1984, p. 86.

36. Edith Kern, "Drama Stripped for Inaction: Beckett's *Godot*," *Yale French Studies* 14 (Winter 1954–55), pp. 41–47.

37. Davis' remark was made with specific reference to *Catastrophe* and *What Where*. See Elaine Carey, "Donald Davis Brings Beckett Back Home," *Toronto Star*, March 10, 1984, sec. H, p. 1.

38. Bair, *Samuel Beckett*, p. 636. To James Knowlson, Beckett wrote in 1974 that *That Time* is a "brother to *Not I*." See Knowlson and Pilling, *Frescoes*, pp. 206, 235.

Chapter Three

1. As reported to this author on separate occasions by S. E. Gontarski and James Knowlson.

2. Patrick Magee to Enoch Brater in May 1976; see also Cohn, *Just Play*, p. 30.

3. Cohn, *Just Play*, p. 172; Knowlson and Pilling, *Frescoes*, p. 219.

4. See Hersh Zeifman, "Being and Non-Being: Samuel Beckett's *Not I*," *Modern Drama* 19 (March 1976), pp. 35–46.

5. Beckett wrote this message on a postcard to Billie Whitelaw, who showed it to Martin Esslin because she couldn't understand the playwright's handwriting. Quoted by Esslin to Enoch Brater in April 1981 and again on March 18, 1985.

6. See S. E. Gontarski, "'Making Yourself All Up Again': the Composition of Samuel Beckett's *That Time*," *Modern Drama* 23 (June 1980), p. 112.

7. Walter D. Asmus, "Rehearsal Notes for the German Première of Beckett's *That Time* and *Footfalls* at the Schiller-Theater Werkstatt, Berlin," trans. Helen Watanabe, *Journal of Beckett Studies* 2 (Summer 1977), p. 94.

8. James Joyce, *Finnegans Wake* (New York, 1959), p. 57.

9. Asmus, "Rehearsal Notes," p. 92.

10. Ibid.

11. *The Unnamable*, p. 300.

12. Asmus, "Rehearsal Notes," p. 92.

13. Reid, *All I Can Manage*, p. 68.

14. Samuel Beckett, *How It Is* (New York , 1964), p. 107.

15. Asmus, "Rehearsal Notes," p. 93.

16. T. S. Eliot, "Poetry and Drama," in *On Poetry and Poets* (London, 1956), pp. 75–95.

17. See Antoni Libera, "Structure and Pattern in *That Time*," *Journal of Beckett Studies* 6 (Autumn 1980), p. 81.

18. Asmus, "Rehearsal Notes," pp. 92, 93.

19. Ibid., p. 93. For the use of "millstone" in the King James Bible, see Mark 9:42, Matthew 18:6, and Luke 17:2. Celia Easton was among the first to suggest to me the correspondence between stones and millstones in the context of this work.

20. *The Waste Land*, in *The Complete Poems and Plays of T. S. Eliot*, p. 65.

21. Samuel Beckett, *Proust* (New York, 1931), p. 49.

22. Schneider, symposium on *Rockaby*.

23. See *Proust*, p. 42.

Chapter Four

1. *All That Fall*, p. 74.

2. Asmus, "Rehearsal Notes," pp. 90–91.

3. The preproduction Faber version of *Footfalls* (London, 1976) reads "*seven steps.*" The authorized change to nine appears in print for the first time in the Faber (1977) and Grove (1976) editions of *Ends and Odds*.

4. *Four Quartets*, in *The Complete Poems and Plays of T. S. Eliot*, p. 171.

5. Beckett had considered calling this play *It all* instead of *Footfalls*. See Knowlson and Pilling, *Frescoes*, p. 220.

6. For information concerning changes in the script of this play, see in particular Knowlson and Pilling, *Frescoes*, pp. 220–28, and Cohn's several fine discussions of *Footfalls* in *Just Play*.

7. Asmus, "Rehearsal Notes," pp. 85, 86.

8. Ibid., p. 86.

9. Ibid., pp. 85, 87.

10. See Ruby Cohn, "Outward Bound Soliloquies," *Journal of Modern Literature* 6 (February 1977), pp. 17–38.

11. Beckett himself acknowledges this pun. See Asmus, "Rehearsal Notes," p. 85.

12. Asmus, "Rehearsal Notes," p. 84.

13. Billie Whitelaw and Beckett as quoted by Sally Brompton, "Billie and Beckett—A Unique Double," *The Times* [London], January 9, 1985.

14. On the change from "his" to "His" in *Footfalls*, see the several published versions of the play: the single-volume Faber edition (London, 1976); the Faber *Ends and Odds: Plays and Sketches* (London, 1977); the Grove *Ends and Odds* (New York, 1976); the Faber and Grove editions of *Collected Shorter Plays of Samuel Beckett*, both 1984; as well as the Faber *Samuel Beckett: The Complete Dramatic Works* (London, 1986). Embedded in "His poor arm" lies a Joycean echo from *Ulysses*: "Cranley's arm. His arm." On the use of such word combinations in Joyce, see Dorrit Cohn, *Transparent Minds: Narrative Modes for Presenting Consciousness in Fiction* (Princeton, N.J., 1978), p. 93.

15. Billie Whitelaw to Enoch Brater, August 12, 1986; Asmus, "Rehearsal Notes," pp. 83, 88.

16. Samuel Beckett, *Fizzles* (New York, 1976), p. 22.

17. See Sighle Kennedy, *Murphy's Bed: A Study of Real Sources and Sur-Real Associations in Samuel Beckett's First Novel* (Lewisburg, Pa., 1971), pp. 64–65; and S. E. Gontarski, *The Intent of "Undoing" in Samuel Beckett's Dramatic Texts* (Bloomington, Ind., 1985), pp. 199–208.

18. Asmus, "Rehearsal Notes," p. 85.

19. See Marjorie Perloff, *The Poetics of Indeterminacy: Rimbaud to Cage* (Princeton, N.J., 1981).

20. Maurice Merleau-Ponty, *Sense and Non-Sense,* trans. Herbert L. and Patricia Allen Dreyfus (Evanston, Ill., 1964), p. 50.

21. *Transition* 27 (1938): 292. Reprinted in Samuel Beckett, *Disjecta: Miscellaneous Writings and a Dramatic Fragment,* ed. Ruby Cohn (London, 1983), pp. 91–94. For a different discussion of the use of infinity in Beckett's work, see Martin Esslin, "Samuel Beckett—Infinity, Eternity," in Brater, *Beckett at 80,* pp. 110–23.

22. Printed in *College Literature* 8 (Fall 1981), p. 312. In this Samuel Beckett special issue the two paragraphs were printed under the heading "Crisscross to Infinity," a title not approved by Beckett. See Breon Mitchell, "A Beckett Bibliography: New Works, 1976–1982," *Modern Fiction Studies* 29 (Spring 1983), p. 146.

23. See Carlton Lake, ed. *No Symbols Where None Intended: A Catalogue of Books, Manuscripts, and Other Material Relating to Samuel Beckett in the Collections of the Humanities Research Center* (Austin, Tex., 1984), pp. 172–74.

24. In Richard Ellmann's Appendix to *Ulysses on the Liffey* (New York, 1972) there is a reproduction of this schema. See also Dorrit Cohn, p. 218.

25. Fletcher, *Student's Guide,* p. 93.

26. *Disjecta,* p. 94; Samuel Beckett, "Dante . . . Bruno. Vico . . Joyce," in *Our Exagmination Round His Factification for Incamination of Work in Progress* (Paris, 1929), p. 8; rpt. New York, 1972.

27. Asmus, "Rehearsal Notes," pp. 83–84; see also *Watt,* p. 248.

28. "Dante. . . Bruno. Vico. . Joyce," p. 14.

29. Ibid., p. 22.

30. Asmus, "Rehearsal Notes," p. 86.

31. Billie Whitelaw in the film of *Rockaby.*

32. Beckett's poem "neither" was printed in the *Journal of Beckett Studies* 4 (Spring 1979), p. vii. Beckett himself calls it a "text." It was written to be set to music by

Morton Feldman in September–October 1976. See Knowlson and Pilling, *Frescoes*, p. 237. The work received its first performance at the Rome opera in June 1977.

33. In Asmus, "Rehearsal Notes," p. 85.

34. Several critics have remarked on Beckett's change in *Footfalls* from seven to nine steps, which took place during rehearsals. See, for example, Knowlson and Pilling, *Frescoes*, p. 236.

35. Asmus, "Rehearsal Notes," p. 88.

36. Ibid., p. 90.

Chapter Five

1. See Zurbrugg, "Beyond Beckett," pp. 37ff.; Perloff, *Poetics*, 288ff.

2. Samuel Beckett, *Embers*, in *Krapp's Last Tape and Other Dramatic Pieces*, p. 101.

3. See Martin Esslin, *Pinter: A Study of His Plays* (London, 1973), pp. 29, 162. My discussion here deals with *Film* as originally directed by Alan Schneider. Beckett's scenario was reshot in color by David Clark, starring Max Wall, in 1979 for the British Film Institute. Clark's film not only uses music from Schubert's "Der Doppelgänger," but includes several opening shots omitted from Schneider's production—those detailing all of the street action before O finally comes into view. See S. E. Gontarski, *"Film* and Formal Integrity," in *Samuel Beckett: Humanistic Perspectives*, ed. Morris Beja, S. E. Gontarski, and Pierre Astier (Columbus, Ohio, 1983), p. 136; see also David R. Clark, *"Film* Refilmed," *The Beckett Circle/Le Cercle de Beckett: The Newsletter of the Samuel Beckett Society* 1, no. 2 (Fall 1978).

4. See Schneider, "On Directing *Film,"* in Samuel Beckett, *Film*, pp. 63ff.

5. See Kennedy, *Murphy's Bed*, p. 113.

6. *Le Soir*, April 15, 1927; quoted in J. H. Matthews, *Surrealism and Film* (Ann Arbor, Mich., 1971), p. 36.

7. Matthews, *Surrealism*, p. 12.

8. The film was originally silent, but a sound track, based on the recordings played at the first performance, was added under Buñuel's supervision in 1960. The music is by Beethoven and Wagner, with extracts from a tango.

9. Matthews, *Surrealism*, p. 88.

10. *L'Age d'or and Un chien andalou*, trans. Marianne Alexandre (New York, 1968) p. 95.

11. See Cohn, *Back to Beckett*, p. viii.

12. Samuel Beckett, *Murphy* (New York, 1957), p. 191.

13. Interview with Elena Poniatowska; quoted in Matthews, *Surrealism*, p. 141.

14. *Film*, p. 11.

15. Quoted by Harold Rosenberg in *Artworks and Packages* (New York, 1969), p. 42. A collection of Klee's writings and visual demonstrations was published under the title *Das bildnerische Denken*, ed. J. Spiller (Basel, 1956), and was issued in English as *The Thinking Eye: The Notebooks of Paul Klee*, ed. J. Spiller and trans. Ralph Manheim (New York, 1961).

16. "On Directing *Film,"* p. 85.

17. As quoted by Matthews, *Surrealism*, p. 64.

18. See Sylvain du Pasquier, "Buster Keaton's Gags," *Journal of Modern Literature* 3 (April 1973), pp. 269–91.

19. Quoted in Matthews, *Surrealism*, pp. 1–2.

20. Jean-Jacques Mayoux, "Samuel Beckett and the Mass Media," *Essays and Studies* 24 (1971), p. 99; Federman, p. 369; Ruth Perlmutter, "Beckett's *Film* and Beckett and Film," *Journal of Modern Literature* 6 (February 1977), pp. 83–94. See also Hugh Kenner's responses to *Film* in *A Reader's Guide to Samuel Beckett*, pp. 167–69, and in *Samuel Beckett: A Critical Study*, 2nd ed. (Berkeley, Calif., 1968), pp. 217–19.

21. See Lawrence E. Harvey, *Samuel Beckett: Poet and Critic* (Princeton, N.J., 1970), pp. 433–34.

22. Ibid., pp. 249–50.

23. *Disjecta*, p. 94.

24. Esslin, Symposium on *Rockaby*.

25. Samuel Beckett, *Ghost Trio*, in *Ends and Odds* (New York, 1976), pp. 55–57.

26. Samuel Beckett, *Eh Joe*, in *Cascando and Other Short Dramatic Pieces*, p. 37.

27. In the film of *Rockaby* we discover an interesting anecdote about the door in *Ghost Trio*. When the assistant stage manager made a move to open it, following the script's directive that it must be "imperceptibily ajar," Beckett is reported to have said, "Where are you going?" When the assistant replied that he was going to open the door, Beckett said, "If it's imperceptibly ajar, it's closed."

28. *Embers*, p. 109.

29. There is a discrepancy between the American and British editions of *Ghost Trio*. The Grove *Ghost Trio* in *Ends and Odds* lists thirty-nine camera movements; the Faber *Ends and Odds* lists forty-one. For clarification of this discrepancy, see S. E. Gontarski, *The Intent of "Undoing,"* p. 125. I want to thank the students in my Senior Seminar on Beckett (University of Michigan, Spring 1983) for their help in working out the complicated camera movements in *Ghost Trio* and . . . *but the clouds* . . . . See Beryl Fletcher, *A Student's Guide*, p. 212.

30. Interview with Tristram Powell.

31. Alan Tyson, "Beethoven," in *Chamber Music*, ed. Alec Robertson (Baltimore, Md., 1957), p. 102. James Knowlson has uncovered Beckett's specific allusion to *Macbeth* in the manuscript versions of *Ghost Trio*. See his *"Ghost Trio/Geister Trio"* in Brater, *Beckett at 80*, p. 200.

32. *Purgatory*, in *The Collected Plays of W. B. Yeats* (New York, 1952), p. 430. *Ulysses* (New York, 1961), p. 188.

33. John Goodwin, ed., *Peter Hall's Diaries: The Story of a Dramatic Battle* (London, 1983), p. 127.

34. "The Tower," in *The Collected Poems of W. B. Yeats* (New York, 1956), p. 197.

35. Symposium on *Rockaby*.

36. . . . *but the clouds* . . . , in *Ends and Odds* (London, 1977), pp. 49–56. The first American publication of this play is in the 1984 Grove edition of *Collected Shorter Plays of Samuel Beckett*.

37. Esslin, symposium on *Rockaby*.

38. *The Complete Poems and Plays of T. S. Eliot*, p. 65.

39. *Endgame*, p. 12. See Beryl Fletcher, *A Student's Guide*, p. 96.

40. *The Collected Plays of W. B. Yeats*, p. 385.

41. See Dietrich Fischer-Dieskau, *The Fischer-Dieskau Book of Lieder*, trans. George Bird and Richard Stokes (New York, 1984), p. 303.

42. *Nacht und Träume*, in *Collected Shorter Plays of Samuel Beckett* (London, 1984), pp. 303–306.

43. *Footfalls,* p. 9; *Endgame,* p. 53.

44. Matthäus von Collin, "Nacht und Träume," in Fischer-Dieskau, p. 303.

45. "Byzantium," in *The Collected Poems of W. B. Yeats,* p. 243.

46. Beckett as quoted by Martha Fehsenfeld in "Beckett's Late Works: An Appraisal," *Modern Drama* 25 (September 1982), p. 360.

47. *Quad,* in *Collected Shorter Plays of Samuel Beckett,* pp. 289–94.

48. In Fehsenfeld, "Beckett's Late Works," p. 360.

49. Ibid.

50. Ibid.

51. Ibid.

52. Ibid.

53. In Esslin, *Samuel Beckett,* p. 21.

54. As told by Martin Esslin to this author, December 1983.

55. See Fehsenfeld, "Beckett's Late Works," p. 360.

56. Quoted by Richard Ellmann in *James Joyce* (New York, 1959), p. 559.

Chapter Six

1. Samuel Beckett, *Still,* in *Collected Shorter Prose,* p. 184.

2. Samuel Beckett, *A Piece of Monologue,* in *Rockaby and Other Short Pieces* (New York, 1981), pp. 76, 77.

3. Quoted by Fehsenfeld in "Beckett's Late Works," p. 356. Produced by Ned Chaillet, an adaptation of Beckett's "text for the stage" was transmitted on BBC Radio 3 in Spring 1986. Ronald Pickup, who played the role of Speaker, observed that Beckett is "a playwright who should go straight into your head." See Malcolm Hay, "Happy Birthday Beckett," *Plays and Players* 393 (June 1986), pp. 5–6.

4. David Warrilow to this author, May 1981.

5. Beckett as quoted by Rosette Lamont to this author, October 1984.

6. John Ashbery, "Paradoxes and Oxymorons," collected in *Shadow Train* (New York, 1981).

7. See Charles Lyons' approach to this problem in "Perceiving *Rockaby*—As a Text, As a Text by Beckett, As a Text for Performance," *Comparative Drama* 16 (Winter 1982–83), pp. 297–311.

8. Wallace Stevens, "Esthétique du Mal," in *Collected Poems* (New York, 1965), p. 324.

9. James Joyce, *Portrait of the Artist as a Young Man* (New York, 1956), p. 11.

10. Linda Ben-Zvi has reached similar conclusions about how age and time are reckoned in this play. See "The Schismatic Self in *A Piece of Monologue,*" *Journal of Beckett Studies* 7 (Spring 1982), p. 11.

11. "Dante . . . Bruno. Vico . . Joyce," p. 19.

12. *Malone Dies,* p. 196.

13. See Kristin Morrison, *Canters and Chronicles: The Use of Narrative in the Plays of Samuel Beckett and Harold Pinter* (Chicago, 1983), p. 107.

14. See Ben-Zvi, "The Schismatic Self," p. 15; Morrison, *Canters and Chronicles,* p. 104.

15. Samuel Beckett, *Heard in the Dark 1* and *Heard in the Dark 2,* in *Collected Shorter Prose,* pp. 201–207.

16. Samuel Beckett, *Ohio Impromptu,* in *Rockaby and Other Short Pieces,* pp. 25–35.

17. Samuel Beckett, Letter to David Warrilow, 1981, and in conversation with Alan Schneider. See also Fehsenfeld, "Beckett's Late Works," pp. 357, 362.

18. Baudelaire, "Au Lecteur," in *Poètes français du dix-neuvième siècle,* ed. Maurice Z. Shroder (Cambridge, Mass., 1964), p. 92.

19. S. E. Gontarski to Enoch Brater, May 1981.

20. Schneider, symposium on *Ohio Impromptu,* May 9, 1981, following the performance of the play at Ohio State University.

21. Beckett as quoted by Martha Fehsenfeld to this author, October 1984.

22. *Ulysses,* p. 17.

23. *Finnegans Wake,* p. 305.

24. Schneider quoted by Diana Barth, "Schneider Directs Beckett," program notes to *Ohio Impromptu, Catastrophe,* and *What Where* at the Harold Clurman Theatre, 1983.

25. See Pierre Astier, "Beckett's *Ohio Impromptu:* A View from the Isle of Swans," *Modern Drama* 25 (September 1982), pp. 331–41.

26. *Proust,* p. 3. For the confluence of what is seen, heard, and experienced in the theater, see Ruby Cohn's neologism "theatereality" as discussed in *Just Play,* pp. 30–31, 273.

27. "Where Knock Is Open Wide," in *The Collected Poems of Theodore Roethke* (Garden City, N.Y., 1975), p. 67.

28. See Ellmann, *James Joyce,* p. 662.

29. See Ruby Cohn, *Back to Beckett,* pp. 220ff.

30. W. H. Auden, "In Memory of W. B. Yeats," in *Collected Poems,* ed. Edward Mendelson (New York, 1976), p. 197.

31. *The Inferno of Dante Alighieri,* trans. J. A. Carlyle, rev. by H. Oelsner (London, 1932), canto IX, l. 130, pp. 98–99.

32. Esslin, *Samuel Beckett,* p. 21.

33. *The Complete Poems and Plays of T. S. Eliot,* p. 63.

34. See *Ulysses,* p. 6.

35. David Bevington, *Action Is Eloquence: Shakespeare's Language of Gesture* (Cambridge, Mass., 1984).

36. *Ulysses,* p. 16.

37. On the symbolic use of numbers in Pythagoras, see A. R. Burn, *The Pelican History of Greece* (London, 1966), especially pp. 126–45.

38. Samuel Beckett, *Rockaby,* in *Rockaby and Other Short Pieces,* p. 16.

Chapter Seven

1. See Rosette Lamont, "New Beckett Plays: A Darkly Brilliant Evening," *Other Stages,* June 16, 1983, p. 3.

2. See *Catastrophe* and *Mistake,* along with accompanying notes, as published in the *Index on Censorship* 13 (February 1984), pp. 11–15.

3. My thanks to Martha Fehsenfeld, who checked copies of the French and English typescripts of *Catastrophe* in her possession on the author's use of the word "explicitation."

4. *Catastrophe,* in *Ohio Impromptu, Catastrophe, and What Where: Three Plays by Samuel Beckett* (New York, 1984), pp. 21–36. "Explicitation," p. 32 of this edition, my correction.

5. See Jean-Paul Sartre, *What Is Literature?* trans. Bernard Frechtman (New York, 1966).

6. *Malone Dies*, p. 236.

7. See Colin Duckworth, "The Making of *Godot*," in *Casebook on Waiting for Godot*, ed. Ruby Cohn (New York, 1967), p. 95.

8. Bair, *Samuel Beckett*, p. 341.

9. See Darko Suvin, "Preparing for *Godot*—or the Purgatory of Individualism," *Tulane Drama Review*, 11 (Summer 1967).

10. Cohn, *Back to Beckett*, p. 129.

11. Bertolt Brecht, *Schriften zum Theater*, vol. 5 (Frankfurt, 1963), p. 208. This passage is quoted and translated by Julian H. Wulbern, *Brecht and Ionesco: Commitment in Context* (Urbana, Ill., 1971), p. 58.

12. Duckworth, "The Making of *Godot*," p. 95.

13. On Beckett's work for the resistance, see Harvey, *Samuel Beckett, Poet and Critic*, pp. 348ff, and Bair, *Samuel Beckett*, pp. 321ff. Beckett makes specific references to World War II in *Molloy*. Moran fears his son may denounce him and later asks if a bicycle belongs to Goering (see p. 196 in the Grove single-volume edition [New York, 1955]). My thanks to Rubin Rabinovitz for calling my attention to this.

14. *Disjecta*, pp. 91, 94.

15. See Normand Berlin, *The Secret Cause: A Discussion of Tragedy* (Amherst, Mass., 1981).

16. Lamont, "New Beckett Plays," p. 3.

17. Ibid.

18. Ibid.

19. For a discussion of this stage situation in Shakespeare, see Michael Goldman, *Acting and Action in Shakespearian Tragedy* (Princeton, N.J., 1985).

20. *Endgame*, pp. 29–30.

21. Samuel Beckett, "something there," in *Collected Poems in English and French* (New York, 1961), p. 63.

22. David Warrilow to this author, April 1986.

23. See Bert O. States, *Great Reckonings in Little Rooms: On the Phenomenology of Theater* (Berkeley, Calif., 1985).

24. Lamont, "New Beckett Plays," p. 3.

25. *Waiting for Godot*, p. 25.

26. Lamont, "New Beckett Plays," p. 3.

27. *How It Is*, p. 33.

28. *Malone Dies*, p. 254.

29. *What Where*, in *Ohio Impromptu, Catastrophe, and What Where*, p. 41.

30. See Barth, "Schneider Directs Beckett."

31. Lamont, "New Beckett Plays," p. 3.

32. See Charles Marowitz, "Paris Log," *Encore* 9 (March–April 1962), p. 44.

33. Though Beckett's diagram does not appear in the Grove edition of *Ohio Impromptu, Catastrophe, and What Where*, it is printed in the *Evergreen Review* 98 (Spring 1984), in the Faber and Grove editions of *Collected Shorter Plays*, and in the Faber *Samuel Beckett: The Complete Dramatic Works*.

34. *The Complete Poems and Plays of T. S. Eliot*, p. 178.

35. Lamont, "New Beckett Plays," p. 3.

36. Alan Schneider to this author, December 1983.

37. See Barth, "Schneider Directs Beckett."

38. *For to End Yet Again* in *Collected Shorter Prose*, pp. 179–82; *The Unnamable*, p. 366.

39. My information about the making of *What Where* (*Was Wo*) comes from two important sources: Martha Fehsenfeld, "Everything Out But the Faces: Beckett's Reshaping of *What Where* for Television," *Modern Drama* 29 (June 1986) pp. 229–40; and Walter D. Asmus, "All Gimmicks Gone?" *Theater Heute*, Heft, April 4, 1986, pp. 28–30. Asmus, who assisted Beckett in Stuttgart when *Was Wo* was being made, presented a public lecture in Paris about his involvement in this project on April 27, 1986. His talk (in English), based on his article in *Theater Heute*, was part of the symposium entitled "Beckett dans le siècle" held at the Centre Pompidou and organized by Tom Bishop. See also Jim Lewis, "Beckett et la caméra," in Chabert, *Revue d'esthétique: Samuel Beckett*, pp. 371–79.

40. Fehsenfeld, "Everything Out But the Faces," p. 234.

41. Jim Lewis, as quoted by Fehsenfeld, "Everything Out But the Faces," p. 232.

42. Rimbaud, "Voyelles," in *Anthologie de la littérature française*, vol. 2, ed. Henri Clouard and Robert Leggewie (New York, 1960), p. 237.

43. *All Strange Away*, p. 128. For an extended discussion of how Rimbaud's "Voyelles" functions in *All Strange Away*, see my essay "Voyelles, Cromlechs, and the Special (W)Rites of *Worstward Ho*" in *Beckett's Later Fiction and Drama: Texts for Company*, ed. James Acheson and Kateryna Arthur (London, 1986).

44. Jim Lewis, as quoted by Fehsenfeld, "Everything Out But the Faces," p. 237.

45. Jim Lewis and Beckett, as quoted by Asmus, "All Gimmicks Gone?" pp. 28–30. Translations my own.

46. *Berceuse* is Beckett's French translation of *Rockaby*. See Samuel Beckett, *Catastrophe et autres dramaticules* (Paris, 1986), pp. 40–55.

47. See, for example, Lamont, "New Beckett Plays," p. 3; and Ned Chaillet, "The Beckett Plays," *Plays and Players* 374 (November 1984), p. 33. Stan Gontarski directed the English-language stage premiere of the 1986 *What Where* at the Magic Theatre in San Francisco, where the play opened on November 4, 1986.

48. Jim Lewis, as quoted by Fehsenfeld, "Everything Out But the Faces," p. 238.

49. Samuel Beckett, *Quoi où*, in *Catastrophe et autres dramaticules*, p. 88; "Byzantium," *The Collected Poems of W. B. Yeats*, p. 260.

Chapter Eight

1. Quoted by Katharine Worth, "Beckett and the Radio Medium," in *British Radio Drama*, ed. John Drakakis (London, 1981), p. 197.

2. Timing my own. Alan Schneider liked to time it to an even thirteen minutes.

3. The dates for this production were as follows: April 8, 9, 10, 11 (Buffalo); April 13, 14, 15 (New York City); April 17 (SUNY College at Purchase).

4. Georg Lukács, *Soul and Form*, trans. Anna Bostock (Cambridge, Mass., 1974), p. 163.

5. My information here is from Daniel Labeille's presentation on March 24, 1984 about the making of *Rockaby* at the conference, "Beckett Translating/Translating Beckett," the University of Texas, Austin.

6. Ruby Cohn, "Alan Schneider and Roger Blin." Irene Worth, however, did offer a dramatic reading of *Rockaby* (without a chair) at the New School for Social Research in New York on April 12, 1986, as part of a celebration in honor of Beckett's eightieth birthday.

7. Schneider, symposium on *Rockaby*.

8. Beckett quoted by Labeille, March 24, 1984.

9. Billie Whitelaw in the film of *Rockaby*.

10. Beckett quoted by Labeille, March 24, 1984.

11. Whitelaw and Schneider in the film of *Rockaby*.

12. See Sally Brompton, "Billie and Beckett—A Unique Double," and Gussow, "Billie Whitelaw's Guide to Performing Beckett," p. 21.

13. Whitelaw in the film of *Rockaby*.

14. Gussow, "Billie Whitelaw's Guide to Performing Beckett," p. 21; Schneider and Whitelaw in the film of *Rockaby*.

15. In February 1986 Billie Whitelaw performed *Rockaby* again, this time at the Riverside Studios in London in a production restaged by Robert Hendry and Rocky Greenberg. Of this interpretation the *Times Literary Supplement* (February 14, 1986) wrote that "voice" and "body gestures are subsumed into physical dimensions of the text." The actress re-created her one-woman show of *Enough, Footfalls,* and *Rockaby* at the four-week Pepsico Festival of the Performing Arts at the State University of New York campus at Purchase, July 12–August 4, 1986.

16. "Beckett's Letters on *Endgame*," in *The Village Voice Reader,* ed. Daniel Wolf and Edwin Fancher (Garden City, N.Y., 1962), p. 185.

17. Beckett as quoted by Lamont, "New Beckett Plays," p. 3.

18. Schneider in the film of *Rockaby*.

19. Schneider, symposium on *Rockaby*.

Bibliography

Abbott, H. Porter. "A Poetics of Radical Displacement." *Texas Studies in Literature and Language* 17 (Spring 1975).

Acheson, James, and Kateryna Arthur, eds. *Beckett's Later Fiction and Drama: Texts for Company*. London: Macmillan, 1986.

Admussen, Richard. "The Manuscripts of Beckett's *Play*." *Modern Drama* 16 (June 1973).

Albright, Daniel. *Representation and the Imagination: Beckett, Nabokov, Kafka, and Schoenberg*. Chicago: University of Chicago Press, 1981.

Alpaugh, David. "*Embers* and the Sea: Beckettian Intimations of Mortality." *Modern Drama* 16 (December 1973).

Arnheim, Rudolf. *Art and Visual Perception*. Berkeley: University of California Press, 1969.

————. *Radio: An Art of Sound*. London: Faber & Faber, 1936.

————. *Visual Thinking*. Berkeley: University of California Press, 1969.

Artaud, Antonin. *The Theater and Its Double*. Trans. Mary C. Richards. New York: Grove Press, 1958.

Ashbery, John. *Shadow Train*. New York: Viking Press, 1981.

Asmus, Walter D. "All Gimmicks Gone?" *Theater Heute*, Heft, April 4, 1986, pp. 28–30.

————. "Rehearsal Notes for the German Première of Beckett's *That Time* and *Footfalls* at the Schiller-Theater Werkstatt, Berlin." Trans. Helen Watanabe. *Journal of Beckett Studies* 2 (Summer 1977).

Astier, Pierre. "Beckett's *Ohio Impromptu*: A View from the Isle of Swans." *Modern Drama* 25 (September 1982).

Auden, W. H., *Collected Poems*. Ed. Edward Mendelson. New York: Random House, 1976.

Bair, Deirdre. *Samuel Beckett: A Biography*. New York: Harcourt, Brace, Jovanovich, 1978.

Barth, Diana. "Schneider Directs Beckett." Program notes to *Ohio Im-*

promptu, Catastrophe, and *What Where* at the Harold Clurman Theatre, 1983.

Barthes, Roland. *Le Degré 0 de l'écriture.* Paris: Editions de Seuil, 1953.

Beckerman, Bernard. *Dynamics of Drama: Theory and Method of Analysis.* New York: Drama Book Specialists, 1979.

Beckett, Samuel, et al. "Statements by Samuel Beckett, Barney Rosset of Grove Press, and Robert Brustein of the American Repertory Theatre." Appended to the program for *Endgame* at the Loeb Drama Center, Cambridge, Mass., December 1984.

Beja, Morris, S. E. Gontarski and Pierre Astier, eds. *Samuel Beckett: Humanistic Perspectives.* Columbus: Ohio State University Press, 1983.

Benedikt, Michael, and George E. Wellwarth, eds. and trans. *Modern French Theatre: The Avant Garde, Dada, and Surrealism.* New York: Dutton, 1966.

Benn, Gottfried. "Artists and Old Age." *Partisan Review* 3 (Summer 1955).

Ben-Zvi, Linda. *Samuel Beckett.* Boston: Twayne, 1986.

———. "The Schismatic Self in *A Piece of Monologue.*" *Journal of Beckett Studies* 7 (Spring 1982).

Berger, John. *About Looking.* New York: Pantheon, 1980.

Berlin, Normand. *The Secret Clause: A Discussion of Tragedy.* Amherst: University of Massachusetts Press, 1981.

Bevington, David. *Action Is Eloquence: Shakespeare's Language of Gesture.* Cambridge: Harvard University Press, 1984.

Blumenthal, Eileen. "The Beckett Stops Here." *Village Voice,* January 1, 1985, p. 71.

Bradby, David. *Modern French Drama, 1940–1980.* Cambridge: Cambridge University Press, 1984.

Brater, Enoch, ed. *Beckett at 80/Beckett in Context.* New York: Oxford University Press, 1986.

Brecht, Bertolt. *Schriften zum Theater.* Vol. 5. Frankfurt: Suhrkamp Verlag, 1963.

Breton, André. *Manifestoes of Surrealism.* Trans. Richard Seaver and Helen R. Lane. Ann Arbor: University of Michigan Press, 1969.

Brompton, Sally. "Billie and Beckett—A Unique Double." *The Times* [London], January 9, 1985.

Brook, Peter. *The Empty Space.* New York: Avon, 1969.

Brown, John Russell. *Theatre Language.* London: Allen Lane, 1972.

Bruns, Gerald L. *Modern Poetry and the Idea of Language.* New Haven: Yale University Press, 1974.

Buñuel, Luis. *L'Age d'or and Un chien andalou.* Trans. Marianne Alexandre. New York: Simon and Schuster, 1968.

Burn, A. R. *The Pelican History of Greece.* London: Pelican, 1966.

Butor, Michel. "Literature, the Ear and the Eye." *Repertoire* III (1968).

Carey, Elaine. "Donald Davis Brings Beckett Back Home." *Toronto Star,* March 10, 1984, sec. H, p. 1.

Chabert, Pierre. "Beckett as Director." *Gambit: International Theatre Review*, no. 28 (1976), pp. 41–63.

——, ed. *Revue d'esthétique: Samuel Beckett*. Privat: Paris and Toulouse, 1986.

Chaillet, Ned. "The Beckett Plays." *Plays and Players* 374 (November 1984), p. 33.

Chipp, Herschel B. *Georges Braque: The Late Paintings, 1940–1963*. Washington, D.C.: The Phillips Collection, 1982.

Clark, David R. "*Film* Refilmed." *The Beckett Circle/Le Cercle de Beckett: Newsletter of the Samuel Beckett Society* 1, no. 2 (Fall 1978).

Clark, Kenneth. *The Artist Grows Old*. London: Cambridge University Press, 1972.

Cleveland, Louise O. "Trials in the Soundscape: the Radio Plays of Samuel Beckett." *Modern Drama* 11 (December 1968).

Clouard, Henri, and Robert Leggewie, eds. *Anthologie de la littérature française*. Vol. 2. New York: Oxford University Press, 1960.

Cohn, Dorrit. *Transparent Minds: Narrative Modes for Presenting Consciousness in Fiction*. Princeton: Princeton University Press, 1978.

Cohn, Ruby. *Back to Beckett*. Princeton: Princeton University Press, 1973.

——. *Samuel Beckett: The Comic Gamut*. New Brunswick: Rutgers University Press, 1962.

——. *Just Play: Beckett's Theater*. Princeton: Princeton University Press, 1980.

——. "Outward Bound Soliloquies." *Journal of Modern Literature* 6 (February, 1977).

——. ed. *Casebook on Waiting for Godot*. New York: Grove Press, 1967.

Cooke, Virginia, ed. *Beckett on File*. London: Methuen, 1985.

Dante. *The Inferno of Dante Alighieri*. Trans. J. A. Carlyle, rev. by H. Oelsner. London: J. M. Dent, 1932.

Dearlove, J. E. *Accommodating the Chaos: Samuel Beckett's Nonrelational Art*. Durham: Duke University Press, 1982.

Deleuze, Gilles. *Différence et répétition*. Paris: Presses universitaires de France, 1968.

——. *La Logique du sens*. Paris: Editions de Minuit, 1969.

de Man, Paul. *Blindness and Insight: Essays in the Rhetoric of Contemporary Criticism*. New York: Oxford University Press, 1971.

Derrida, Jacques. "The Law of Genre." In *On Narrative*. Ed. W. J. T. Mitchell. Chicago: University of Chicago Press, 1981.

Diamond, Elin. "The Fictionalizers in Beckett's Plays." In *Samuel Beckett*. Ed. Ruby Cohn. New York: McGraw-Hill, 1975.

Driver, Tom. "Beckett by the Madeleine." *Columbia University Forum* 4 (Summer 1961).

du Pasquier, Sylvain. "Buster Keaton's Gags." *Journal of Modern Literature* 3 (April 1973).

Duckworth, Colin. *Angels of Darkness: Dramatic Effect in Samuel Beckett with Special Reference to Eugène Ionesco*. London: George Allen and Unwin, 1972.

Edelstein, David. "Rockaby Billie." *Village Voice*, March 20, 1984, pp. 81, 86.

Elam, Keir. *The Semiotics of Theatre and Drama*. London: Methuen, 1980.

Eliot, T. S. *The Complete Poems and Plays*. London: Faber & Faber, 1969.

————. "Poetry and Drama." In *On Poetry and Poets*. London: Faber & Faber, 1956.

Ellmann, Richard. *James Joyce*. New York: Oxford University Press, 1959.

————. *Ulysses on the Liffey*. New York: Oxford University Press, 1972.

Esslin, Martin. *Mediations: Essays on Brecht, Beckett, and the Media*. Baton Rouge: Louisiana State University Press, 1980.

————. *Pinter: A Study of His Plays*. London: Methuen, 1973.

————, ed. *Samuel Beckett: A Collection of Critical Essays*. Englewood Cliffs, N.J.: Prentice-Hall, 1965.

Federman, Raymond. "Samuel Beckett's Film on the Agony of Perceived-ness." *James Joyce Quarterly* 8 (Summer 1971).

Fehsenfeld, Martha. "Beckett's Late Works: An Appraisal." *Modern Drama* 25 (September 1982).

————. "Everything Out But the Faces: Beckett's Reshaping of *What Where* for Television." *Modern Drama* 29 (June 1986).

————, and Dougald McMillan. *Beckett in the Theatre*. London: Calder, in press.

Finney, Brian H. *Since "how it is": A Study of Samuel Beckett's Later Fiction*. London: Covent Garden, 1972.

Fischer-Dieskau, Dietrich. *The Fischer-Dieskau Book of Lieder*. Trans. George Bird and Richard Stokes. New York: Limelight Editions, 1984.

Fletcher, Beryl, et al. *A Student's Guide to the Plays of Samuel Beckett*. London: Faber & Faber, 1978. Rev. ed. 1985.

Fletcher, John. "Roger Blin at Work." *Modern Drama* 9 (February 1966).

Foucault, Michel. *Les Mots et les choses*. Paris: Gallimard, 1966.

————. *This Is Not a Pipe*. Trans. and ed. James Harkness. Berkeley: University of California Press, 1983.

Fowler, Alastair. *Kinds of Literature: An Introduction to the Theory of Genres and Modes*. Cambridge: Harvard University Press, 1982.

Freedman, Samuel G. "Criticism of Beckett Cast Protested." *New York Times*, January 9, 1985, p. 23.

Friedman, Alan W., Charles Rossman, and Dina Sherzer, eds. *Beckett Translating/Translating Beckett*. University Park: Pennsylvania State University Press, in press.

Gantner, Joseph. "Der alte Künstler," in *Festschrift für Herbert von Einem*. Berlin, 1965.

Gold, Sylviane. "The Beckett Brouhaha." *The Wall Street Journal*, December 28, 1984.

Goldman, Michael. *Acting and Action in Shakespearean Tragedy*. Princeton:

Princeton University Press, 1985.

―――. *The Actor's Freedom: Toward a Theory of Drama*. New York: Viking Press, 1975.

Gombrich, E. H. *Art and Illusion: A Study in the Psychology of Pictorial Representation*. Princeton: Princeton University Press, 1960.

Gontarski, S. E. *The Intent of "Undoing" in Samuel Beckett's Dramatic Texts*. Bloomington: Indiana University Press, 1985.

―――. "Beckett's Voice Crying in the Wilderness, from "Kilcool" to *Not I*." *Papers of the Bibliographical Society of America* 74 (1980).

―――. "'Making Yourself All Up Again': The Composition of Samuel Beckett's *That Time*." *Modern Drama* 23 (June 1980).

―――, ed. *On Beckett: Essays and Criticism*. New York: Grove Press, 1986.

Goodman, Randolph, ed. *From Script to Stage: Eight Modern Plays*. San Francisco: Rinehart Press, 1971.

Goodwin, John, ed. *Peter Hall's Diaries: The Story of a Dramatic Battle*. London: Hamisch Hamilton, 1983.

Gussow, Mel. "'Endgame' in Disputed Production." *New York Times,* December 20, 1984.

―――. "Billie Whitelaw's Guide to Performing Beckett." *New York Times,* February 14, 1984, p. 21.

Harding, M. Esther. *The "I" and the "Not-I": A Study in the Development of Consciousness*. Princeton: Princeton University Press, 1965.

Harvey, Lawrence E. *Samuel Beckett, Poet and Critic*. Princeton: Princeton University Press, 1970.

Hassan, Ihab. *The Literature of Silence: Henry Miller and Samuel Beckett*. New York: Knopf, 1967.

Havel, Vaclav. *Mistake*. Trans. George Theiner. *Index on Censorship* 13 (February 1984), pp. 13–14.

Hay, Malcolm. "Happy Birthday Beckett." *Plays and Players* 393 (June 1986), pp. 5–6.

Hayward, Susan. "The Use of Refrain in Beckett's Plays." *Language and Style* 8 (Fall 1975).

Hernadi, Paul. *Beyond Genre*. Ithaca: Cornell University Press, 1972.

Homan, Sidney. *Beckett's Theaters: Interpretations for Performance*. Lewisburg: Bucknell University Press, 1984.

Hubert, Renée Riese. "Beckett's *Play* Between Poetry and Performance." *Modern Drama* 9 (December 1966).

Humphrey, Doris. *The Art of Making Dances*. New York: Grove Press, 1959.

Iser, Wolfgang. *The Implied Reader: Patterns of Communication in Prose Fiction from Bunyan to Beckett*. Baltimore: Johns Hopkins University Press, 1974.

Joyce, James. *Finnegans Wake*. New York: Viking Press, 1959.

―――. *Portrait of the Artist as a Young Man*. New York: Viking Press, 1956.

―――. *Ulysses*. New York: Random House, 1961.

Kane, Leslie. *The Language of Silence: On the Unspoken and the Unspeak-able in Modern Drama.* Rutherford: Fairleigh Dickinson University Press; and Cranbury: Associated University Presses, 1984.

Kennedy, Andrew. *Dramatic Dialogue: The Duologue of Personal Encoun-ter.* London: Cambridge University Press, 1983.

————. *Six Dramatists in Search of a Language.* London: Cambridge Uni-versity Press, 1975.

Kennedy, Sighle. *Murphy's Bed: A Study of Real Sources and Sur-Real As-sociations in Samuel Beckett's First Novel.* Lewisburg: Bucknell University Press, 1971.

Kenner, Hugh. *Samuel Beckett: A Critical Study.* 2nd ed. Berkeley: University of California Press, 1968.

————. *Flaubert, Joyce, and Beckett: The Stoic Comedians.* Boston: Beacon Press, 1962.

————. *A Reader's Guide to Samuel Beckett.* New York: Farrar, Straus and Giroux, 1973.

Kern, Edith. "Drama Stripped for Inaction: Beckett's *Godot.*" *Yale French Studies* 14 (Winter 1954–55).

Klee, Paul. *The Thinking Eye: The Notebooks of Paul Klee.* Ed. J. Spiller and trans. Ralph Manheim. New York: G. Wittenborn, 1961.

Knapp, Mark. *Essentials of Nonverbal Communication.* New York: Holt, Rinehart and Winston, 1980.

Knowlson, James. *Light and Darkness in the Theatre of Samuel Beckett.* Lon-don: Turret Books, 1972.

————, ed. *Happy Days: The Production Notebook of Samuel Beckett.* New York: Grove Press, 1985.

Knowlson, James, and John Pilling. *Frescoes of the Skull: the Later Prose and Drama of Samuel Beckett.* London: Calder, 1979.

Lake, Carlton, ed. *No Symbols Where None Intended: A Catalogue of Books, Manuscripts, and Other Material Relating to Samuel Beckett in the Collections of the Humanities Research Center.* Austin: Humanities Research Center, University of Texas, 1984.

Lamont, Rosette. "New Beckett Plays: A Darkly Brilliant Evening." *Other Stages,* June 16, 1983, p. 3.

Libera, Antoni. "Structure and Pattern in *That Time.*" *Journal of Beckett Stud-ies* 6 (Autumn 1980).

Lipking, Lawrence. *The Life of the Poet: Beginning and Ending Poetic Ca-reers.* Chicago: University of Chicago Press, 1981.

Lukács, Georg. *Soul and Form.* Trans. Anna Bostock. Cambridge: M.I.T. Press, 1974.

Lyons, Charles. "Perceiving *Rockaby*—As a Text, As a Text by Samuel Beckett, As a Text for Performance." *Comparative Drama* 16 (Winter 1982–83).

————. *Samuel Beckett.* New York: Grove Press, 1983.

Marowitz, Charles. "Paris Log." *Encore* 9 (March–April, 1962).

Masheck, Joseph, ed. *Marcel Duchamp in Perspective.* Englewood Cliffs,
    N.J.: Prentice-Hall, 1975.
Mast, Gerald. *The Comic Mind: Comedy and the Movies.* New York: Bobbs-
    Merrill, 1973.
————. *A Short History of the Movies.* New York: Bobbs-Merrill, 1971.
Matthews, J. H. *Surrealism and Film.* Ann Arbor: University of Michigan
    Press, 1971.
————. *Theatre in Dada and Surrealism.* Syracuse: Syracuse University Press,
    1974.
Mayoux, Jean-Jacques. "Samuel Beckett and the Mass Media." *Essays and
    Studies* 24 (1971).
McLaughlin, Jeff. "Controversy Over *Endgame.*" *Boston Globe,* December
    10, 1984.
————. "Play Goes On, With a Beckett Disclaimer." *Boston Globe,* Decem-
    ber 13, 1984.
McMillan, Dougald. *Transition: The History of a Literary Era, 1927–38.* New
    York: George Braziller, 1976.
McWhinnie, Donald. *The Art of Radio.* London: Faber & Faber, 1959.
Merleau-Ponty, Maurice. *The Primacy of Perception and Other Essays on
    Phenomenological Psychology, the Philosophy of Art, History and
    Politics.* Trans. James M. Edie. Evanston: Northwestern University
    Press, 1964.
————. *Sense and Non-Sense.* Trans. Herbert L. and Patricia Allen Dreyfus.
    Evanston: Northwestern University Press, 1964.
Mitchell, Breon. "A Beckett Bibliography: New Works, 1976–1982." *Mod-
    ern Fiction Studies* 29 (Spring 1983).
Morot-Sir, Edward, Howard Harper, and Dougald McMillan, eds. *Samuel
    Beckett: The Art of Rhetoric.* North Carolina Studies in the Romance
    Languages and Literatures, no.5. Chapel Hill: University of North
    Carolina Press, 1976.
Morrison, Kristin. *Canters and Chronicles: The Use of Narrative in the Plays
    of Samuel Beckett and Harold Pinter.* Chicago: University of Chi-
    cago Press, 1983.
Murray, Edward. *The Cinematic Imagination.* New York: Frederick Ungar,
    1972.
Nightingale, Benedict. "A British Grand Dame Comes Into Her Own." *New
    York Times,* January 20, 1985, sec. 2, pp. 1, 4.
O'Brien, Eoin. *The Beckett Country: Samuel Beckett's Ireland.* Dublin: Black
    Cat Press; London: Faber & Faber, 1986.
Perlmutter, Ruth. "Beckett's *Film* and Beckett and Film." *Journal of Modern
    Literature* 6 (February 1977).
Perloff, Marjorie. *The Poetics of Indeterminacy: Rimbaud to Cage.* Princeton:
    Princeton University Press, 1981.
Pilling, John. *Samuel Beckett.* London: Routledge and Kegan Paul, 1976.
Reid, Alec. *All I Can Manage, More Than I Could: An Approach to the Plays*

of Samuel Beckett. Dublin: Dolmen, 1968.

Riffaterre, Michael. *Semiotics of Poetry*. Bloomington: Indiana University Press, 1978.

Roethke, Theodore. *The Collected Poems of Theodore Roethke*. Garden City, N.Y.: Doubleday, 1975.

Rollins, Ronald G. "Old Men and Memories: Yeats and Beckett." *Eire* 13 (Fall 1978).

Rosenberg, Harold. *The Anxious Object: Art Today and Its Audience*. New York: Collier, 1964.

———. *Artworks and Packages*. New York: Dell, 1969.

Rosenthal, Gertrude, ed. *From El Greco to Pollock: Early and Late Works of European and American Masters*. Baltimore: Baltimore Museum of Art, 1968.

Rubin, William S. *Dada, Surrealism, and Their Heritage*. New York: The Museum of Modern Art, 1968.

———, ed. *Cézanne: The Late Work*. New York: The Museum of Modern Art, 1977.

Sandrow, Nahma. *Surrealism: Theater, Arts, Ideas*. New York: Harper & Row, 1972.

Sartre, Jean-Paul. *What Is Literature?* Trans. Bernard Frechtman. New York: Washington Square Press, 1966.

Schneider, Alan. *Entrances: An American Director's Journey*. New York: Viking Press, 1986.

———. "I Hope to Be Going On With Sam Beckett—And He With Me." *New York Times*, December 18, 1977.

———. "On Directing *Film*." In Samuel Beckett, *Film*. New York: Grove Press, 1969.

Shroder, Maurice Z., ed. *Poètes français du dix-neuvième siècle*. Cambridge, Mass.: Schoenhof's Foreign Books, 1964.

Smith, Barbara Herrnstein. *Poetic Closure: A Study of How Poems End*. Chicago: University of Chicago Press, 1968.

Solomon, Alisa. "For Interpretation." *Village Voice*, January 1, 1985, p. 71.

States, Bert O. *Great Reckonings in Little Rooms: On the Phenomenology of Theater*. Berkeley: University of California Press, 1985.

———. *The Shape of Paradox: An Essay on 'Waiting for Godot'*. Berkeley: University of California Press, 1978.

Stevens, Wallace. *Collected Poems*. New York: Knopf, 1965.

Stewart, Susan. *Nonsense: Aspects of Intertextuality in Folklore and Literature*. Baltimore: Johns Hopkins University Press, 1980.

———. *On Longing: Narratives of the Miniature, the Gigantic, the Souvenir, the Collection*. Baltimore: Johns Hopkins University Press, 1984.

Styan, J. L. *The Elements of Drama*. London: Cambridge University Press, 1960.

———. *Max Reinhardt*. London: Cambridge University Press, 1982.

Suvin, Darko. "Preparing for *Godot*—or the Purgatory of Individualism." *Tulane Drama Review* 11 (Summer 1967).

Takahashi, Yasunari. "The Theatre of Mind: Samuel Beckett and the Noh." *Encounter* 58 (April 1982), pp. 66–73.

Todorov, Tzvetan. *The Poetics of Prose*. Trans. Richard Howard. Ithaca: Cornell University Press, 1977.

—————. *Theories of the Symbol*. Trans. Catherine Porter. Ithaca: Cornell University Press, 1982.

Tyson, Alan. "Beethoven." In *Chamber Music*. Ed. Alec Robertson. Baltimore, Md.: Penguin, 1957.

—————. *Beethoven Studies*. New York: Norton, 1973.

—————. "Stages in the Composition of Beethoven's Piano Trio, Op. 70, No. 1." In *Proceedings of the Royal Music Association*. Ed. Edward Olleson. Vol. 97 (1970–71).

Wardle, Irving. *The Theatres of George Devine*. London: Jonathan Cape, 1978.

Whitaker, Thomas R. *Fields of Play in Modern Drama*. Princeton: Princeton University Press, 1977.

Whitman, Cedric. *The Heroic Paradox: Essays on Homer, Sophocles, and Aristophanes*. Ed. Charles Segal. Ithaca: Cornell University Press, 1982.

Wiles, Timothy J. *The Theater Event: Modern Theories of Performance*. Chicago: University of Chicago Press, 1980.

Wolf, Daniel, and Edwin Fancher, eds. *The Village Voice Reader*. Garden City, N.Y.: Doubleday, 1962.

Worth, Katharine: "Beckett and the Radio Medium." In *British Radio Drama*. Ed. John Drakakis. London: Cambridge University Press, 1981.

—————. *The Irish Drama of Europe from Yeats to Beckett*. London: Athlone Press, 1978.

Worthen, William B. *The Idea of the Actor: Drama and the Ethics of Performance*. Princeton: Princeton University Press, 1984.

Wulbern, Julian H. *Brecht and Ionesco: Commitment in Context*. Urbana: University of Illinois Press, 1971.

Yeats, W. B. *The Collected Plays of W. B. Yeats*. New York: Macmillan, 1952.

—————. *The Collected Poems of W. B. Yeats*. New York: Macmillan, 1956.

Zeifman, Hersh. "Being and Non-Being: Samuel Beckett's *Not I*." *Modern Drama* 19 (March 1976).

Zilliacus, Clas. *Beckett and Broadcasting*. Abo, Finland: Acta Academiae Aboensis, Ser. A. Humaniora, 51, no. 2, 1976.

Zurbrugg, Nicholas. "Beyond Beckett: Reckless Writing and the Concept of the Avant-Garde within Post-Modern Literature." *Yearbook of Comparative and General Literature* 30 (1981).

Index